FOOD & WINE.
One Pot Meals

BY THE EDITORS OF *FOOD & WINE*

STEAK-AND-SHRIMP
HOT POT (P. 46)

FOOD & WINE
BOOKS

FOOD & WINE® MAGAZINE
EDITOR IN CHIEF **Hunter Lewis**
EXECUTIVE DIRECTOR, CONTENT STRATEGY **Michelle Edelbaum**
DEPUTY EDITOR **Melanie Hansche**
EXECUTIVE EDITOR **Karen Shimizu**
EXECUTIVE WINE EDITOR **Ray Isle**
MANAGING EDITOR **Caitlin Murphree Miller**

FOOD & EDITORIAL
SENIOR FOOD EDITOR **Mary-Frances Heck**
FOOD EDITOR **Josh Miller**
ASSOCIATE FOOD EDITOR **Kelsey Youngman**
ASSOCIATE CULTURE EDITOR **Oset Babur**
ASSOCIATE FEATURES EDITOR **Nina Friend**
BUSINESS MANAGER **Alice Eldridge Summerville**

COPY & RESEARCH
RESTAURANT EDITOR **Khushbu Shah**
COPY EDITOR **Erin Clyburn**
COPY EDITOR **Winn Duvall**

ART
CREATIVE DIRECTOR **Winslow Taft**
ART FELLOW **Rachel Carney**

PHOTO
PHOTO DIRECTOR **Tori Katherman**
PHOTO EDITOR **Dan Bailey**

PRODUCTION
PRODUCTION DIRECTOR **Liz Rhoades**

DIGITAL
SENIOR ENGAGEMENT EDITOR **Sam Gutierrez**
SENIOR EDITOR **Kat Kinsman**
SENIOR EDITOR **Margaret Eby**
RESTAURANT EDITOR **Maria Yagoda**
ASSOCIATE NEWS EDITOR **Adam Campbell-Schmitt**
DIGITAL REPORTER **Bridget Hallinan**
DIGITAL PHOTO EDITOR **Sarah Crowder**
DIGITAL OPERATIONS EDITOR **Elsa Säätelä**
ASSOCIATE DIGITAL EDITOR **Megan Soll**

CONTRIBUTORS
CULINARY DIRECTOR AT LARGE **Justin Chapple**

MEREDITH CORPORATION CONSUMER MARKETING
DIRECTOR OF DIRECT MARKETING-BOOKS **Daniel Fagan**
MARKETING OPERATIONS MANAGER **Max Daily**
ASSISTANT MARKETING MANAGER **Kylie Dazzo**
CONTENT MANAGER **Julie Doll**
SENIOR PRODUCTION MANAGER **Liza Ward**

WATERBURY PUBLICATIONS, INC.
EDITORIAL DIRECTOR **Lisa Kingsley**
CREATIVE DIRECTOR **Ken Carlson**
ASSOCIATE EDITOR **Tricia Bergman**
ASSOCIATE EDITOR **Maggie Glisan**
ASSOCIATE DESIGN DIRECTOR **Doug Samuelson**
PRODUCTION ASSISTANT **Mindy Samuelson**
CONTRIBUTING COPY EDITOR **Peg Smith**
CONTRIBUTING PROOFREADER **Carrie Truesdell**
CONTRIBUTING INDEXER **Mary Williams**

MEREDITH CORPORATION
PRESIDENT AND CEO **Tom Harty**
CHAIRMAN **Stephen M. Lacy**
VICE CHAIRMAN **Mell Meredith Frazier**

CONTENTS

ONE-POT PERFECTION

IN NEARLY EVERY CULTURE in the world, there is a tradition of the one-pot meal—some combination of protein, vegetables, herbs, seasonings, rice, noodles, potatoes and/or roots—all simmered, sautéed, stir-fried, or roasted (or eaten raw) until the resulting sum is so much greater than the parts. There is shakshuka, all manner of frittatas, curries, pho, donburi, ramen, gumbo, and soto ayam, the Indonesian chicken soup, to name just the tiniest few.

This book celebrates the beauty of the one-pot meal. We love one-pot meals because they're usually relatively uncomplicated to make (although just because they're simple doesn't mean they can't be sophisticated) and are a perfect fit for a variety of circumstances and occasions.

The more than 200 recipes in this book run the gamut, from homey comfort-food classics such as Braised Beef and Handmade Noodles (page 33) to company-ready Wine-Braised Beef with Green-Garlic Soubise and Young Chicories (page 41).

They are for every season, from Quick Skillet-Roasted Chicken with Spring Vegetables (page 112) to the freshest, lightest Classic Ceviche (page 161) for the heat of summer, to Hunter's Sausage-and-Sauerkraut Stew (page 121) when the weather turns cool, to warm-you-up Spicy Cumin-Braised Pork (page 74) when it's downright cold.

There are meatless one-pot meals that put a fresh spin on classics such as Spaghetti with Cacio e Pepper Butter, with a pop of crisp-tender broccoli rabe (page 200), and Mushroom-Chickpea Pozole (page 216). A chapter devoted to sheet-pan recipes provides a range of super-simple dishes with an array of flavor profiles—Sheet Pan Hanger Steak and Bok Choy with Lemon-Miso Butter (page 236) and Ancho-Rubbed Turkey Breast with Vegetables (page 244) among them.

The lion's share of the recipes in the book are complete meals that include meat, poultry, fish or seafood, legumes, and vegetables. In the rare instance when they don't, a simple salad or steamed or roasted vegetable on the side rounds out the menu.

Simplicity is a thread that runs through all of these recipes, but so—as in *Food & Wine* fashion—does a commitment to superb flavor and a transcendent eating experience.

HUNTER LEWIS
@NOTESFROMACOOK
HUNTER@FOODANDWINE.COM

PICK A POT

For the purposes of this book, the term "pot" is broadly defined. Cooking vessels utilized in its pages include those that meet the strict definition of a pot—Dutch ovens and saucepans, for instance—but also skillets, woks, and sheet pans. Even if a recipe calls for a few pieces of additional equipment for prep—a mixing bowl here or a small skillet there—ultimately, all of the ingredients are simmered, roasted, baked, braised, or stir-fried in a single cooking vessel to create delicious, one-pot meals. These are the basic types of "pots" used in this book.

DUTCH OVEN
This stovetop-to-oven pot is essential for soups, stews, and braises. Usually made of a heavy material, such as cast iron, you can brown foods and bake or braise in the same vessel. An enamel coating (over cast iron) helps prevent the metal from reacting with acidic foods, such as tomatoes.

SAUCEPAN
These tall, straight-sided pots with tight-fitting lids and long handles generally range in size from 1 quart to 4 quarts—

ideally, your kitchen will be equipped with at least three sizes.

COOKING POT OR STOCKPOT
These large, straight-sided pots have two small handles for lifting them on and off the stovetop. They're primarily used for soups, stews, and—as the name implies—making homemade stock.

SKILLET
Like the Dutch oven, skillets made of oven-safe materials (see page 9) can be used to sear meats and vegetables to

brown the exteriors, then transferred to the oven to finish cooking through. Or they can simply be used to make quick stir-fries.

SHEET PANS
The most common sheet-pan sizes for home kitchens are the half-sheet (18- ×13-inches) and quarter-sheet (13- ×9-inches). It's a good idea to have a couple of each size for larger-yield recipes. If you overcrowd a sheet pan, foods tend to steam rather than roast. Look for sturdy, rimmed sheet pans.

MATERIAL MATTERS

What a cooking vessel is made from has an impact on how it cooks and, consequently, on your final results.

TEFLON NONSTICK
While these pans—which have an infused or bonded coating on their cooking surfaces—prevent foods from sticking and require minimal cleanup, they generally are not the best for getting a really good sear on foods. They are fairly essential for eggs, though, which are notorious for sticking. Use nonmetal utensils such as wood or silicone to avoid scratching.

CERAMIC NONSTICK (PFOA-FREE)
These pots are made from aluminum coated with a nonstick ceramic surface that's free from perfluorooctanoic acid (PFOA), which may cause health problems. They do a good job of conducting heat, and the nonreactive surface cleans up well. Lightly brush with oil to boost the nonstick capability.

HARD-ANODIZED ALUMINUM
While straight-up aluminum reacts with acidic foods, this type of pot is processed to create a nonreactive surface. Heavier aluminum pots cook more evenly than lighter-weight ones.

STAINLESS STEEL
While pots made of stainless steel are sturdy and resist scratching and denting, they are less efficient at conducting heat compared to other materials. For more even heating, choose one that has a core of aluminum or copper, called tri-ply.

CAST IRON
There's a reason this classic material has stood the test of time—many cooks won't use anything else. Cast-iron pots and skillets are heavy and require a bit of extra care, but they're nearly indestructible and absorb, conduct, and retain heat well. Some cast iron requires seasoning before use, which creates a nonstick finish. Avoid using soap on cast-iron pots—just give them a good scrubbing with hot water and wipe down thoroughly.

CERAMIC-COATED CAST IRON
A hard, shiny glazed layer is applied over cast-iron to protect it from rust and from reacting with acidic foods. Avoid using ceramic-coated cast-iron pots over very high heat, as extreme heat can cause the surface to crack.

COPPER
These beautiful, gleaming, and sturdy pots are the priciest on the market—and for good reason. Copper is superior to other metals for conducting heat. Copper pots—which oxidize over time—require polishing to maintain their shine, but the patina of age and use is beautiful, too. They're usually lined with stainless steel to make them nonreactive.

WISE SIZE: THE RIGHT POT FOR THE JOB

2-QUART
This small pot is scaled for sauces and quick-cooking side dishes such as grains and vegetables.

3-QUART
A medium-size pot for making small-batch soups, and stews and for cooking pasta. A 3-quart oven-safe sauté pan, which is shallower than a saucepan, can also be used to make pot pies and small roasts.

4- TO 5-QUART
Braise large roasts and simmer large-batch soups, stews, and sauces in this versatile pot.

BREAKFAST
& BRUNCH

ZA'ATAR BAKED EGGS (P. 21)

CANDIED GINGER, COCONUT, AND QUINOA GRANOLA

"Quinoa gives granola a nice, unconventional little crunch," says Amanda Rockman, pastry chef at Chicago's Nico Osteria and the force behind many of the hotel restaurant's great brunch dishes. She serves her granola with creamy ricotta; plain yogurt is great, too.

ACTIVE 15 MIN; TOTAL 45 MIN; MAKES ABOUT 5½ CUPS

¾ cup rolled oats

½ cup quinoa, rinsed and drained

⅓ cup pumpkin seeds

⅓ cup sliced almonds

⅓ cup sweetened shredded coconut

¼ cup light brown sugar

1 tsp. ground cinnamon

1 tsp. ground ginger

1 tsp. kosher salt

½ cup applesauce

¼ cup honey

2 Tbsp. coconut oil

¼ cup each dried cranberries and halved dried cherries

¼ cup crystallized ginger, finely chopped

Fresh ricotta cheese or plain Greek yogurt, and mixed berries, for serving

1 Preheat oven to 325°F. On a parchment paper-lined baking sheet combine oats, quinoa, pumpkin seeds, almonds, coconut, brown sugar, cinnamon, ground ginger and salt. In a small bowl whisk the applesauce, honey, and coconut oil. Add applesauce mixture to the dry ingredients and toss to coat. Scatter in an even layer. Bake 30 minutes, stirring occasionally, until golden brown and crisp. Let cool completely.

2 Stir in dried cranberries and cherries and the crystallized ginger. Serve in bowls with ricotta and mixed berries.

PEACHES AND CREAM BAKED QUINOA AND OATMEAL

What to do with an abundance of late-summer peaches? Bake them into and on top of quinoa and steel-cut oats. Top it with heavy cream for an indulgent seasonal breakfast.

ACTIVE 45 MIN; TOTAL 1 HR 15 MIN; SERVES 6

- 1 cup quinoa, rinsed
- 1 cup steel-cut oats
- Kosher salt
- 1 Tbsp. cinnamon
- 1 cup brown sugar, plus 2 Tbsp. for sprinkling
- 1 tsp. unsalted butter, for greasing the pan
- 2 eggs, lightly beaten
- 1 Tbsp. baking powder
- 2 ripe peaches, 1 cut into ¼-inch pieces, 1 thinly sliced
- 3 cups heavy cream, for serving

1 Bring quinoa, oats, ½ teaspoon kosher salt, and 4 cups water to a rolling boil in a large pot. Reduce heat, and add the cinnamon and 1 cup brown sugar; stir. Simmer 10 to 15 minutes, stirring occasionally, until water is absorbed. Remove from heat; let cool 10 minutes.

2 Preheat oven to 350°F. Butter an 8- × 8-inch or 11- × 7-inch baking dish (or 6 individual 6- to 8-ounce ramekins); set aside. Slowly add eggs to quinoa mixture, stirring constantly. Add baking powder and peach pieces; mix well. Transfer mixture to the baking dish(es), cover with peach slices, and sprinkle with 2 tablespoons brown sugar. Bake, uncovered, 25 to 35 minutes or until bubbly. Let stand 5 to 10 minutes. Pour ½ cup cream over each serving. —EMILY FARRIS

MAKE AHEAD The quinoa and steel-cut oats can be made a day ahead and refrigerated. Add eggs, baking powder, and peaches before baking.

BANANA-WALNUT BAKED QUINOA AND OATMEAL

This banana-nut baked quinoa and oatmeal breakfast casserole is a wonderful way to use overripe bananas.

ACTIVE 45 MIN; TOTAL 1 HR 15 MIN; SERVES 6

- 1 cup quinoa, rinsed
- 1 cup steel-cut oats
- Kosher salt
- 1 Tbsp. cinnamon
- 1 cup brown sugar, plus 2 Tbsp. for sprinkling
- 1 tsp. unsalted butter, for greasing the pan
- 2 eggs, lightly beaten
- 1 Tbsp. baking powder
- 2 overripe bananas, cut into ½-inch pieces
- 1½ cups (about 6 oz.) raw walnuts, chopped
- Milk or cream and fresh berries, for serving

1 Bring quinoa, oats, ½ teaspoon kosher salt, and 4 cups water to a rolling boil in a large pot. Reduce heat; add cinnamon and 1 cup brown sugar. Stir. Simmer until water is absorbed, stirring occasionally, 10 to 15 minutes. When water is absorbed, remove from heat; let cool 10 minutes.

2 Preheat oven to 350°F. Butter an 8- × 8-inch or 11- × 7-inch baking dish or two loaf pans; set aside. Slowly add eggs to quinoa and oats mixture, stirring constantly. Add baking powder, banana pieces, and 1 cup walnuts; mix well. Transfer mixture to the baking dish(es); sprinkle with 2 tablespoons brown sugar and remaining walnuts. Bake, uncovered, until bubbly and brown on top, 25 to 35 minutes. Let stand 5 to 10 minutes. — EMILY FARRIS

MAKE AHEAD The quinoa and steel-cut oats can be made a day ahead and refrigerated. Add eggs, baking powder, walnuts and freshly-sliced bananas before baking.

STEEL-CUT OATMEAL WITH SOY MILK

Art Smith of Washington, D.C.'s Art and Soul restaurant says that eating breakfast speeds up his metabolism and also fuels his intense workouts. He swears by steel-cut oatmeal, which has an appealing chewy texture.

TOTAL 40 MIN; SERVES 4

2 cups soy milk or skim milk
1 cup steel-cut oats
1 cup fresh berries
1 cup plain fat-free Greek yogurt
¼ cup sliced raw almonds

In a medium saucepan bring 2 cups water and the soy milk to a boil. Add oats; cover and simmer over low until oats are tender, about 30 minutes. Uncover and cook over medium, stirring, until the oatmeal is creamy, about 3 minutes. Spoon oatmeal into bowls and top with berries, yogurt, and almonds. —ART SMITH

MAKE AHEAD The oatmeal can be refrigerated up to 5 days. Reheat over low, stirring occasionally.

CINNAMON-RAISIN BREAD CUSTARD WITH FRESH BERRIES

Chef Bradley Ogden's 1987 recipe for ultra-rich bread pudding is perfect for brunch or dessert. It can be made with store-bought bread, but it's best made with a fresh bakery loaf, sliced ½ inch thick.

ACTIVE 15 MIN; TOTAL 40 MIN; SERVES 6 TO 8

16 slices cinnamon-raisin bread
6 Tbsp. unsalted butter, melted and cooled slightly
4 large eggs
2 large egg yolks
¾ cup granulated sugar
3 cups milk
1 cup heavy cream
1 Tbsp. vanilla extract
Confectioners' sugar
Fresh berries, for serving

1 Preheat oven to 350°F. Butter a 13- × 9-inch glass or ceramic baking dish. Brush both sides of bread with melted butter. Arrange bread in prepared dish in 2 even rows.

2 Whisk together whole eggs and egg yolks until blended in a large bowl. Whisk in granulated sugar, milk, heavy cream, and vanilla. Strain milk mixture over the bread, pressing slices to evenly moisten.

3 Place baking dish in a larger roasting pan; add warm water to reach halfway up side of dish. Bake in the upper third of the oven until lightly browned and custard is set, about 25 minutes. Transfer baking dish to a wire rack; let stand 15 minutes. Sift confectioners' sugar over custard; cut into servings. Serve with berries. —BRADLEY OGDEN

MAKE AHEAD The bread custard can be prepared through Step 2. Cover with plastic wrap and refrigerate overnight.

KRU NID'S KHAO TOM
(THAI BREAKFAST PORRIDGE WITH BACON)

This comforting, creamy rice porridge shines with punchy, savory toppings for a hearty meal. Traditional toppings can include Chinese sausage, dried shrimp, or eggs, but food writer Kat Thompson's favorite version of her auntie's dish is topped with fermented mustard greens and crispy bacon.

ACTIVE 20 MIN; TOTAL 1 HR; SERVES 6

1 cup uncooked jasmine rice

Kosher salt or fish sauce, to taste

6 (1-oz.) thick-cut maple bacon slices, cut into 2-inch pieces

Fermented mustard greens (such as Pigeon Brand)

Sliced scallions and sliced fresh red Thai chiles, for garnish

1 Place rice in a large saucepan; add enough water to just cover rice. Swirl water in pan to rinse rice, and drain. Repeat rinsing and draining process until water runs clear, 8 to 10 times. Add 6 cups water to drained rice in saucepan; bring to a boil over high. Stir in salt or fish sauce to taste. Reduce heat to medium-low; cover and cook, undisturbed, until rice is tender and creamy, 30 minutes. Remove from heat; let rice stand, covered, until thickened, about 10 minutes.

2 While rice cooks, cook bacon in a large skillet over medium-high, turning occasionally, until crispy, 8 to 10 minutes. Drain on a paper towel–lined plate.

3 Divide porridge among 6 shallow bowls. Sprinkle with bacon; garnish with fermented mustard greens, scallions, and chiles. —ORANIJ PROMSATIT

MAKE AHEAD Porridge can be refrigerated in an airtight container up to 2 days.

WINE Richer-style French rosé: 2019 Château de Trinquevedel Tavel

NOTE Find canned fermented mustard greens at Asian markets or online.

CHRISTMAS-MORNING CASSEROLE

Chef Bryan Voltaggio loves this make-ahead dish: a classic baked bread-and-egg casserole with bites of pepperoni, mushrooms, and gooey cheese. It's as good for dinner as it is for breakfast.

ACTIVE 40 MIN; TOTAL 1 HR 40 MIN, PLUS 8 HOUR REFRIGERATION; SERVES 8

Butter, for greasing

2 Tbsp. extra-virgin olive oil

½ cup finely diced pepperoni (2 oz.)

½ lb. shiitake mushrooms, stems discarded and caps cut into ¾-inch pieces

1 medium onion, minced

1 red bell pepper, cut into ½-inch pieces

2 tsp. kosher salt, plus more for seasoning

8 large eggs

3 cups whole milk

1 Tbsp. Dijon mustard

1 Tbsp. soy sauce

½ tsp. black pepper

¾ lb. day-old challah, sliced 1 inch thick and cut into 1-inch dice (10 cups)

6 oz. Black Forest ham, finely diced (1¼ cups)

4 oz. Monterey Jack cheese, shredded (1 cup)

4 oz. aged white cheddar cheese, shredded (1 cup)

½ cup finely chopped scallions, plus thinly sliced scallions for garnish

Hot sauce, for serving

1 Butter a 13- × 9-inch baking dish. Heat olive oil in a large skillet over medium. Add pepperoni and cook until fat is rendered, about 3 minutes. Add mushrooms and cook until lightly browned and tender, about 5 minutes. Add onion, bell pepper, and a generous pinch of salt. Cook, stirring occasionally, until softened and browned, about 7 minutes. Let cool completely.

2 In a large bowl whisk together eggs, milk, mustard, soy sauce, pepper, and 2 teaspoons salt. Add cooled vegetables, challah, ham, cheeses, and chopped scallions to egg mixture; mix well. Transfer to prepared baking dish; cover with plastic wrap; refrigerate 8 hours.

3 Preheat oven to 350°F. Uncover casserole. Bake just until set and top is browned, about 50 minutes. Let stand 10 minutes. Top with thinly sliced scallions and serve with hot sauce. —BRYAN VOLTAGGIO

ZA'ATAR BAKED EGGS

One go-to brunch for Bravo Top Chef *judge and cookbook author Gail Simmons is baked eggs in a cherry tomato-pepper mix seasoned with the Mediterranean spice blend za'atar.*

TOTAL 30 MIN; SERVES 4

- 3 Tbsp. extra-virgin olive oil, plus more for drizzling
- 1 medium yellow onion, thinly sliced
  Kosher salt
  Black pepper
- 2 pints cherry tomatoes
- 2 red bell peppers, chopped
- ¼ cup plus 2 tsp. finely chopped parsley, plus more for garnish
- 2 tsp. za'atar, plus more for garnish
- 4 large eggs
- 1 cup plain yogurt
- ½ cup finely chopped seeded English cucumber
- 1 Tbsp. fresh lemon juice, plus more for drizzling
- ½ tsp. sumac
- 2 tsp. finely chopped fresh mint

1 Preheat oven to 375°F. In a large oven-going skillet heat 3 tablespoons olive oil until shimmering. Add onion; season with salt and black pepper. Cook over medium, stirring occasionally, until softened, about 5 minutes. Add tomatoes and cook, stirring occasionally, until some of them burst, 5 to 7 minutes. Add bell peppers and cook, stirring occasionally, until peppers are softened and tomatoes have burst, about 10 minutes. Remove from heat; stir in ¼ cup parsley and 1½ teaspoons za'atar. Season tomato sauce with salt and black pepper.

2 Using a spoon, make 4 wells in the tomato sauce, then crack an egg into each one; season with salt and black pepper. Transfer skillet to oven. Bake 10 to 12 minutes, until egg whites are just set and yolks are still runny.

3 Meanwhile, in a small bowl, mix yogurt with cucumber, the 1 tablespoon lemon juice, the sumac, mint, remaining 2 teaspoons parsley, and ½ teaspoon za'atar. Season with salt and garnish with additional za'atar. Drizzle eggs with olive oil and garnish with additional parsley. Drizzle tomato sauce with lemon juice. Serve with cucumber yogurt. —GAIL SIMMONS

EGGS BAKED OVER SAUTÉED MUSHROOMS AND SPINACH

Drinking wine with eggs at lunch always feels so French to food writer Kristin Donnelly, likely thanks to Elizabeth David's famous essay, "An Omelette and a Glass of Wine."

ACTIVE 20 MIN; TOTAL 45 MIN; SERVES 4

- 1 Tbsp. olive oil
- 1 large leek, white and light green parts only, cut into ½-inch pieces
- 1 Tbsp. unsalted butter
- 1 lb. white or cremini mushrooms, thinly sliced (about 6 cups)
- 1 Tbsp. soy sauce
- ¼ cup dry red wine
- 5 oz. baby spinach
  Salt and freshly ground black pepper
- 4 large eggs
- 4 slices whole-grain toast

1 Preheat oven to 350°F. Heat olive oil in a deep skillet over medium. Add leek and cook, stirring, until softened, about 3 minutes. Stir in butter and mushrooms. Cook, covered, stirring occasionally, until mushrooms are softened and liquid is released, about 7 minutes. Add soy sauce and red wine. Cook, uncovered, over medium-high, stirring, until liquid is reduced to 2 tablespoons, about 5 minutes. Add spinach and stir until wilted, 2 minutes. Season with salt and pepper.

2 Coat four 1-cup ramekins or small gratin dishes with additional oil. Transfer mushrooms and spinach to ramekins, then crack an egg on top of each. Bake until egg whites are barely set and yolks are runny, 10 to 12 minutes. Let stand 2 minutes. Serve with toast. —KRISTIN DONNELLY

WINE Fruity Gamay from France's Beaujolais region

MEXICAN EGGS BAKED IN TOMATO SAUCE

Food & Wine's *Kay Chun uses fresh tomatoes as well as canned tomato sauce to amp up the flavor in her simple and delicious breakfast bake.*

TOTAL 40 MIN; SERVES 4

2 Tbsp. extra-virgin olive oil

3 poblano chiles, seeded and sliced ½ inch thick

3 garlic cloves, chopped

1 (15 oz.) can tomato sauce

2 cups halved cherry tomatoes (12 oz.)

1 tsp. dried oregano

4 large eggs

1 cup crumbled queso fresco (5 oz.)

Chopped cilantro and sliced jalapeños, for garnish

Warm corn tortillas, for serving

1 Preheat oven to 425°F. Heat olive oil in a large cast-iron skillet. Add poblanos and garlic; cook over medium, stirring, until golden, 5 minutes. Stir in tomato sauce, tomatoes, and oregano; cook over low until thickened, about 10 minutes.

2 Carefully crack eggs in tomato sauce and top with cheese. Bake until set, about 12 minutes. Garnish with cilantro and jalapeños. Serve with corn tortillas.
—KAY CHUN

BAKED EGGS WITH CHORIZO AND POTATOES

Chef David Kinch says that this hearty combination of crumbled chorizo, chunks of crispy potatoes, and eggs—all cooked together in a big cast-iron skillet—is his Mexican-Californian twist on rösti, the classic Swiss fried-potato breakfast.

ACTIVE 30 MIN; TOTAL 45 MIN; SERVES 8

2 lb. medium Yukon Gold potatoes

1½ lb. fresh chorizo, casings removed

1 large onion, finely chopped

2 Tbsp. extra-virgin olive oil

Salt and freshly ground black pepper

8 large eggs

Toast and hot sauce, for serving

1 Preheat oven to 375°F. Place potatoes in a large saucepan and cover with cold water. Bring to a boil and cook over medium until tender, about 25 minutes; drain and let cool. Peel potatoes and cut into ¾-inch pieces.

2 Meanwhile, cook chorizo in a large cast-iron skillet over medium until cooked through and lightly browned, about 8 minutes. Add onion and cook, stirring, until softened, about 5 minutes. Transfer chorizo mixture to a bowl; wipe out skillet.

3 Add oil to skillet and heat over medium. Add potatoes; season with salt and pepper. Cook, turning occasionally, until golden and crispy, about 6 minutes. Stir in the chorizo mixture. Remove skillet from heat.

4 Using a ladle, make 8 indentations about 1 inch apart in the potato-chorizo mixture; crack an egg into each. Transfer skillet to the oven. Bake until egg whites are just set and yolks are still runny, about 12 minutes. Serve with toast and hot sauce. —DAVID KINCH

MAKE AHEAD The potatoes can be boiled one day ahead and refrigerated.

MEXICAN EGGS BAKED
IN TOMATO SAUCE

CHIPOTLE CHILAQUILES

Chilaquiles is a simple Mexican dish created to use leftovers like tortillas, chiles, shredded chicken, and cheese. Chef Rick Bayless keeps the recipe simple by doctoring canned tomatoes with chipotles in adobo.

TOTAL 40 MIN; SERVES 4

1 (28-oz.) can whole tomatoes, drained and ½ cup liquid reserved

2 canned chipotles in adobo

1½ Tbsp. vegetable oil

1 large white onion, thinly sliced

3 garlic cloves, very finely chopped

1½ cups chicken stock or low-sodium broth

Salt

8 oz. tortilla chips

1½ cups shredded chicken

¼ cup freshly grated Parmesan cheese or queso añejo (see Note)

⅓ cup sour cream

¼ cup finely chopped fresh cilantro leaves

1 In a blender combine tomatoes with reserved ½ cup liquid and the chipotles; blend until almost smooth.

2 Heat oil in an extra-large deep skillet. Add two-thirds of the onion and cook over medium-high until browned around the edges, about 6 minutes. Add garlic and cook 1 minute. Pour in tomato puree and simmer, stirring, until slightly thickened, about 5 minutes. Stir in stock. Boil sauce over medium-high until slightly thickened, about 2 minutes. Season with salt and remove from heat.

3 Gently stir tortilla chips into sauce until well coated. Top with the remaining onion, the shredded chicken, and Parmesan cheese. Spoon sour cream over chilaquiles; sprinkle with cilantro and serve immediately. —RICK BAYLESS

MAKE AHEAD The recipe can be prepared through Step 2 and refrigerated overnight. Reheat chipotle-tomato sauce before proceeding.

NOTE Queso añejo is an aged, slightly salty Spanish white cheese.

WINE Zinfandels from warm regions like Sonoma's Dry Creek Valley

CHEESY GRITS CASSEROLE

Clothing designer Billy Reid says, "Folks in the South start eating grits young. You learn to love them as a kid and it never goes away." Using old-fashioned, stone-ground grits gives the casserole better texture and flavor than quick-cooking grits.

ACTIVE 45 MIN; TOTAL 2 HR 20 MIN; SERVES 12

2 cups coarse, stone-ground white grits (not instant) (12 oz.), rinsed

Salt and freshly ground black pepper

1 stick unsalted butter, cut into chunks, plus more for greasing

½ lb. sharp white cheddar cheese, coarsely shredded

3 large eggs, beaten

1 Preheat oven to 350°F. Butter a 13- × 9-inch baking dish. In a large, heavy pot bring 8 cups water to a boil. Sprinkle grits into water, stirring constantly, and return to a boil. Cook over low, stirring frequently, just until grits are tender, about 30 minutes. Season generously with salt and pepper, and cook, stirring, until grits are very thick and tender, about 10 minutes longer. Remove from heat; stir in butter and cheese until combined. Stir in eggs.

2 Pour mixture into the prepared dish. Bake until bubbling and top is golden, about 1 hour. Let cool 20 minutes before serving. —BILLY REID

MAKE AHEAD The baked casserole can be refrigerated overnight. Reheat before serving.

MONTE CRISTO STRATA

In this rich and hearty dish, bread, ham, and cheese are baked in an eggy custard. Grainy mustard and tarragon add lovely vibrant flavor.

ACTIVE 10 MIN; TOTAL 1 HR; SERVES 8

Softened butter, for greasing

1 (1¼-lb.) loaf bakery white bread, crusts removed and bread sliced (about 18 slices)

¼ cup grainy mustard

1 lb. thinly sliced Virginia ham

2 Tbsp. chopped fresh tarragon, plus more for garnish

¾ lb. Gruyère cheese, coarsely shredded (3 cups)

3 cups milk

4 large eggs

Freshly ground black pepper

1 Preheat oven to 375°F with a rack in center of oven. Butter a 13- × 9-inch baking dish. Arrange one-third of the bread in dish; spread with 2 tablespoons mustard. Top with half the ham, 1 tablespoon tarragon, and 1 cup cheese. Repeat layers, reserving the last 1 cup cheese.

2 In a medium bowl whisk milk with eggs; season generously with pepper. Pour milk mixture evenly over layers in the dish, gently press bread to absorb liquid. Pat remaining cheese on top; cover with buttered parchment paper.

3 Bake strata in center of oven until bubbling and browned around the edges, 30 to 35 minutes. Remove parchment paper. Turn on broiler. Broil about 3 minutes, just until top is golden and bubbling. Let rest 10 minutes. —GRACE PARISI

MAKE AHEAD The unbaked strata can be refrigerated overnight.

WINE Fruity sparkling: Col Mesian "Nove Cento Dieci" Spumante Extra Dry NV

SAUSAGE AND APPLE FRITTATA WITH DILL

Instead of serving the breakfast sausages on the side of her eggs, Food & Wine's Kay Chun bakes them right into her delicious egg frittata. To give the baked eggs more flavor, she includes sweet bites of apple and sharp cheddar cheese. This is the perfect brunch or lunch dish, but it's also great for dinner with a simple salad and sparking Cava.

ACTIVE 15 MIN; TOTAL 45 MIN; SERVES 4

- 1 Tbsp. extra-virgin olive oil
- ½ lb. breakfast sausage links
- 1 dozen large eggs, beaten
- ¼ cup whole milk
- 1 Granny Smith apple, peeled and cut into ¼-inch pieces
- 1 cup grated sharp cheddar cheese
- ½ cup chopped dill
- Salt and black pepper

Preheat oven to 375°F. Heat oil in a 9-inch ovenproof nonstick skillet. Add sausage and cook over medium, turning, until golden, about 5 minutes. Stir in eggs, milk, apple, cheese, and dill. Season with salt and pepper. Bake until golden and set, about 30 minutes. –KAY CHUN

WINE Fresh, green apple–scented cava.

POTATO FRITTATA WITH PROSCIUTTO AND GRUYÈRE

This cheesy frittata is the kind of dish—fast, flexible, and easy to reheat—that chef and restaurant owner Tom Valenti likes to have around for all kinds of holiday eating.

ACTIVE 25 MIN; TOTAL 40 MIN; SERVES 10

- 1 dozen large eggs
- Salt and freshly ground black pepper
- 1 packed cup shredded Gruyère cheese
- 4 oz. prosciutto, sliced ¼ inch thick and cut into ¼-inch dice
- ¼ cup extra-virgin olive oil
- 1 lb. Yukon Gold potatoes, peeled and cut into ½-inch dice
- 2 scallions, thinly sliced

1 Preheat oven to 375°F. In a bowl beat eggs with 2 tablespoons water; season with ¾ teaspoon salt and ½ teaspoon pepper. Beat in cheese and prosciutto.

2 Heat olive oil in a large nonstick oven-going skillet. Add potatoes and cook over medium-high, stirring occasionally, until tender and golden brown, about 7 minutes. Add scallions and cook 1 minute. Stir egg mixture then add to skillet. Stir to combine. Cook just until bottom is set, about 3 minutes; lift frittata to allow uncooked eggs to run underneath.

3 Bake frittata until nearly set in the center, about 10 minutes.

4 Preheat broiler. Broil frittata 8 inches from heat 1 minute, or just until top begins to brown. Cut frittata into wedges and serve hot or at room temperature.
—TOM VALENTI

SAUSAGE AND APPLE
FRITTATA WITH DILL

BEEF, LAMB
& GAME

HUNGARIAN GOULASH (P. 42)

GLAZED BEEF SHANKS WITH COFFEE AND PEANUTS

Mashama Bailey, head chef and co-owner of The Grey in Savannah, Georgia, roasts these hefty beef shanks in a ginger- and spice-spiked tomato sauce then finishes with a generous dollop of thick and creamy peanut butter. She garnishes with Microplane-grated coffee beans; you can grind the beans in a coffee grinder for chunky texture.

ACTIVE 1 HR 15 MIN; TOTAL 5 HR 30 MIN; SERVES 6 TO 8

- 4 (about 1½-lb.) osso buco-cut Angus beef shanks (about 2 inches thick), tied
- 2½ Tbsp. kosher salt, plus more to taste
- ¼ cup peanut oil
- 1 (28-oz.) can whole peeled plum tomatoes (such as Cento), undrained
- 1 large yellow onion, sliced
- ¾ cup ¼-inch-thick unpeeled fresh ginger slices
- ¾ cup garlic cloves, peeled and smashed
- 1 (6-oz.) can tomato paste
- 1 red Fresno chile, unseeded and halved lengthwise
- 5 chiles de árbol
- 3 cups strong-brewed coffee
- 2 tsp. toasted coriander seeds
- 1½ tsp. toasted cumin seeds
- ½ tsp. toasted fenugreek seeds
- 1 toasted cinnamon stick
- 4 toasted Tellicherry peppercorns
- ¾ cup creamy peanut butter
- Finely crushed roasted peanuts, finely ground coffee beans, and fresh cilantro leaves, for garnish

1 Sprinkle beef all over with salt. Let stand at room temperature 1 hour, or chill, uncovered, at least 8 hours or up to overnight.

2 Preheat oven to 300°F. (If beef was chilled overnight, let stand at room temperature 30 minutes.) Heat oil in a roasting pan over medium-high until starting to smoke. Add beef; cook, turning occasionally, until browned on all sides, 15 to 20 minutes. Remove from pan. While beef browns, process plum tomatoes in a blender until smooth, about 15 seconds; set aside.

3 Reduce heat under roasting pan to medium. Add onion, ginger, and garlic; cook, stirring occasionally and scraping bottom of pan to loosen any browned bits, until onion is softened, 6 to 8 minutes. Stir in tomato paste, Fresno chile, and chiles de árbol; cook, stirring often, until mixture is fragrant, about 3 minutes. Stir in coffee and pureed tomatoes. Bring mixture to a boil over medium; boil, stirring occasionally, 2 minutes.

4 Return beef to pan, nestling into tomato mixture. Add 1½ cups water, the coriander, cumin, fenugreek, cinnamon stick, and peppercorns. Return mixture to a boil over medium. Cover pan tightly with aluminum foil. Transfer to preheated oven; roast until beef is fork-tender, 2 hours and 30 minutes to 3 hours. Uncover and continue to roast 30 minutes.

5 Remove from oven; let stand 15 minutes. Remove beef from pan, and cover beef with foil to keep warm. Pour braising liquid in pan through a fine wire-mesh strainer into a heatproof bowl; discard solids. Wipe pan clean. Return braising liquid to pan. Bring to a boil over medium-high; reduce heat to medium-low, and simmer, stirring occasionally, until liquid is slightly thickened and reduced to about 5 cups, 15 to 20 minutes.

6 Whisk peanut butter into reduced sauce in pan until smooth; season with salt to taste. Return beef to pan; cook over medium-low, basting occasionally, until warmed through, 8 to 10 minutes. Garnish with crushed peanuts, ground coffee beans, and cilantro. Serve immediately. —MASHAMA BAILEY

MAKE AHEAD Prepare recipe as directed through Step 4. Let beef cool in pan 1 hour. Cover and chill mixture overnight or up to 2 days. Uncover and skim hardened fat from surface. Cover and reheat in a 300°F oven until warmed through, about 1 hour. Proceed with Steps 5 and 6 as directed.

WINE Luscious, oak-edged Merlot: 2016 Chappellet Napa Valley

BRAISED BEEF AND HANDMADE NOODLES

Tender and hearty handmade noodles—simply made with flour, eggs, and whole-milk yogurt—add texture to the stew and thicken the broth. Store the noodles and broth separately to prevent the noodles from dissolving.

ACTIVE 50 MIN; TOTAL 6 HR 10 MIN; SERVES 4

- 2 Tbsp. olive oil
- 2 cups (about 8½ oz.) plus 1 Tbsp. all-purpose flour, divided, plus more for work surface
- 1 (3-lb.) boneless chuck roast, beef brisket, or bottom round roast, trimmed
- 1½ Tbsp. kosher salt, divided, plus more to taste
- 1½ tsp. black pepper, divided, plus more to taste
- 1 bunch celery, stalks cut into large pieces (about 8 cups)
- 2 large eggs, beaten
- ¼ cup plain whole-milk yogurt
- ¼ cup dry red wine (optional)

1 Preheat oven to 300°F. Heat oil in a large Dutch oven over medium. Place 1 tablespoon flour in a fine wire-mesh strainer, and sprinkle all over beef. Season with 1 tablespoon salt and 1 teaspoon pepper. Add beef to Dutch oven; cook, turning occasionally, until deeply browned on all sides, 20 to 25 minutes. Add celery and 9 cups water (water should come to just below top of meat). Bring to a simmer over medium-high; cover and transfer to oven. Braise until meat is fork-tender, about 3 hours. Transfer beef to a work surface and shred with 2 forks into large pieces. Using a slotted spoon, remove and discard celery from broth. Set aside broth in Dutch oven.

2 While meat cooks, stir together eggs, yogurt, 1 teaspoon salt, remaining 2 cups flour, and remaining ½ teaspoon pepper in a medium bowl just until dough comes together. Turn dough out onto a floured work surface; knead until it forms a ball. Continue to knead 4 minutes (dough will be sticky and elastic). Wrap in plastic wrap, and chill 2 hours.

3 Remove plastic wrap. Roll dough out on a floured surface into a 14-inch square (⅛ to ¼ inch thick). Lightly sprinkle flour over dough. Using a sharp knife or pizza cutter, cut dough into ¼-inch-wide noodles. Arrange noodles in a single layer on a parchment-paper-lined baking sheet. Add wine to reserved broth and bring to a simmer over medium-high. Add noodles to broth, and return to a simmer. Cook noodles until tender and just cooked through, 3 to 4 minutes. (You should not see a white center when you bite into cooked pasta.) Return shredded beef to pot. Stir in remaining ½ teaspoon salt. Add salt and pepper to taste, if needed. —ILIANA REGAN

MAKE AHEAD Beef can be cooked, shredded, and stored in broth in refrigerator up to 2 days ahead.

WINE Full-bodied, peppery Syrah: 2016 Ramey Sonoma Coast

RIB EYE AND RADISHES IN BAGNA CAUDA BUTTER

The trick to this amazingly delicious steak by Food & Wine's *Kay Chun is basting it with garlicky anchovy butter while it roasts.*

TOTAL 1 HR; SERVES 4

1 stick unsalted butter, at room temperature

5 oil-packed anchovies, minced

1 large garlic clove, minced

¼ cup chopped fresh flat-leaf parsley

Kosher salt and black pepper

1 Tbsp. extra-virgin olive oil

1 (1¾-lb.) bone-in rib eye steak (2 inches thick), at room temperature for 1 hour

2 fresh rosemary sprigs

2 bunches radishes

1 Preheat oven to 450°F. In a medium bowl stir together butter, anchovies, garlic, and 2 tablespoons parsley. Season with salt and pepper; mix well.

2 In a large cast-iron skillet heat olive oil until shimmering. Season steak with salt and pepper. Add steak and rosemary to skillet; sear over medium until steak is browned, about 2 minutes per side. Add radishes and half the butter mixture. Roast 18 to 20 minutes, basting every 3 minutes, until a thermometer inserted in steak registers 125°F for medium rare. Transfer to a board to rest 15 minutes. Discard rosemary.

3 Thinly slice steak and transfer to a platter along with the radishes. Sprinkle with remaining parsley and serve with remaining butter mixture. —KAY CHUN

WINE Herby, cassis-scented Cabernet Franc: 2011 Couly-Dutheil La Baronnie Madeleine Chinon

FRAGRANT SOUTH INDIAN BEEF CURRY

This warming curry has a good bit of heat to it. Serve it with lots of rice to round out the meal.

ACTIVE 20 MIN; TOTAL 2 HR 15 MIN; SERVES 4

2 Tbsp. canola oil

1 medium onion, thinly sliced

12 fresh curry leaves or 2 bay leaves

6 garlic cloves, grated

4 tsp. finely grated peeled fresh ginger

1 Tbsp. tomato paste dissolved in ½ cup water

2 tsp. ground coriander

1 tsp. garam masala

1 tsp. cayenne pepper

½ tsp. ground turmeric

4 small dried hot chiles

4 star anise pods

2 (3-inch) cinnamon sticks

1¾ lb. boneless beef short ribs, cut into ¾-inch pieces

Salt

Hot cooked rice, for serving

1 In a medium-size enameled cast-iron casserole, heat oil until shimmering. Add onion and curry leaves; cook over medium until lightly browned, about 7 minutes. Add garlic and ginger; cook until fragrant, 1 minute. Stir in dissolved tomato paste, coriander, garam masala, cayenne, turmeric, dried chiles, star anise, and cinnamon sticks. Add ribs, season with salt, and stir until coated with spices.

2 Cook, partially covered, over very low heat until meat is tender, about 1 hour 30 minutes. Use a spoon to remove as much fat as possible. Discard star anise, cinnamon sticks, and bay leaves. Serve with hot cooked rice. —ASHA GOMEZ

SPICY POT ROAST WITH ORANGES, SWEET POTATOES, AND CALABRIAN CHILE GREMOLATA

Whole orange segments and freshly squeezed orange juice and zest give this hearty winter braise a burst of fresh citrus flavor. Creamy sweet potatoes and celery root along with tender beef chuck fill out this satisfyingly hearty meal.

ACTIVE 40 MIN; TOTAL 3 HR 10 MIN; SERVES 8

½ cup olive oil, divided

1 (4-lb.) boneless chuck roast, trimmed

4 tsp. kosher salt, plus more to taste

1 tsp. black pepper, plus more to taste

2 oranges, divided

1 medium yellow onion, thinly sliced

2 cups unsalted beef stock or water

1 (28-oz.) can whole peeled San Marzano plum tomatoes, crushed

3 whole Calabrian chiles in oil, divided

1 large sweet potato, peeled and cut into 1-inch pieces

1 lb. celery root, turnips, or rutabagas, peeled and cut into 1-inch pieces

½ cup packed chopped fresh flat-leaf parsley

Crusty bread, for serving

1 Preheat oven to 300°F. Heat ¼ cup oil in a large Dutch oven over medium-high. Season roast with salt and pepper. Add roast to Dutch oven and sear, turning occasionally, until browned on all sides, 15 to 20 minutes. Transfer to a plate, and set aside.

2 Scrub 1 orange and cut into 8 wedges; discard seeds and core, and set aside. Add onion to Dutch oven; cook over medium, stirring and scraping bottom of pan often with a wooden spoon, until onion is soft and translucent, about 8 minutes. (Add ¼ cup water while cooking onion if too many browned bits accumulate.) Add beef stock, tomatoes, 1 chile, and orange wedges; bring to a boil. Return chuck roast and any accumulated juices to pan; bring to a simmer over high.

3 Cover and transfer to preheated oven; braise 1 hour 30 minutes. Uncover and stir in sweet potato and celery root. Return to oven, and braise, uncovered, until meat and vegetables are tender but not falling apart, 1 hour to 1 hour 30 minutes. Remove from oven, and let rest 15 minutes. Transfer chuck roast to a work surface; shred into large pieces. Skim off and discard fat from Dutch oven. Return shredded beef to Dutch oven.

4 While meat rests, zest remaining orange to equal 1 tablespoon zest and squeeze to yield 3 tablespoons juice. Finely chop remaining 2 chiles to equal 1 tablespoon. Stir together parsley, orange zest and juice, chopped chiles, and remaining ¼ cup oil; season with salt and pepper to taste. Divide roast mixture evenly among bowls; top with gremolata. Serve with crusty bread. —JUSTIN SMILLIE

MAKE AHEAD After roast is shredded and returned to Dutch oven, let cool to room temperature. Cover and refrigerate up to 2 days. Gently reheat over low.

WINE Earthy Calabrian red: 2015 Librandi Duca Sanfelice Cirò Rosso Riserva

NOTE We like the Tutto Calabria brand of Calabrian chiles.

JAMAICAN BRAISED OXTAILS
WITH CARROTS AND CHILES

This Jamaican braised oxtail recipe, by Novelist Bryan Washington, is an homage to one prepared by his mother. Perfumed by plenty of warming spices, hot Scotch bonnet chiles, and fresh thyme, this dish is rounded out with sweet carrots and creamy beans.

ACTIVE 1 HR 20 MIN; TOTAL 3 HR 20 MIN, PLUS 8 HR REFRIGERATION; SERVES 4

- 2 lb. oxtails, cut into 2-inch pieces
- 2 small yellow onions, finely chopped
- 1 cup thinly sliced scallions (white and light green parts), plus sliced dark green tops, for garnish
- ⅓ cup packed light brown sugar
- 2 Tbsp. soy sauce
- 2 Tbsp. ground allspice
- 1 Tbsp. black pepper
- 1 Tbsp. Worcestershire sauce
- 2½ tsp. kosher salt, or to taste
- 4 medium garlic cloves, smashed
- 2 fresh Scotch bonnet chiles, stemmed and chopped
- 1¼ cups dried butter beans
- 2 Tbsp. vegetable oil
- 4 cups water, divided
- 2 tsp. fresh thyme leaves
- 3 medium carrots, chopped into 1½-inch pieces

1 Combine oxtails, onions, white and light green scallion slices, brown sugar, soy sauce, allspice, black pepper, Worcestershire sauce, salt, garlic, and chiles in a large bowl; toss to coat. Cover with plastic wrap. Place beans in a separate large bowl; add cold water to cover by about 3 inches. Cover with plastic wrap. Place both bowls in refrigerator for at least 8 hours or up to 12 hours.

2 Drain beans; set aside until ready to use. Heat oil in a large Dutch oven over medium-high until shimmering. Using a slotted spoon or tongs, add oxtails, reserving marinade in bowl. Cook oxtails, turning occasionally, until evenly browned on all sides, about 15 minutes. Remove from heat.

3 Remove oxtails from Dutch oven, and set aside. Discard drippings, and return oxtails to Dutch oven. Add beans, reserved oxtail marinade, 3 cups water, and the thyme.

4 Cover Dutch oven; cook over low, stirring mixture and turning oxtails every 30 minutes and adjusting heat as needed to maintain a very low simmer, until meat is tender when pierced with a paring knife but not yet falling apart, about 2 hours.

5 Add carrots to oxtail mixture; uncover and cook over low, undisturbed, adjusting heat as needed to maintain a very low simmer, until carrots are tender, meat easily pulls away from bone with a fork, and sauce starts to thicken, about 45 minutes, skimming fat from surface as needed. Gradually stir in up to remaining 1 cup water as needed until sauce reaches a gravy consistency.

6 If desired, remove oxtails from pot; shred meat and discard bones. Stir shredded meat back into pot. Divide mixture evenly among bowls; garnish with reserved dark green scallion slices. —BRYAN WASHINGTON

MAKE AHEAD Oxtails can be made up to 3 days ahead.

BEER Crisp Jamaican beer: Red Stripe Lager

WINE-BRAISED BEEF WITH GREEN-GARLIC SOUBISE AND YOUNG CHICORIES

Suzanne Goin, the chef at the famed Lucques in Los Angeles, marked 20 years of business in 2018 with a dinner that celebrated her now-classic blend of French cuisine and California produce. Beef cheeks add to the glistening, wine-fortified sauce.

ACTIVE 1 HR 20 MIN; TOTAL 14 HR 40 MIN; SERVES 6

WINE-BRAISED BEEF

- 3 lb. cleaned beef cheeks or chuck roast, cut into 2-inch cubes
- 1 Tbsp. fresh thyme leaves
- 1 Tbsp. plus ⅛ tsp. cracked black pepper, divided
- 4 thyme sprigs
- 1 Tbsp. plus ¼ tsp. kosher salt, divided
- ¼ cup extra-virgin olive oil, divided
- 1 medium yellow onion, chopped
- 1 medium carrot, chopped
- 1 celery stalk, chopped
- 2½ cups hearty red wine (such as Burgundy)
- 1½ cups ruby port
- 2 Tbsp. balsamic vinegar
- 6 cups beef or veal stock
- 4 fresh flat-leaf parsley sprigs
- 2 bay leaves
- 8 loosely packed cups mixed baby chicories (such as radicchio, treviso, dandelion, and baby kale)
- 1 Tbsp. fresh lemon juice

GREEN-GARLIC SOUBISE

- ¼ cup cold unsalted butter, cubed
- 6 cups thinly sliced white onion
- 1 cup chopped white onion
- 1 Tbsp. fresh thyme leaves
- 2 tsp. kosher salt, plus more to taste
- Freshly ground black pepper
- ¼ cup uncooked Arborio rice
- ⅓ cup heavy cream
- 4 oz. Gruyère cheese, grated
- ½ cup thinly diagonally sliced green garlic, or 3 garlic cloves, sliced
- 2 Tbsp. chopped fresh flat-leaf parsley

1 **Make the wine-braised beef:** Place beef cheeks on a wire rack set inside a rimmed baking sheet; season with thyme leaves and 1 tablespoon pepper. Place thyme sprigs on top of beef cheeks. Cover and chill 8 hours or overnight. Let beef cheeks stand at room temperature 1 hour 30 minutes before cooking.

2 Sprinkle beef cheeks with 1 tablespoon salt. Preheat oven to 325°F. Heat 3 tablespoons oil in a large Dutch oven, until oil is fragrant and almost smoking. Add beef cheeks, and sear, turning occasionally, until deeply browned on all sides, 15 to 20 minutes; transfer to a plate. Reduce heat to medium-high; add onion, carrot, and celery, and cook, stirring occasionally, until vegetables are lightly caramelized, about 5 minutes. Stir in red wine, port, and vinegar, scraping bottom of Dutch oven to loosen any browned bits. Bring to a boil over high, and cook, stirring occasionally, until reduced by three-fourths, about 15 minutes. Add stock, and bring to a boil.

3 Add parsley, bay leaves, and beef cheeks and their juices. Cover Dutch oven tightly with aluminum foil; cover with lid. Braise until meat is tender and easily pierced with a paring knife, about 3 hours. Remove from oven, uncover, and set aside. Increase oven temperature to 400°F.

4 Let meat rest 30 minutes in juices, then transfer meat to a large plate. Pour braising liquid through a fine wire-mesh strainer over a bowl; discard solids. Let strained liquid stand 5 minutes; skim off and discard fat. Return beef cheeks and strained braising liquid to Dutch oven.

5 Roast, uncovered, at 400°F until meat is hot and caramelized on top, about 15 minutes.

6 Toss together chicories, lemon juice, and remaining 1 tablespoon oil. Season with remaining ⅛ teaspoon pepper and ¼ teaspoon salt.

7 To serve, divide hot Green-Garlic Soubise evenly among 6 large bowls; top evenly with dressed chicories. Place beef cheeks on chicories, and ladle some braising liquid over each serving.

8 **Make the Green-Garlic Soubise:** Preheat oven to 350°F. Melt butter in a Dutch oven over medium. When butter foams, add onions, thyme, salt, and pepper. Cook, stirring occasionally, until onions soften but do not color, about 12 minutes. Remove from heat.

9 While onions are cooking, bring a small pot of water to a boil over medium-high. Add rice, and cook 5 minutes. Drain and stir rice into onions.

10 Cover Dutch oven with aluminum foil; cover with lid. Bake 30 minutes. Remove from oven; let stand, covered, until rice is tender, about 15 minutes. Stir heavy cream and Gruyère into hot onion mixture until cheese is melted and mixture is creamy. Season to taste. Stir in garlic and parsley until combined. —SUZANNE GOIN

WINE Earthy, herbal Cabernet Franc: 2016 Russiz Superiore Collio

HUNGARIAN GOULASH

Hungarian paprika and caraway seeds jump-start the flavor of this comforting stew.

ACTIVE 1 HR; TOTAL 3 HR 30 MIN; SERVES 8

6 oz. thinly sliced bacon, chopped

2½ lb. well-marbled boneless beef chuck, cut into 1½-inch pieces

Kosher salt and black pepper

2 onions, chopped

¼ cup Hungarian sweet paprika

1 Tbsp. tomato paste

½ tsp. caraway seeds

2 Tbsp. apple cider vinegar, divided

1½ lb. small Yukon Gold potatoes, cut into 1-inch pieces

1 green bell pepper, chopped

2 tsp. fish sauce, optional

Sour cream and toasted rye bread, for serving

1 In a large Dutch oven cook bacon over medium until crisp, about 7 minutes. Using a slotted spoon, transfer bacon to a plate, leaving fat in pan.

2 Season beef with salt and pepper. In batches, add beef to pot, and cook in bacon fat over medium-high until browned all over, about 5 minutes per batch. Using a slotted spoon, transfer beef to plate with bacon.

3 Add ¼ cup water and the onions to pot. Cook, stirring with a wooden spoon and scraping up browned bits, until all liquid is evaporated and onion is softened, about 6 minutes. Add paprika, tomato paste, and caraway seeds; cook, stirring, 1 minute.

4 Add 7 cups of water and 1 tablespoon apple cider vinegar; return meat and any accumulated juices to pot. Bring goulash to a boil, cover partially, and simmer over low 1 hour 30 minutes.

5 Add potatoes and bell pepper to pot. Simmer, partially covered, over low until beef is very tender and sauce is slightly thickened, about 1 hour.

6 Stir in fish sauce, if using, and remaining 1 tablespoon apple cider vinegar. Season with salt and pepper. Ladle into bowls and serve with sour cream and rye bread.

—ANTHONY BOURDAIN

SPICED BEEF PHO WITH SESAME-CHILE OIL

This rice vermicelli-based soup is a staple all over Vietnam and this spicy beef version is the specialty of Hanoi. At home in Connecticut, cookbook author Marcia Kiesel often eats it for breakfast, as the Vietnamese do.

ACTIVE 1 HR; TOTAL 3 HR; SERVES 6

BEEF BROTH

- 4 lb. oxtails or beef short ribs
- 1 tsp. vegetable oil
- 1 medium onion, halved
- 1 (3-inch) piece unpeeled fresh ginger, halved lengthwise
- 2 bay leaves
- 2 (3-inch) cinnamon sticks, broken into pieces
- 1 (2-inch) piece rock sugar or 6 sugar cubes (see Note)
- Kosher salt
- 4 whole cloves
- 4 star anise pods, broken into pieces
- 2 tsp. fennel seeds

SESAME-CHILE OIL

- ¼ cup vegetable oil
- 3 large garlic cloves, chopped
- 2 Tbsp. crushed red pepper
- 1½ tsp. sesame seeds
- ½ tsp. Asian sesame oil
- Kosher salt

- 1 lb. rice vermicelli
- 1 lb. beef round, partially frozen and very thinly sliced across the grain

CONDIMENTS

- Asian fish sauce
- Asian sesame oil
- Sriracha chile sauce
- Lime wedges
- Fresh cilantro sprigs
- Fresh basil leaves
- Sliced onion
- Sliced chiles
- Escarole leaves
- Mung bean sprouts

1 **Make the beef broth:** In a large soup pot cover oxtails with cold water and bring to a boil over high. Drain off water. Add 18 cups water and bring to a boil.

2 Meanwhile, heat oil in a small nonstick skillet. Add onion and ginger, cut-sides down, and cook over medium until richly browned, about 5 minutes. Add onion and ginger, bay leaves, cinnamon sticks, rock sugar, and 1 tablespoon kosher salt to pot.

3 Place cloves, star anise, and fennel seeds in a tea ball or tie them up in a piece of cheesecloth. Add to pot and simmer, skimming occasionally, until oxtails are tender, about 2 hours. Strain broth in a large sieve set over a heatproof bowl. Remove meat from oxtails. Refrigerate broth and meat separately overnight.

4 **Make the Sesame-Chile Oil:** Heat ¼ cup vegetable oil in a small saucepan. Add garlic and cook over medium until golden, about 2 minutes. Add crushed red pepper and sesame seeds, and cook 1 minute; transfer to a bowl. Stir in sesame oil and a pinch of salt.

5 Place vermicelli in a large bowl and cover with cold water. Let vermicelli soak until pliable, about 20 minutes.

6 Skim and discard fat from surface of broth. Bring broth to a simmer over medium. Bring a large saucepan of water to a boil.

7 Place thinly sliced raw beef in a large strainer and lower it into the simmering broth for 4 seconds; transfer the meat to 6 soup bowls. Drain vermicelli. Working in 6 batches, put vermicelli in strainer and lower it into the boiling water for 30 seconds, or until the vermicelli is barely tender. Drain and transfer to bowls. Ladle about 1½ cups of the broth over each bowl of vermicelli and add chilled oxtail meat.

8 Place condiments in separate bowls, or arrange vegetables and herbs together on a platter. Serve soup with condiments and sesame-chile oil. —MARCIA KIESEL

MAKE AHEAD The beef broth and oxtail meat can be refrigerated up to 3 days. The Sesame-Chile Oil can be refrigerated overnight. Return both to room temperature before serving.

BEER A bottle of cold and refreshing Hue or "33" Export, both light Vietnamese lagers

NOTE Rock sugar is in large amber crystals and is less sweet than refined granulated white sugar. It is available at Asian markets.

ROPA VIEJA

Cuban-born photographer Romulo Yanes shares a recipe for classic Cuban Ropa Vieja, which literally translates as "old clothes." Skirt steak braises until tender in the pressure cooker before being shredded and stewed in a rich tomato sauce.

ACTIVE 50 MIN; TOTAL 1 HR 40 MIN; SERVES 8

6 Tbsp. olive oil, divided

2½ lb. skirt steak, cut along the grain into 6-inch pieces

3½ tsp. kosher salt, divided

2 large white onions, halved

2 large green bell peppers, halved

1 bay leaf

3 garlic cloves, peeled and smashed, divided

1 tsp. ground cumin

1 tsp. dried oregano

⅓ cup dry white wine

2 cups crushed tomatoes (canned or fresh)

1 Heat 2 tablespoons oil in an uncovered pressure cooker over medium-high. Sprinkle steak with 2 teaspoons salt. Working in batches, sear steak pieces until well browned, 2 to 3 minutes per side. Transfer to a medium bowl. Add 1 onion half and 1 bell pepper half to pressure cooker; cook, stirring after 2 minutes, until browned in spots, about 5 minutes. Return steak to pressure cooker; add 5 cups water, bay leaf, and 1 garlic clove. Lock lid into place and set pressure to HIGH (15 pounds); bring up to pressure over high heat. When pressurized, reduce heat to medium and cook 20 minutes. Remove from heat, release pressure, and let stand until pressure is completely released.

2 When pressure cooker unlocks, transfer steak to a bowl; cool 10 minutes. When cool enough to handle, shred steak by hand. (Pieces do not need to be uniform.) Return shredded meat to bowl. Pour cooking liquid through a fine wire-mesh strainer into a bowl; reserve 2 cups liquid. Discard solids and remaining liquid.

3 Thinly slice remaining onion and bell pepper halves. Heat remaining ¼ cup oil in a large high-sided skillet over medium. Add sliced onions, peppers, and remaining 2 garlic cloves to skillet. Cook, stirring often, until onions are translucent, about 10 minutes. Stir in cumin and oregano. Add wine. Bring to a simmer; add shredded steak and remaining 1½ teaspoons salt. Fold to incorporate with vegetables.

4 Simmer until meat is warmed through, about 5 minutes. Add tomatoes and 2 cups reserved cooking liquid. Bring to a simmer, stirring. Cover and reduce heat to medium-low. Gently simmer, stirring every 5 minutes, until meat is tender and liquid is thickened, about 20 minutes. If necessary, uncover and cook several minutes to thicken sauce. —ROMULO YANES

WINE Robust, dark-fruited Zinfandel: 2015 Ridge Vineyard Ponzo

STEAK-AND-SHRIMP HOT POT

Cooking tender rib eye, fresh mushrooms, and sweet shrimp tableside makes for an interactive holiday meal. The broth—already seasoned and spiced with fresh aromatics, oils, and sauces—deepens in flavor as you cook vegetables, meats, and, eventually, noodles throughout the night. Keep the broth at a simmer to safely cook each ingredient.

TOTAL 45 MIN; SERVES 8

Hot Pot Broth (recipe follows)

1 lb. baby bok choy (about 7 heads), cut into small pieces

2 fresh enoki mushroom bunches (about 8 oz.), trimmed and cut into small bundles

1 lb. daikon, peeled and cut into ¼-inch-thick half-moons (about 3 cups)

1 (14-oz.) pkg. firm tofu, drained, halved lengthwise, and cut crosswise into ¼-inch-thick slices

1 lb. peeled and deveined tail-on raw medium shrimp

½ lb. sea scallops, sliced crosswise

1 (1½-lb., 1½-inch-thick) rib eye steak, frozen until firm and thinly sliced crosswise with a sharp chef's knife

Hot Pot Dipping Sauce (recipe follows)

3 (6-oz.) pkg. frozen steamed dumplings (such as Bibigo Pork & Vegetable Steamed Dumplings) (about 16 dumplings)

2 lb. uncooked refrigerated udon noodles

1 Place broth in a one-compartment electric shabu-shabu hot pot (or shallow stockpot). Place hot pot in center of dinner table and heat according to manufacturer's instructions (or place stockpot on a hot plate in center of table). Bring broth to a gentle simmer in pot; maintain during cooking. (To help maintain simmer, do not overcrowd ingredients.) Place vegetables, tofu, seafood, and steak on serving trays on dinner table.

2 Using chopsticks, small hot pot strainers, and small tongs, dip, cook, and eat items in batches; serve with dipping sauce. Cook bok choy and mushrooms until crisp-tender, 1 to 2 minutes; cook daikon pieces until crisp-tender, 3 to 4 minutes; cook tofu until just warmed through, about 30 seconds; cook shrimp and scallops until just cooked through and opaque, 2 to 3 minutes; cook steak to desired degree of doneness. When all the meat and vegetables have been eaten, add dumplings to broth, and cook according to package directions. Remove dumplings, and add noodles to broth. Cook noodles according to package directions. (The noodles will absorb and help thicken the broth.) Divide noodles and dumplings among bowls. Ladle thickened broth into bowls. —NICK WONG

MAKE AHEAD Vegetables can be prepped and refrigerated up to 1 day in advance.

WINE Bright, spicy red: 2017 Fratelli Alessandria Speziale Verduno Pelaverga

HOT POT BROTH

Infusing chicken stock with fresh herbs and aromatics, as well as classic condiments like hot chile-sesame oil and chile bean sauce, quickly adds layers of flavor. Keep additional salt light—the broth will become saltier as you cook the ingredients.

TOTAL 50 MIN; MAKES 8 CUPS

2 Tbsp. sesame oil

2 Tbsp. Chiu Chow-style chile oil (such as Lee Kum Kee) or hot chile-sesame oil

9 garlic cloves, smashed

1 (3-inch) piece fresh ginger, thinly sliced (about ¼ cup)

1 (5-oz.) bunch scallions, quartered

6 whole star anise

3 black cardamom pods

2 Tbsp. toban djan or chile bean sauce (such as Lee Kum Kee)

3 qt. best-quality lower-sodium chicken broth (such as Imagine)

2 Tbsp. soy sauce, plus more to taste

1 Heat sesame oil and chile oil in a large saucepan over medium; add garlic, ginger, and scallions. Cook, stirring often, until scallion mixture is wilted and ginger is caramelized in spots, 5 to 7 minutes. Add star anise and cardamom; cook, stirring constantly, until fragrant, about 1 minute. Add chile bean sauce, and stir to coat. Add chicken broth, and bring to a boil over high.

2 Reduce heat to low, and simmer, stirring and scraping bottom of pan occasionally, until broth is spicy, aromatic, and has a slight smokiness from the cardamom, about 20 minutes. Strain broth; discard solids. Stir in soy sauce, adding more to taste. —NW

MAKE AHEAD Broth can be made 2 days in advance, or frozen up to 3 months.

NOTE Chile oil, black cardamom, and toban djan can be found at Asian grocery stores.

HOT POT DIPPING SAUCE

Using pasteurized eggs makes this dipping sauce safe to eat raw and thickens the sauce to a luxurious consistency.

TOTAL 15 MIN; SERVES 8

3 large pasteurized eggs

⅓ cup sliced scallions

6 Tbsp. hoisin sauce

6 Tbsp. seasoned rice wine vinegar

3 Tbsp. soy sauce

3 Tbsp. satay sauce (such as Lee Kum Kee)

3 Tbsp. sriracha

1 Tbsp. grated peeled fresh ginger

1 Tbsp. finely chopped garlic

1 Tbsp. sesame oil

Whisk together eggs in a medium bowl until thoroughly blended. Whisk in scallions, hoisin sauce, rice wine vinegar, soy sauce, satay sauce, sriracha, ginger, garlic, and sesame oil until well combined. —NW

BO KHO (VIET BEEF STEW WITH STAR ANISE AND LEMONGRASS)

This French-inspired stew, with the aromas of lemongrass and star anise wafting through your home, is a dream simmering on your stovetop. You can enjoy the same flavor in about half the time with help from your electric pressure cooker.

ACTIVE 1 HR; TOTAL 3 HR 30 MIN; SERVES 4 TO 6

- 1 (2-lb.) boneless chuck roast, trimmed and cut into 1½-inch chunks
- 3 oz. lemongrass stalks (2 large or 3 medium stalks), trimmed, cut into 3-inch pieces, and gently smashed with a mallet or heavy saucepan
- 3 Tbsp. fish sauce (such as Three Crabs), plus more to taste
- 2 tsp. light or dark brown sugar
- 1½ tsp. five-spice powder
- ¼ cup canola oil or other neutral oil (such as grapeseed), divided
- 1 cup chopped shallots or yellow onion
- 3 Tbsp. minced peeled fresh ginger
- 1 Tbsp. finely chopped garlic
- 1½ cups canned crushed tomatoes
- 2 whole star anise
- 1 fresh bay leaf
- ½ tsp. fine sea salt, plus more to taste
- 1 lb. carrots, peeled and cut into 1-inch pieces
- ¼ cup coarsely chopped fresh cilantro, mint, or basil

1 Toss together beef, lemongrass, fish sauce, brown sugar, and five-spice in a large bowl. Let beef marinate at room temperature 30 minutes.

2 Heat a Dutch oven over high until very hot; add 1 tablespoon oil. Remove one-third of beef from marinade, and add to Dutch oven. Cook, stirring often, until lightly browned on 2 to 3 sides, 2 to 3 minutes. Transfer seared beef to a plate. Repeat process twice with 2 tablespoons oil and remaining beef, reserving marinade in bowl. (If there is excessive browning on bottom of Dutch oven, reduce heat to medium.)

3 Reduce heat to medium-low. Add shallots, ginger, garlic, and remaining 1 tablespoon oil; cook, stirring often, until fragrant, 3 to 4 minutes. Stir in tomatoes, star anise, bay leaf, and salt. Bring mixture to a simmer; cover and cook, stirring occasionally, until mixture reduces and thickens slightly, 12 to 14 minutes.

4 Return beef and accumulated juices on plate to Dutch oven; stir in reserved beef marinade. Cook, stirring often, until tomato mixture thickens and coats beef, about 5 minutes. Stir in 5 cups water; bring to a boil over high. Reduce heat to low; cover and simmer until beef yields slightly when pierced with a knife, about 1 hour 15 minutes.

5 Skim and discard fat from surface of stew. Stir carrots into stew; bring to a boil over high. Reduce heat to low; simmer, uncovered, until beef and carrots are tender and sauce has thickened and coats the back of a spoon, about 45 minutes. Remove from heat; let stand, uncovered, 5 to 10 minutes.

6 Taste stew; if needed, add more fish sauce or salt to intensify flavor, or add a few splashes of water to lighten flavors. Remove and discard lemongrass, star anise, and bay leaf. Divide stew among shallow bowls; sprinkle with cilantro.
—ANDREA NGUYEN

MAKE AHEAD This stew develops fabulous flavor when made 1 or 2 days ahead. Store, covered, in refrigerator.

WINE Spicy, light-bodied red: 2016 Feudo di Santa Tresa Frappato

BELGIAN BEEF STEW

Chef Andrew Zimmern calls this recipe "a one-pot rock-star beef stew that will warm you from the inside out."

ACTIVE 45 MIN; TOTAL 2 HR 45 MIN; SERVES 6

3 lb. trimmed beef chuck, cut into 1½-inch pieces

Kosher salt

Ground white pepper

1½ cups all-purpose flour

6 Tbsp. canola oil

3 medium onions, thinly sliced

4 garlic cloves, minced

1 (12-oz.) bottle Duvel or other Belgian golden ale

1 qt. beef stock or low-sodium broth

3 thyme sprigs, 3 parsley sprigs, and 1 bay leaf, tied in cheesecloth

10 new potatoes, halved

2 large carrots, cut into ½-inch pieces

1 Tbsp. Dijon mustard

2 Tbsp. red wine vinegar

Chopped fresh flat-leaf parsley, for garnish

1 Preheat oven to 325°F. Season beef with salt and white pepper. In a large zip-top plastic bag combine beef and flour; shake well. Remove beef from bag, shaking off excess flour. Heat 2 tablespoons canola oil in a large enameled cast-iron casserole. Add one-third of the beef and cook over medium until browned all over, about 5 minutes; transfer to a plate. Repeat with remaining oil and beef.

2 Pour off all but 2 tablespoons fat from casserole. Add onions; season with salt and white pepper. Cook over medium, stirring, until softened and browned, about 8 minutes. Add garlic and cook until fragrant, about 1 minute. Add beer and cook, scraping up any browned bits. Return meat to casserole; add stock and herb bundle. Bring to a boil; remove from heat. Bake, covered, 1 hour 30 minutes or until meat is tender.

3 Add potatoes and carrots to the meat. Bake, covered, until tender, about 25 minutes more. Discard herb bundle. Stir in mustard and vinegar; season with salt and white pepper. Garnish with parsley. —ANDREW ZIMMERN

WINE Dark-fruited Italian red: 2011 Di Majo Norante Ramitello

SWISS ARMY STEW

We love this dish for its simplicity. Everything goes into one pot; a few hours later a meal ideal for the depths of winter emerges. It's just the right kind of healthy eating for that post-holiday detox, without sacrificing flavor and satisfaction.

ACTIVE 35 MIN; TOTAL 2 HR 5 MIN; SERVES 8

2 qt. beef broth

2 lb. beef chuck roast, trimmed of excess fat and cut into 1-inch pieces

1 Tbsp. plus 1 tsp. kosher salt, plus more to taste

2 bay leaves (preferably fresh)

4 whole cloves

1 large onion, halved

¾ tsp. black pepper

½ tsp. freshly grated nutmeg

1 (1½-lb.) small head Savoy cabbage, cored and coarsely shredded

1 lb. waxy baby potatoes, halved

5 medium carrots, trimmed and cut into ¾-inch pieces (about 1½ cups)

1 medium celery root, peeled and cut into ¾-inch pieces (about 2½ cups)

3 celery stalks, trimmed and cut into ¾-inch pieces (about 1¾ cups)

1 leek, white and light green parts only, cut into ¼-inch slices (about 1 cup)

2 Tbsp. apple cider vinegar

2 Tbsp. minced fresh chives

Sliced hearty brown bread, for serving

1 Bring broth and 1 quart water to a boil in a large stockpot over high. Season beef with 1 teaspoon salt. Stud each bay leaf with 2 cloves.

2 Place seasoned beef, clove-studded bay leaves, onion halves, black pepper, nutmeg, and remaining 1 tablespoon salt in boiling broth mixture. Reduce heat to medium-low to maintain a steady simmer; cook 1 hour.

3 Remove and discard onion halves and clove-studded bay leaves. Add cabbage, potatoes, carrots, celery root, celery, leek, and vinegar to beef mixture; return to a steady simmer over medium-low. Cook until vegetables are very tender but not falling apart, 30 to 40 minutes. Add salt to taste. Serve stew sprinkled with chives and with slices of brown bread on the side. —ANDREA SLONECKER

SMOKED BRISKET NOODLE SOUP

This down-home bowl comes from the brain of Griffin Bufkin, proprietor of Southern Soul Barbeque in St. Simons Island, Georgia, who showcases his restaurant's fantastic barbecued brisket—paired with tender egg noodles, okra, corn, and lima beans—in each smoky bite.

ACTIVE 1 HR; TOTAL 1 HR 25 MIN; SERVES 6 TO 8

1 Tbsp. unsalted butter

2 lb. smoked beef brisket, cut into 2-inch pieces

½ medium sweet onion, chopped

1 medium celery stalk, chopped

1 medium carrot, chopped

1 large garlic clove, finely chopped

¼ cup tomato paste

¼ cup (2 oz.) ruby port

4 qt. lower-sodium chicken broth

1 cup shelled fresh or frozen field peas or butter peas

1 bay leaf

1 fresh thyme sprig

1½ cups fresh or frozen okra slices (about 6 oz.)

1 cup fresh or frozen lima beans or butter beans (6 oz.)

1 cup fresh or frozen corn kernels (from 1 ear fresh corn)

Kosher salt and black pepper, to taste

8 oz. uncooked medium egg noodles, cooked

1 Melt butter in a large Dutch oven over medium-high. Add brisket and cook, stirring occasionally, until browned, about 6 minutes. Stir in onion, celery, carrot, and garlic; cook, stirring occasionally, just until softened, about 6 minutes. Add tomato paste; cook, stirring often, until mixture turns rusty brown, about 2 minutes.

2 Add port and stir, scraping up any browned bits from bottom of pan. Stir in broth, field peas, bay leaf, and thyme, and bring to a simmer. Cook 30 minutes.

3 Add okra, lima beans, and corn, and cook, stirring occasionally, until vegetables are tender and flavors have melded, about 40 minutes. Season with salt and pepper to taste. Discard bay leaf and thyme sprig. Serve hot soup over cooked egg noodles. —GRIFFIN BUFKIN

BEEF AND FARRO SOUP

Chef and TV personality Hugh Acheson uses miso to add umami to this hearty and exceptionally savory soup.

ACTIVE 30 MIN; TOTAL 2 HR 40 MIN; SERVES 6

2 Tbsp. canola oil

1½ lb. beef chuck, cut into 1-inch pieces
   Kosher salt and black pepper

9 cups chicken stock

1 head garlic, pierced all over with a knife

3 fresh thyme sprigs

3 bay leaves

1 cup farro

2 medium tomatoes, chopped

1 leek, light green and white parts only, thinly sliced

2 celery ribs, thinly sliced

3 small carrots, chopped

1 small bunch Tuscan kale, chopped (3 cups)

2 Tbsp. white miso

1 tsp. smoked paprika
   Freshly shaved Parmigiano-Reggiano cheese, for garnish

1 Heat canola oil in a large enameled cast-iron casserole. Season meat with salt and pepper; add half to the casserole and cook over medium, turning, until browned, about 5 minutes. Transfer to a large plate, and repeat with remaining meat.

2 Pour off all the oil from the casserole. Add 1 cup stock and stir, scraping up any browned bits. Add the remaining 8 cups of stock along with the meat, garlic, thyme, and bay leaves; bring to a simmer. Cover and cook over low, stirring occasionally, until meat is tender, 1 hour 30 minutes.

3 Stir in farro and bring to a simmer. Cook, covered, over medium until farro is almost tender, 20 minutes. Stir in the tomatoes, leek, celery, carrots, kale, miso, and paprika. Cook, covered, until vegetables are tender, about 10 minutes. Discard garlic, thyme sprigs, and bay leaves. Season with salt and pepper. Ladle soup into bowls; garnish with cheese. —HUGH ACHESON

BEEF CHILI WITH BEANS

This smoky, spicy chili is a slightly modified version of Grant Achatz's mother's chili, made with ancho, pasilla, and chipotle powders, plus a homemade blend of seasonings and fresh herbs.

ACTIVE 30 MIN; TOTAL 2 HR 30 MIN; SERVES 8

3 Tbsp. vegetable oil

3 lb. ground beef chuck

2 large onions, finely chopped

1 green bell pepper, finely chopped

5 garlic cloves, minced

3 Tbsp. ancho chile powder

3 Tbsp. pasilla chile powder

3 Tbsp. ground cumin

2 Tbsp. ground coriander

1 Tbsp. sugar

2 tsp. chopped fresh thyme

2 tsp. chopped fresh oregano

1 tsp. freshly ground black pepper

1 tsp. cayenne pepper

3 cups low-sodium beef broth

1 (15-oz.) can pinto beans

1 (14-oz.) can diced tomatoes with the juices

5 chipotle chiles in adobo, seeded and finely chopped

1 cup tomato sauce

¼ cup tomato paste

1 Tbsp. cider vinegar

Juice of 1 lime

Salt, to taste

1 Heat oil in a large heavy pot or a medium enameled cast-iron casserole. Add half the ground beef and cook over high, breaking it up with a wooden spoon, until browned, about 5 minutes. Transfer beef to a bowl with a slotted spoon. Brown remaining ground beef. Return first batch of browned beef to the pot.

2 Add onions and bell pepper to the pot and cook over medium, stirring occasionally, until onions are translucent, about 8 minutes. Add garlic, chile powders, cumin, coriander, sugar, thyme, oregano, black pepper, and cayenne. Cook 10 minutes, stirring occasionally.

3 Stir in broth, pinto beans, tomatoes, chipotles, tomato sauce, tomato paste, and vinegar. Simmer chili over low 1 hour 30 minutes, stirring occasionally. Add lime juice and season with salt. —GRANT ACHATZ

MAKE AHEAD The chili can be refrigerated up to 3 days.

WINE California Zinfandel that can stand up to bold flavors

PASTRAMI PAD KEE MAO (DRUNKEN NOODLES)

Tender wide rice noodles pick up color and peppery meaty flavor when charred in a wok with thick slices of pastrami. This speedy flavor-packed dish cooks up quickly, so have all the ingredients at the ready before heating the wok.

ACTIVE 20 MIN; TOTAL 25 MIN; SERVES 4

- 2 Tbsp. plus 1 tsp. vegetable oil, divided
- 8 oz. pastrami, trimmed and cut against the grain into ¼-inch-thick slices
- 1 tsp. finely chopped garlic
- ½ to 1 tsp. finely chopped fresh green or red Thai chiles
- 1 cup sliced red bell pepper (¼-inch-wide strips)
- 2 medium jalapeños, stemmed, seeded, and cut lengthwise into ⅛-inch-wide strips (about ⅓ cup)
- 1 lb. fresh wide rice noodles (about ⅓ inch wide), noodles uncoiled and separated
- 2 Tbsp. granulated sugar
- 2 Tbsp. oyster sauce
- 2 Tbsp. black soy sauce
- ½ cup packed fresh Thai basil leaves (about ½ oz.)
- 2 tsp. fish sauce
- 1 tsp. ground white pepper
- Brined green peppercorns, for garnish (optional)

1 Heat a wok over high until it begins to smoke; drizzle 1 teaspoon oil around wok edge. Add pastrami in a single layer around sides of wok. Cook until pastrami is warmed through and fat begins to render, about 1 minute per side. Transfer to a plate lined with paper towels to drain. Cut pastrami into bite-size (about 2-inch) pieces. Carefully wipe wok clean.

2 Return wok to heat over high until it begins to smoke; add remaining 2 tablespoons oil. Add garlic and Thai chiles; cook, stirring constantly, until fragrant, 10 to 15 seconds. Add bell pepper and jalapeños; cook, stirring constantly, until slightly softened, 1 minute to 1 minute and 30 seconds. Add noodles, sugar, oyster sauce, and black soy sauce; toss to evenly coat. Cook, stirring occasionally, until noodles are tender and peppers are softened, 2 to 4 minutes. Add pastrami pieces; cook, stirring often, until heated through, 30 seconds to 1 minute. Remove from heat. Stir in Thai basil, fish sauce, and white pepper. Garnish with green peppercorns, if desired. Serve immediately.

—KRIS YENBAMROONG

WINE Robust red from the Loire Valley: 2019 Clos du Tue-Boeuf Pineau d'Aunis

SOBORO DONBURI (GINGERY GROUND BEEF WITH PEAS OVER RICE)

This hearty Japanese rice bowl features soboro (finely ground meat simmered in soy sauce, dashi, and sake) served over rice to make a hearty meal. Dashi granules or powder for instant dashi broth can be found at well-stocked grocery stores or Asian markets.

ACTIVE 25 MIN; TOTAL 40 MIN; SERVES 4

- 1 lb. 90% lean ground beef
- ⅓ cup sake
- ¼ cup soy sauce
- ¼ cup dashi broth or water
- 1½ Tbsp. granulated sugar
- ½ cup frozen English peas, thawed
- 1 Tbsp. grated peeled fresh ginger
- 5 cups hot cooked rice
- 2 large tomatoes, sliced, or 2 Tbsp. beni shoga (Japanese pickled ginger)

1 Stir together ground beef, sake, soy sauce, dashi, and sugar in a small Dutch oven or medium-size, heavy saucepan. Cook over medium-high, stirring often to break up beef, 5 minutes. Stir in peas and ginger. Cook, stirring occasionally, until liquid is mostly evaporated and beef is no longer pink, about 4 minutes. Remove from heat.

2 Divide rice evenly among 4 large bowls. Spoon ½ cup beef mixture over each. Garnish with pickled ginger. —ELIZABETH ANDOH

SPICY BLACK BEAN STEW WITH LAMB SAUSAGE

Award-winning chef JJ Johnson's feijoada-inspired stew of smoky, spicy black beans and lamb sausage is highly adaptable: Use whatever sausage or meat you have on hand.

ACTIVE 30 MIN; TOTAL 2 HR 30 MIN; SERVES 6

- 2 Tbsp. olive oil
- 1 lb. spicy lamb sausage, casings removed and meat crumbled
- 1 red onion, chopped
- 1 large carrot, chopped
- 1 celery stalk, chopped
- 1 jalapeño, seeded and thinly sliced
  Salt
- 4 garlic cloves, finely chopped
- ½ tsp. ground cumin
- 1 lb. dried black beans, soaked overnight and drained
- 1 chipotle in adobo with sauce, minced
- 2 Tbsp. lime juice
  Steamed rice, chopped fresh cilantro, and orange wedges, for serving

1 Heat oil in a large enameled cast-iron Dutch oven or heavy pot over medium-high. Add sausage and cook, stirring and breaking up meat, until browned, 6 to 8 minutes. Transfer sausage to a paper-towel-lined plate to drain. Add onion, carrot, celery, jalapeño, and ½ teaspoon salt to pot. Cook over medium, stirring occasionally, until softened, about 8 minutes. Add garlic and cumin; cook, stirring, until fragrant, about 1 minute. Stir in beans, chipotle, and sausage. Add 6 cups water and bring to a simmer. Cook, covered, over medium-low until beans are tender, 1 hour 30 minutes to 2 hours.

2 Mash some beans with the back of a fork to make the stew creamy; stir in lime juice and season with salt. Serve stew over steamed rice with cilantro and orange wedges. —JOSEPH JOHNSON

SLOW-ROASTED LAMB SHOULDER
WITH SHALLOTS AND WHITE WINE

Pre-salting the lamb (the longer the better) deepens its flavor and increases moisture and tenderness in the meat. Afterward, a simple sear then braise renders fork-tender shreds of meat. A spoonful of garlicky gremolata heightens those long-cooked flavors.

ACTIVE 50 MIN; TOTAL 4 HR 20 MIN; SERVES 6 TO 8

LAMB

- 1 (6- to 7-lb.) bone-in lamb shoulder, or 1 (4- to 5-lb.) boneless lamb shoulder, tied
- 2 Tbsp. plus 1 tsp. fine sea salt, divided
- 1 Tbsp. black pepper
- ¼ cup plus 2 Tbsp. extra-virgin olive oil, divided
- 1 medium-size yellow onion, roughly chopped
- 6 large shallots, halved lengthwise
- 1 large carrot, roughly chopped
- 2 large celery stalks, roughly chopped
- 1 large garlic head, halved crosswise
- 1 bunch fresh thyme sprigs
- 1 cup dry white wine
- 1 cup fresh orange juice
- 1 Tbsp. wildflower honey
- 1 Tbsp. apple cider vinegar
- 2 (3-inch) orange peel strips

LEMON-OREGANO GREMOLATA

- ½ cup packed finely chopped fresh flat-leaf parsley
- ¼ cup plus 2 Tbsp. extra-virgin olive oil
- 2 Tbsp. apple cider vinegar
- 1 Tbsp. finely chopped fresh oregano
- 1 tsp. lemon zest plus 2 Tbsp. fresh lemon juice
- 1 tsp. fine sea salt, plus more to taste
- 1 tsp. crushed red pepper
- 1 large garlic clove, grated

1 **Make the lamb:** Sprinkle lamb evenly with 2 tablespoons salt and black pepper. Let stand at room temperature 1 hour, or chill, uncovered, at least 8 hours or overnight. (If lamb chills overnight, let stand at room temperature 30 minutes before cooking.)

2 Preheat oven to 350°F with rack in lower third position. Heat ¼ cup oil in a large Dutch oven over medium-high. Add lamb, fat-side down; cook, undisturbed, until deep golden brown, 12 to 15 minutes. Carefully turn lamb over; cook, turning occasionally, until golden on all sides, 12 to 15 minutes. Remove lamb from Dutch oven. Discard drippings. Wipe Dutch oven clean.

3 Add remaining 2 tablespoons oil to Dutch oven; heat over medium. Add onion, shallots, carrot, celery, and remaining 1 teaspoon salt. Cook, stirring occasionally, until vegetables soften and begin to brown, 10 to 12 minutes. Reduce heat to low. Add garlic and thyme; cook, stirring often, until garlic is fragrant, about 1 minute. Stir in wine, orange juice, honey, vinegar, and orange peel strips. Nestle lamb, fat-side up, on vegetable mixture; bring to a boil over medium. Remove from heat, and cover. Transfer to preheated oven, and roast until lamb is fork-tender, 2 hours to 2 hours 30 minutes.

4 **Make the Lemon-Oregano Gremolata:** Stir together all gremolata ingredients in a bowl. Let stand 10 minutes. Season with salt to taste.

5 Remove lamb from Dutch oven and transfer to a platter. Tent with aluminum foil; let rest 30 minutes before slicing. Serve with gremolata. —ARIA ALPERT ADJAN

WINE Earthy, emphatic Pinot Noir: 2018 Marine Layer Gravenstein Vineyard

HARISSA LAMB SKILLET LASAGNA

Chicken broth dials up the richness of this stovetop lasagna, while harissa and ground lamb add a modern, Middle Eastern twist.

ACTIVE 35 MIN; TOTAL 1 HR; SERVES 6

- 1 Tbsp. extra-virgin olive oil
- 1 lb. ground lamb
- 1 tsp. kosher salt, divided
- ¾ tsp. black pepper, divided
- 1 yellow onion, finely chopped
- 2 Tbsp. harissa paste (such as Dea Harissa)
- 3 medium garlic cloves, sliced
- 6 cups fresh spinach leaves
- 1 lb. uncooked dried lasagna noodles, broken into 1- to 2-inch pieces
- 3 cups jarred marinara sauce
- 2 cups chicken stock
- 1¼ cups whole-milk ricotta cheese
- ¾ oz. Parmesan cheese, finely grated (about ½ cup), plus more for serving
- Chopped fresh flat-leaf parsley

1 Heat oil in a deep 12- to 14-inch skillet over medium-high until shimmering. Add lamb, and season with ½ teaspoon salt and ½ teaspoon pepper. Cook, breaking up meat with a spoon, until fat has rendered and meat is browned, 6 to 8 minutes. Using a slotted spoon, transfer lamb to a bowl, and set aside. Spoon off and discard all but 1 tablespoon rendered drippings from skillet.

2 Reduce heat to medium and add onion, harissa, garlic, remaining ½ teaspoon salt, and remaining ¼ teaspoon pepper. Cook, stirring occasionally, until onion is softened, about 8 minutes. Stir in spinach until just wilted, 1 to 2 minutes. Stir in lasagna noodles, marinara, stock, and reserved lamb (it's OK if noodles aren't completely submerged). Bring to a simmer over high; reduce heat to medium-low, cover, and cook until pasta is al dente and most of the sauce is absorbed, 20 to 25 minutes, stirring once after 10 minutes.

3 Dollop ricotta over lasagna, and sprinkle with Parmesan. Cover and cook over medium-low until cheese is hot and melted, about 5 minutes. Garnish with parsley and additional Parmesan. Serve with a big green salad and garlic bread.
—JUSTIN CHAPPLE

RED WINE VENISON STEW

Made with venison, this stew is intensely flavored and has a silky, thick sauce that clings to the vegetables and meat as they slowly cook together. Beef chuck roast works very well here, too, but may add more fat, so be sure to skim the final stew before serving.

ACTIVE 1 HR 50 MIN; TOTAL 4 HR; SERVES 8

¼ cup all-purpose flour

1 Tbsp. kosher salt, plus more to taste

½ tsp. black pepper, plus more to taste

1 (4-lb.) boneless venison or chuck roast, trimmed and cut into 2-inch cubes

7 to 8 Tbsp. bacon drippings (from about 1 lb. thick-cut bacon, cooked) or vegetable oil, divided

8 fresh thyme sprigs

4 whole cloves, crushed

8 juniper berries, crushed

3 bay leaves

3 (2-inch) lemon peel strips plus 3 Tbsp. fresh lemon juice (from 2 lemons), divided

3 medium yellow onions, large diced (about 5 cups)

4 medium carrots, peeled and large diced (about 1½ cups)

10 oz. sliced fresh cremini mushrooms (about 3½ cups)

4 large garlic cloves, chopped

1 (28-oz.) can whole peeled plum tomatoes, crushed

4 cups beef bone broth (such as Brodo)

1½ cups full-bodied, robust red wine (such as Cabernet Sauvignon or Syrah)

Cooked egg noodles

Chopped fresh flat-leaf parsley and sour cream, for serving

1 Preheat oven to 350°F. Toss together flour, salt, and pepper in a large bowl; add venison, and toss to coat.

2 Heat 2 tablespoons bacon drippings in a large Dutch oven over medium. Working in four batches, add venison and cook, turning occasionally, until well browned, about 15 minutes per batch. Transfer venison to a plate. Add more bacon drippings, 1 tablespoon at a time, between batches as needed. (If necessary, deglaze Dutch oven with water [save this water and return to pan when adding broth], and wipe clean, then start next batch with 2 tablespoons bacon drippings.)

3 Place thyme, cloves, juniper berries, bay leaves, and lemon peel strips in a double layer of cheesecloth. Gather edges of cheesecloth; tie securely with kitchen twine, and set aside.

4 Add onions, carrots, mushrooms, garlic, and remaining 2 tablespoons bacon drippings to Dutch oven. Cook, stirring occasionally, until onions are softened, about 15 minutes. Add tomatoes, broth, cheesecloth bundle, lemon juice, and browned venison along with any drippings accumulated on plate. Return to a simmer over medium-high; transfer to preheated oven. Braise, uncovered, until venison is fork-tender, about 2 hours, stirring in wine after 1 hour.

5 Return Dutch oven to stovetop and bring to a simmer over medium. Reduce heat to low and gently simmer until sauce has thickened slightly, 10 to 15 minutes. Remove from heat; skim and discard fat from surface of stew. Remove and discard cheesecloth bundle. Season with salt and pepper to taste. Serve over egg noodles and top with parsley and sour cream. —RAY ISLE

PORK

GEERA PORK (SPICY CUMIN-BRAISED PORK) (P. 74)

MISO-CRUSTED PORK ROAST WITH APPLES

White Rose Miso makes a sweet potato miso that Baltimore chef Spike Gjerde loves to feature; substitute red miso if you can't find it. If the pork shoulder comes pre-tied, untie before rubbing with miso, then re-tie.

ACTIVE 25 MIN; TOTAL 11 HR 50 MIN, INCLUDING 8 HR REFRIGERATION; SERVES 6

½ cup sweet potato miso (such as White Rose Miso) or red miso

3 Tbsp. canola oil

2 Tbsp. granulated sugar

1 tsp. fish pepper flakes or crushed red pepper

1 (2-lb.) boneless pork shoulder

2 medium yellow onions, cut crosswise into ½-inch-thick slices

4 medium Pink Lady apples, cut into ¾-inch wedges

2 Tbsp. unsalted butter, melted

¼ tsp. medium-grind sea salt

⅛ tsp. black pepper

1 Stir together miso, oil, sugar, and fish pepper flakes in a small bowl. Rub mixture all over pork shoulder. Using kitchen twine, tie pork shoulder to shape into a uniform size. Wrap tightly in plastic wrap and chill 8 hours or overnight.

2 Preheat oven to 300°F. Arrange onion slices in a single layer in a large cast-iron skillet. Unwrap pork shoulder; place on onions. Tent pork with parchment paper; cover with aluminum foil. Roast 2 hours. Uncover pork, and roast until a thermometer inserted in center registers 150°F, about 30 minutes.

3 Toss apples with butter, salt, and black pepper. Scatter apples around pork, and roast until a thermometer inserted in pork registers 180°F and apples are crisp-tender, about 45 minutes, stirring apples halfway through roasting time. (Tent pork with foil if meat is getting too dark.) Transfer pork to a cutting board and let rest 10 minutes before slicing. Serve pork with apples and onions. —SPIKE GJERDE

WINE Savory, substantial Chilean red: 2016 Montes Alpha Syrah

SLOW-COOKED PORK BELLY
WITH POTATOES, ONIONS, AND GARLIC

Pre-seasoning the pork belly with salt not only flavors the meat itself but also creates a crispy crust, while dry white wine balances the richly fatty meat. Save rendered fat for searing vegetables or making onion confit.

ACTIVE 50 MIN; TOTAL 28 HR, INCLUDING 24 HR REFRIGERATION; SERVES 4

1 (2½-lb.) slab bone-in, skinless pork belly, scored, if desired

2½ tsp. kosher salt

¼ cup unsalted butter (2 oz.)

½ cup dry white wine

20 fresh or thawed frozen pearl onions (about ¾ cup)

12 garlic cloves

30 small fingerling potatoes (about 1 lb.)

1 Sprinkle pork evenly with salt. Place pork on a wire rack set in a rimmed baking sheet. Chill, uncovered, 24 hours.

2 Preheat oven to 200°F. Melt butter in a large Dutch oven over low until sizzling. Add pork; cook, turning occasionally, until browned on 3 sides (do not brown side with bones), about 25 minutes. Remove from heat; pour off drippings from Dutch oven. Add wine, onions, and garlic to Dutch oven. Cover and transfer to preheated oven; bake 2 hours.

3 Remove pork from oven; uncover and add potatoes, stirring to coat. Increase oven temperature to 225°F. Cover and bake until a thermometer inserted in thickest portion of pork registers 195°F, 1 hour to 1 hour and 30 minutes. Remove from oven; let rest 20 minutes.

4 Transfer pork to a cutting board; remove and discard rib bone. Slice pork crosswise. Using a slotted spoon, lift potatoes, onions, and garlic from drippings, and divide them among dinner plates. Top with pork belly. —JACQUES THOREL

WINE Loire Cabernet Franc: 2016 Charles Joguet Cuvée Terroir Chinon

MISO-CRUSTED PORK
ROAST WITH APPLES

PORTUGUESE BRAISED PORK AND CLAMS

This simple braise is a mainstay along the coast of Portugal. With clams from the sea and pork from the nearby mountains, it speaks to the landscape as well as the diet of Portugal. Its garlicky broth pairs well with crusty bread and dry Portuguese wine.

ACTIVE 45 MIN; TOTAL 2 HR 50 MIN, PLUS 8 HR MARINATION; SERVES 8

2 lb. boneless pork shoulder, cut into 1½-inch cubes

2¾ tsp. kosher salt, divided

¾ tsp. black pepper, divided

6 garlic cloves, divided

1 cup dry white wine

2 bay leaves

1 Tbsp. Pimentón de la Vera dulce

1 Tbsp. extra-virgin olive oil, divided

1 medium-size (9-oz.) yellow onion, thinly sliced

1 (28-oz.) can whole peeled tomatoes, drained and crushed by hand

½ tsp. crushed red pepper

2 cups chicken stock or lower-sodium chicken broth, divided

2 lb. baby Yukon Gold potatoes, halved

2 lb. Manila clams or cockles, scrubbed

Chopped fresh cilantro, for garnish

Lemon wedges and crusty bread, for serving

1 Season pork all over with 1¼ teaspoons salt and ½ teaspoon black pepper. Place meat in a large zip-top plastic bag. Smash 3 garlic cloves and add to bag along with wine, bay leaves, and Pimentón. Seal and refrigerate 8 hours or overnight.

2 Preheat oven to 350°F. Remove pork from marinade and pat dry. Remove and discard garlic and bay leaves; reserve remaining marinade. Heat 1½ teaspoons oil in a large Dutch oven over medium-high. Add half the pork and cook, stirring once or twice, until lightly browned, about 5 minutes. Transfer pork to a plate. Repeat with remaining pork. Chop remaining 3 garlic cloves and add to Dutch oven with onion and remaining 1½ teaspoons oil; cook, stirring often, until golden, about 6 minutes. Stir in crushed tomatoes, red pepper, and reserved marinade.

3 Bring to a boil; reduce heat to medium-low and simmer, stirring often, 3 minutes. Return cooked pork to Dutch oven; stir in 1 cup stock until pork is mostly submerged. Cover and bake until pork is fork-tender, 1 hour and 30 minutes to 2 hours.

4 Stir in potatoes and remaining 1 cup stock. Cover and bake until potatoes are tender, about 30 minutes.

5 Transfer Dutch oven to stovetop over high; add clams. Cover and cook until clams open, 3 to 5 minutes. (Remove and discard any unopened clams.) Season with remaining 1½ teaspoons salt and remaining ¼ teaspoon black pepper. Garnish with cilantro. Serve with lemon wedges and crusty bread.

MAKE AHEAD Pork may be prepared through Step 3 and refrigerated overnight. Reheat before proceeding with Step 4.

WINE Robust Portuguese red: 2012 Júlio Bastos Dona Maria Grande Reserva Alentejo

PORK CHOP AU POIVRE
WITH RED WINE–SHALLOT SAUCE

This bone-in pork chop riff on the classic French au poivre steak preparation is so good, we may never go back to beef. Using a blend of peppercorns adds floral notes and vegetal spice to this simple dish. Splurge on the Pierre Poivre N.7 from La Boîte master spice blender Lior Lev Sercarz, or grind your own. Be sure to grind the peppercorns just before cooking to release their fresh aroma.

ACTIVE 25 MIN; TOTAL 35 MIN; SERVES 2

- 1 (1-lb.) bone-in pork loin chop (1 inch thick)
- 1 tsp. kosher salt
- 1 tsp. freshly ground peppercorn blend
- 2 tsp. neutral oil (such as grapeseed)
- 3 Tbsp. unsalted butter, divided
- 1 small shallot, chopped
- ¼ cup (2 oz.) dry red wine
- Steamed baby Yukon Gold potatoes, for serving

1 Preheat oven to 350°F. Place pork chop on a plate; pierce with a fork at ¼-inch intervals. Flip pork, and pierce opposite side. Press salt and peppercorn blend evenly onto both sides.

2 Heat oil in a 10-inch ovenproof skillet over high. Add pork chop; cook until browned, about 3 minutes per side. Transfer skillet with pork to preheated oven. Roast until a thermometer inserted in thickest portion of meat registers 130°F, about 10 minutes.

3 Remove skillet from oven; transfer pork to a plate or carving board. Return skillet to heat over medium; add 1 tablespoon butter, and let melt. Add shallot; cook, stirring occasionally, until aromatic and translucent, about 1 minute. Add wine; bring to a simmer over medium. Simmer, undisturbed, until reduced by half, about 3 minutes. Add remaining 2 tablespoons butter; remove from heat, and swirl skillet until butter is melted and emulsified into sauce. Carve pork; serve with sauce and potatoes.

WINE Peppery, herbaceous Corsican red: 2016 Domaine U Stiliccionu Antica

NOTE Peppercorn blend is available at laboiteny.com.

GEERA PORK (SPICY CUMIN-BRAISED PORK)

PHOTO P. 67

Just a tablespoon of Onwuachi's Pepper Sauce brings plenty of heat to this reverse-braised pork shoulder. As the liquid and delicious fat from the pork cook off, the resulting Geera Pork is coated in a richly seasoned paste, perfect to eat with rice or leftover bara flatbreads.

TOTAL 5 HR, INCLUDING 3 HR MARINATION; SERVES 4 TO 6

- 1 (3-lb.) boneless pork shoulder, cut into 1½-inch pieces
- 1 medium plum tomato, roughly chopped
- ¼ cup Green Seasoning (recipe follows)
- 2 Tbsp. curry powder
- 3 Tbsp. canola oil, divided
- 1 Tbsp. Scotch Bonnet Pepper Sauce (recipe follows) or finely chopped fresh Scotch bonnet chile
- 1 medium yellow onion, finely chopped
- 5 medium garlic cloves, finely chopped
- 2 Tbsp. ground cumin
- 1 Tbsp. granulated sugar
- 2½ tsp. kosher salt, plus more to taste
- 1½ Tbsp. fresh lime juice
- 1 Tbsp. chopped fresh cilantro

1 Combine pork, tomato, green seasoning, curry powder, 2 tablespoons oil, and pepper sauce in a large zip-top plastic bag; seal and toss to evenly coat. Chill at least 3 hours or up to 24 hours.

2 Heat remaining 1 tablespoon oil in a large Dutch oven over medium. Add onion, garlic, cumin, and sugar; cook, stirring often, until onion is softened, 4 to 6 minutes. Stir in pork and marinade. Reduce heat to medium-low; cover and cook, stirring occasionally, until pork is almost tender, 50 minutes to 1 hour. Stir in salt. Cook, uncovered, over medium-low, stirring to scrape bottom of Dutch oven often, until liquid is completely reduced and pork is tender and coated in a coarse paste, 50 minutes to 1 hour. Stir in lime juice; season with salt. Transfer braised pork to a serving platter; sprinkle with cilantro. —KWAME ONWUACHI

BEER Dark, malty Trinidadian beer: Black Wolf Howling Dark Lager

GREEN SEASONING

This blend of fresh herbs and aromatics is certainly spicy, yet well-balanced by cooling celery and cilantro.

TOTAL 10 MIN; MAKES 1½ CUPS

1½ cups loosely packed fresh cilantro leaves and tender stems (about 2 oz.)

¾ cup chopped yellow onion

½ cup chopped celery

9 fresh Scotch bonnet chiles; stems, seeds, and ribs removed; chopped (about ½ cup)

½ cup canola oil

2 Tbsp. plus 2 tsp. fresh thyme leaves

2 Tbsp. grated peeled fresh ginger

1½ Tbsp. grated garlic

Combine all ingredients in a blender. Process on low speed, gradually increasing speed to high, until very smooth, about 1 minute and 30 seconds. —KO

MAKE AHEAD Seasoning mixture may be stored in an airtight container in refrigerator up to 2 weeks.

SCOTCH BONNET PEPPER SAUCE

Onwuachi's family recipe for pepper sauce highlights the sweet, floral notes of Scotch bonnet peppers with an upfront heat that doesn't linger, and lets other flavors shine. Try leftovers on eggs, grilled fish, or in a creamy cabbage slaw.

TOTAL 10 MIN; MAKES ABOUT 1½ CUPS

1 cup white balsamic vinegar

½ cup packed fresh cilantro leaves and tender stems

7 fresh Scotch bonnet chiles; stems, seeds, and ribs removed; chopped (about ⅓ cup)

¼ cup chopped yellow onion

5 medium garlic cloves

½ tsp. kosher salt

Combine all ingredients in a blender. Process on low speed, gradually increasing speed to high, until very smooth, about 45 seconds. Stir before using. — KO

PORK-AND-POTATO CURRY

This deeply flavorful curry is one of the many delicious staff meals prepared by chef Katianna Hong at The Charter Oak restaurant in St. Helena, California. She makes it with ingredients from the Napa Valley—like white wine, citrus leaves, and spices.

ACTIVE 35 MIN; TOTAL 1 HR 15 MIN; SERVES 4 TO 6

2 Tbsp. vegetable oil

⅓ cup finely chopped shallots

1 jalapeño, seeded and minced

4 garlic cloves, finely chopped

1 Tbsp. finely grated fresh ginger

Kosher salt

2 tsp. crushed red pepper

1 cup dry white wine

1½ cups pork or chicken stock

2 Tbsp. packed dark brown sugar

1 Tbsp. Asian fish sauce

1 Tbsp. ground coriander

2 tsp. ground cumin

1 tsp. ground turmeric

1 tsp. ground cinnamon

2 kaffir lime leaves

2 lb. boneless pork shoulder, cut into 1-inch pieces

1 lb. Yukon Gold potatoes, peeled and cut into 1½-inch pieces

1 (15-oz.) can unsweetened coconut milk

3 Tbsp. fresh lime juice

Cilantro, mint, Thai basil, and sliced scallions, for garnish

Steamed rice, for serving

1 In a large enameled cast-iron casserole heat oil until shimmering. Add shallots, jalapeño, garlic, ginger, and a generous pinch of salt. Cook over medium-high until softened, stirring, about 3 minutes. Stir in red pepper and cook 30 seconds. Add wine and simmer until reduced by half, about 5 minutes.

2 Add stock, brown sugar, fish sauce, coriander, cumin, turmeric, cinnamon, and lime leaves to the casserole and bring to a boil. Stir in pork. Cook, partially covered, and simmer over medium-low until pork is nearly tender, about 25 minutes. Stir in potatoes. Cook, partially covered, and simmer until pork and potatoes are tender, about 20 minutes.

3 Stir coconut milk and lime juice into curry and bring to a boil. Season with salt. Discard lime leaves. Garnish with cilantro, mint, basil, and scallions. Serve with steamed rice. —KATIANNA HONG

MAKE AHEAD The curry can be refrigerated overnight. Reheat gently.

WINE Full-bodied, spicy Gewürztraminer: 2016 Paul Blanck

PORK AND CIDER STEW

This hearty stew from chef Fernanda Milanezi is super-simple to make for a crowd.
It's finished with heavy cream, which amplifies the wonderful apple flavor.

ACTIVE 35 MIN; TOTAL 3 HR 30 MIN; SERVES 10 TO 12

- 3 Tbsp. unsalted butter
- 3 Tbsp. extra-virgin olive oil
- 5 lb. trimmed boneless pork shoulder, cut into 1½-inch cubes
- Kosher salt and pepper
- 10 oz. skinless, meaty slab bacon, cut into ½-inch dice
- 1 large onion, thinly sliced
- 5 garlic cloves, finely chopped
- 1 (750-ml) bottle sparkling dry apple cider
- 1 quart chicken stock or low-sodium broth
- 2 bay leaves
- ¼ cup cornstarch
- 1 cup heavy cream
- 3 Tbsp. grainy mustard
- 2 tsp. finely chopped sage leaves

1 In a large enameled cast-iron casserole melt 1 tablespoon butter with 1 tablespoon oil. Season pork with salt and pepper. Add one-third of pork to the casserole and cook over medium-high, stirring occasionally, until well browned, about 8 minutes. Transfer pork to a baking sheet. Repeat twice with remaining butter, oil, and pork.

2 Add bacon to the casserole and cook until golden; add to the pork on a baking sheet. Add onion and garlic to the casserole; cook over medium, stirring, until golden and softened, 5 minutes. Add pork, bacon, cider, stock, and bay leaves to the casserole; bring to a simmer. Simmer, covered, until pork is tender, 2½ hours. Discard bay leaves.

3 In a small bowl whisk cornstarch with ¼ cup water. Add cornstarch mixture and cream to stew; simmer until liquid is thickened, 5 minutes. Stir in mustard and sage, season with salt and pepper, and serve. —FERNANDA MILANEZI

MAKE AHEAD The stew can be refrigerated up to 3 days.

CIDER Earthy artisanal hard cider: Farnum Hill Semi-Dry

MILLION DOLLAR STEW

It's said that eating collards and black-eyed peas on New Year's Day will bring good luck. Food & Wine's Justin Chapple includes both in his hearty and rich pork stew.

ACTIVE 40 MIN; TOTAL 2 HR 5 MIN; SERVES 10 TO 12

- 3 lb. boneless pork shoulder, cut into 1-inch pieces
  Kosher salt and pepper
- 2 Tbsp. canola oil
- 2 large onions, 1 finely chopped and 1 quartered
- 16 garlic cloves, 8 finely chopped and 8 whole
- 1 (15-oz.) can whole peeled tomatoes, crushed by hand
- 2 chipotle chiles in adobo sauce, seeded and minced
- 1 Tbsp. chili powder
- 2 tsp. ground cumin
- 1 tsp. dried oregano
- 3 qt. chicken stock or low-sodium broth
- ½ lb. black-eyed peas, picked over
- 2 lb. collard greens, stemmed and chopped

1 Season the pork with salt and pepper. In a large enameled cast-iron casserole heat the oil until shimmering. Add half the pork and cook over medium-high, turning occasionally, until browned all over, about 8 minutes. Using a slotted spoon, transfer to a plate. Repeat with remaining pork.

2 Add chopped onion, chopped garlic, and a generous pinch of salt to the casserole. Cook over medium, stirring occasionally, until softened and lightly browned, 5 to 7 minutes. Stir in tomatoes, chipotles, chili powder, cumin, and oregano; cook until bubbling. Stir in stock and bring to a boil over high. Stir in pork. Cook, covered, and simmer over low until tender, about 1 hour.

3 Meanwhile, in a large saucepan combine black-eyed peas with the quartered onion, whole garlic cloves, and 12 cups of water. Bring to a boil; reduce heat and simmer over low until peas are tender, about 45 minutes. Remove from heat; add 1 tablespoon salt and let stand 5 minutes. Drain well and discard onion and garlic.

4 Stir collard greens into stew in large handfuls, letting greens wilt slightly before adding more. Cook, covered, over low until pork is very tender and collards are just softened, about 20 minutes. Stir in peas; cover and simmer until hot, about 5 minutes. Ladle into bowls and serve. —JUSTIN CHAPPLE

MAKE AHEAD The stew and black-eyed peas can be refrigerated separately overnight. Reheat the stew before adding the peas.

WINE Robust California Syrah: 2014 Martinelli Terra Felice

PORK-AND-BRISKET CHILI

Kansas City, Missouri, chef Colby Garrelts makes a giant pot of chili for his family's Sunday supper, often using venison that he has hunted himself. Here, he uses a mix of pork shoulder and brisket for a super-decadent and satisfying bowl of chili.

ACTIVE 1 HR 45 MIN; TOTAL 4 HR, PLUS OVERNIGHT SOAKING; SERVES 10 TO 12

BEANS

- 1 lb. small dried pink beans, such as Rancho Gordo's Pinquitos, soaked overnight and drained
- 5 garlic cloves
- 1 small yellow onion, quartered through the core
- 1 medium carrot, halved crosswise
- 1 celery rib, halved crosswise
- 1½ Tbsp. kosher salt

CHILI

- 3½ lb. boneless pork shoulder, cut into 1½-inch pieces
- 2 lb. brisket, cut into 1½-inch pieces
  Kosher salt and pepper
- 3 Tbsp. vegetable oil
- 3 medium yellow onions, chopped
- 1 green bell pepper—stemmed, seeded and chopped
- 10 garlic cloves, chopped
- ¼ cup tomato paste
- ¼ cup chili powder
- 2 Tbsp. light brown sugar
- 1 Tbsp. mustard powder
- 1 Tbsp. ground cumin
- 1 (16-oz.) jar roasted green Hatch chiles
- 1 (16-oz.) can crushed tomatoes
- 5 qt. chicken stock or low-sodium broth
- ¼ cup oregano leaves
  Sour cream, shredded cheese, and thinly sliced scallions, for serving

1 **Make the beans:** Place all ingredients in a large saucepan and cover with 4 quarts of water. Bring to a boil. Simmer over medium-low just until the beans are tender, about 1 hour. Drain well and discard vegetables.

2 **Make the chili:** Season pork and brisket generously with salt and pepper. In a large pot heat vegetable oil until shimmering. In batches, cook pork and brisket over medium-high, turning occasionally, until browned all over, about 10 minutes per batch. Using a slotted spoon, transfer meat to a baking sheet.

3 Add onions, bell pepper, garlic, and a generous pinch of salt to pot. Cook over medium-high, stirring frequently, just until starting to soften and brown, about 5 minutes. Add tomato paste, chili powder, brown sugar, mustard powder, and cumin. Cook, stirring, until fragrant and vegetables are coated, about 3 minutes. Add Hatch chiles and tomatoes. Cook, stirring, until bubbling, about 5 minutes. Add chicken stock and bring to a boil. Add meat and oregano. Simmer over medium, stirring occasionally, just until meat is tender, about 1 hour.

4 Stir beans into chili and simmer over medium, stirring occasionally, until meat and beans are tender, about 1 hour and 15 minutes longer. Serve hot with sour cream, cheese, and scallions. —COLBY GARRELTS

MAKE AHEAD The chili can be refrigerated up to 5 days. Reheat gently before serving.

WINE Robust California Syrah: 2015 Eberle Steinbeck Vineyard

CAMBODIAN RICE NOODLE SOUP

Kuy teav, a rice noodle soup traditionally served for breakfast in Cambodia, takes on layers of flavor from shrimp, pork, and vegetables. In Deana Saukam's version, the rich stock is layered over crisp lettuce leaves and rice noodles, then topped with herbs, sliced chiles, soy sauce, and lime.

ACTIVE 1 HR 45 MIN; TOTAL 3 HR 45 MIN; SERVES 8

1½ cups dried shrimp, divided

2 lb. pork neck bones

1 lb. pork tenderloin

4 chicken drumsticks (about 1 lb.)

2 bunches scallions, plus more, thinly sliced, for serving

1 small white onion, coarsely chopped

1 small sweet potato, diced

1 carrot, coarsely chopped

1 small head bok choy, coarsely chopped

½ medium daikon, diced (about 6 oz.)

1 head garlic, halved crosswise, plus 8 garlic cloves, chopped

2 Tbsp. soy sauce, plus more for serving

1 Tbsp. fish sauce

1 Tbsp. granulated sugar, plus more for serving

7 Tbsp. extra-virgin olive oil, divided

1 lb. ground pork

Kosher salt

Freshly ground black pepper

12 oz. bean sprouts

16 raw large shrimp, peeled and deveined

1 lb. dried rice vermicelli

8 green lettuce leaves

Fresh cilantro leaves, pickled green Thai chiles, thinly sliced Thai bird chiles, chile paste, and lime wedges, for serving

1 Place 1 cup dried shrimp in a small bowl. Add warm water to cover, and let stand for 30 minutes; drain.

2 Combine soaked shrimp, pork bones, pork tenderloin, chicken drumsticks, 2 bunches whole scallions, onion, sweet potato, carrot, bok choy, daikon, garlic head halves, 2 tablespoons soy sauce, fish sauce, and 1 tablespoon sugar in a stockpot. Add 6 quarts water and bring to a boil over high. Reduce heat to medium-low and simmer until an instant-read thermometer inserted in thickest portion of tenderloin registers 140°F, about 30 minutes. Using tongs, transfer tenderloin to a plate and let cool slightly; cover and refrigerate. Continue to simmer broth until well flavored, about 2 hours and 30 minutes.

3 Meanwhile, place a fine wire-mesh strainer over a small heatproof bowl. Heat ¼ cup oil in a small skillet over medium-high. Add chopped garlic and cook, stirring occasionally, until garlic is golden and oil is hot and fragrant, about 3 minutes. Strain into prepared bowl. Reserve fried garlic.

4 Heat 2 tablespoons olive oil in a large skillet over medium. Add ground pork; season with salt and pepper. Cook, stirring occasionally, until cooked through and browned, about 10 minutes. Transfer to a medium bowl. In the same skillet heat remaining 1 tablespoon olive oil. Add remaining ½ cup dried shrimp; cook over medium-high, stirring often, until shrimp are bright pink and crisp, about 2 minutes.

5 Fill a large pot with water and fit with a colander. Bring to a boil. Blanch bean sprouts 10 seconds; transfer to a medium bowl. Return water to a boil and add raw shrimp; cook just until pink, 2 to 3 minutes. Drain and transfer to a medium bowl.

6 Using tongs, remove scallions and chicken drumsticks from stockpot and transfer to a medium bowl. Pour broth through a fine wire-mesh strainer into a large pot; discard solids. Bring to a simmer and season with salt. Add tenderloin and cook until warmed through, about 5 minutes. Transfer tenderloin to a work surface and thinly slice. Coarsely shred chicken meat, and discard skin and bones.

7 Cook vermicelli in a large pot of boiling water until al dente; drain. Rinse under cool water. Pat dry. Toss with reserved garlic oil and 1 teaspoon reserved fried garlic.

8 Divide lettuce leaves among 8 large bowls. Top each leaf with noodles, and ladle broth over noodles. Top with sliced pork tenderloin, shredded chicken, ground pork, cooked shrimp, dried shrimp, whole scallions, and remaining fried garlic. Serve with bean sprouts, sliced scallions, cilantro, pickled chiles, sliced chiles, chile paste, lime wedges, soy sauce, sugar, salt, and pepper. —DEANA SAUKAM

WINE Lemon-zesty Sauvignon Blanc: 2016 Errazuriz Max Reserva

CORSICAN BEAN SOUP WITH GREENS AND PORK

Full of winter vegetables, this comforting soup is hearty without being heavy. Dried beans are key to the satisfying richness of the broth. If you use canned beans to save time, stir two 15-ounce cans in at the end of cooking.

ACTIVE 30 MIN; TOTAL 10 HR 15 MIN, INCLUDING 8 HR SOAKING; SERVES 8

- 8 oz. dried cannellini beans
- 2 Tbsp. olive oil
- 1 small (2-lb.) green cabbage, chopped (about 8 cups)
- 4 medium russet potatoes, peeled and cut into ¼-inch-thick rounds (about 4 cups)
- 4 cups stemmed and chopped Swiss chard
- 2 medium leeks, white parts only, chopped (about 2 cups)
- 2 large carrots, cut into ¼-inch-thick rounds (about 1 cup)
- 3 large garlic cloves, thinly sliced
- 2 Tbsp. kosher salt
- 1 tsp. black pepper
- 1 bouquet garni (1 bay leaf, 2 thyme sprigs, and 3 flat-leaf parsley sprigs, tied together with kitchen twine)
- 1 (15-oz.) can whole peeled tomatoes, drained and finely chopped
- 1 ham bone
- 8 oz. pork cheek or boneless pork shoulder

1 Place beans in a bowl; add cold water to cover. Cover bowl; let soak 8 hours or overnight.

2 Heat oil in a Dutch oven over medium-high; add cabbage, potatoes, chard, leeks, carrots, garlic, salt, and pepper. Cook, stirring often, until vegetables are wilted, about 10 minutes. Add 14 cups water to cover vegetables. Reduce heat to low, and simmer gently while preparing beans.

3 Meanwhile, drain beans. Transfer beans to a large pot; add water to cover by 2 inches. Add bouquet garni; bring to a boil over high. Reduce heat to medium-low; simmer 15 minutes. Drain.

4 Add drained beans and bouquet garni to vegetable mixture in Dutch oven. Add tomatoes, ham bone, and pork cheek. Bring to a boil over high. Reduce heat to low; simmer, stirring occasionally, until beans and vegetables are very tender, about 1 hour and 30 minutes. Remove and discard bouquet garni and ham bone. Ladle soup into bowls and serve.

COLLARD GREENS RAMEN

Riffing on a memorable bowl of yaka-mein that he had as a child, Todd Richards' soup begins with a pot of collards and a generous pour of bourbon, which cooks down into an intense potlikker. Shichimi togarashi, a Japanese spice blend of dried orange peel, ginger, sesame seeds, nori, and a mix of dried chiles, finishes each bowl.

ACTIVE 40 MIN; TOTAL 2 HR; SERVES 4

- 1 (1½-lb.) bunch collard greens
- 1 Tbsp. olive oil
- 4 bacon slices
- 2 large yellow onions, thinly sliced (about 5 cups)
- 4 large garlic cloves, thinly sliced
- 1 lb. smoked ham hocks, at room temperature
- ¼ cup (2 oz.) bourbon or other whiskey
- 2 Tbsp. apple cider vinegar
- 8 cups cold water
- 4 tsp. kosher salt
- ½ tsp. black pepper
- ¼ cup lower-sodium soy sauce
- 12 oz. uncooked instant ramen noodles, cooked
- 4 large hard-cooked eggs, peeled and halved
- 8 scallions, thinly sliced
- 1 lime, cut into wedges
- 2 tsp. shichimi togarashi

1 Using a sharp knife, remove stems from collard greens. Cut leaves into 2-inch squares, then rinse in cold water.

2 Heat olive oil in a 4-quart stockpot over medium. Add bacon; cook until crisp, about 10 minutes. Transfer bacon to paper towels to drain, reserving drippings in pot. Crumble bacon and set aside.

3 Add onions and garlic to hot drippings in pot; cook over medium, stirring often, until golden brown, about 25 minutes. Add ham hocks and cook until browned on all sides, about 5 minutes, turning ham hocks every 45 seconds. Add bourbon and vinegar; cook, stirring and scraping up browned bits on bottom of pot, until liquid is reduced by half, about 30 seconds. Add 8 cups cold water; bring to a simmer.

4 Add salt and pepper to soup. Add collards in large handfuls, stirring each addition until wilted, 2 to 3 minutes, before adding next handful. Return to a simmer; cover and cook until collards are tender, about 1 hour.

5 Remove ham hocks; cool slightly. Pull meat from bones and chop meat. Discard bones and skin.

6 Divide soy sauce evenly among 4 serving bowls. Ladle 1¼ cups liquid from cooked collards into each bowl. Divide noodles evenly among the bowls, then stir noodles twice in broth to combine.

7 Top bowls evenly with ham hock meat, collards, eggs, bacon, scallions, lime wedges, and shichimi togarashi. —TODD RICHARDS

WINE Peppery, Syrah-based red: 2016 Delas Saint-Esprit Côtes-du-Rhône

SPICY KIMCHI TOFU STEW

SPICY KIMCHI TOFU STEW

Stop at a Korean market on the way home from work to have this soothing, vibrant dish on the table in 30 minutes.

TOTAL 30 MIN; SERVES 4

½ lb. pork belly, cut into ½-inch pieces

1 (16-oz.) jar kimchi, drained, ¼ cup liquid reserved

½ onion, thinly sliced

4 oz. shiitake mushrooms, thinly sliced

2 Tbsp. gochujang (Korean red pepper paste)

1 Tbsp. gochugaru (Korean red pepper flakes)

Kosher salt

1 (14-oz.) container silken tofu, cut into large pieces

Steamed short-grain rice, for serving

1 Cook pork belly in a medium-size nonreactive pot over medium, stirring occasionally, until fat is sizzling and pork is light golden, about 8 minutes. Add kimchi and onion. Cook, stirring occasionally, until onion is softened, about 5 minutes.

2 Add reserved kimchi liquid, mushrooms, gochujang, gochugaru, and 4 cups water, and bring to a boil. Reduce heat to medium-low; cook 10 minutes.

3 Season stew with salt. Stir in tofu, breaking it up slightly with a spoon; bring to a boil; remove from heat. Serve stew hot with steamed rice. —ANTHONY BOURDAIN

WINE Off-dry French Chenin Blanc: 2015 François Pinon Les Trois Argiles

MAPO TOFU

"This is totally my way of making this dish," chef Kuniko Yagi says. "I'm sure Chinese people wouldn't let me call this mapo tofu." Yagi's version has more meat than tofu, yet she still relies on jarred toban djan, the chile-bean paste that gives this Chinese takeout staple its signature heat and deeply savory flavor.

TOTAL 15 MIN; SERVES 4

1 tsp. canola oil

½ lb. ground beef chuck (85 percent lean)

½ lb. ground pork

Kosher salt

2 Tbsp. chile-bean sauce, preferably toban djan

2 Tbsp. hoisin sauce or tenmenjan (soybean paste)

1 Tbsp. soy sauce

1 (14-oz.) pkg. soft tofu, finely diced

1½ tsp. cornstarch

3 scallions, finely chopped

White rice, for serving

1 Heat a large skillet until hot. Add oil, beef, and pork; season with salt. Cook over high, stirring and breaking up the meat, until crumbly and lightly browned, about 3 minutes.

2 Stir in chile-bean sauce, hoisin, and soy sauce . Cook, stirring, 3 minutes. Gently fold in tofu. In a small bowl whisk cornstarch into ½ cup water. Add to skillet and simmer, stirring, until sauce thickens, about 2 minutes. Stir in the scallions and serve with rice. —KUNIKO YAGI

BEER Citrusy blond Belgian ale: Brasserie Lefebvre Blanche de Bruxelles

PORK MEATBALL STEW WITH CARROTS AND PICKLED MUSTARD GREENS

Rich pork broth made with pork butt and smoked ham is the flavorful base in this comforting stew from brothers Andrew and Eric Dayton of the Minneapolis restaurant, The Bachelor Farmer.

ACTIVE 1 HR 40 MIN; TOTAL 3 HR 40 MIN; SERVES 4

BROTH

- 1 lb. lean pork butt, cut into 1-inch pieces
- 1 (¼-lb.) piece ham or prosciutto ends, cut into 1-inch pieces
- 1 onion, chopped
- 1 large carrot, chopped
- 2 celery stalks, chopped
- 1 bulb garlic, halved
- 5 fresh thyme sprigs
- 2 dried bay leaves
- 1½ tsp. black peppercorns
- ½ tsp. coriander seeds
- Kosher salt

VEGETABLES

- ½ lb. mustard greens, stemmed and chopped
- 1 tsp. granulated sugar
- Kosher salt
- 1¼ lb. carrots, peeled and cut into 1-inch pieces
- 2 Tbsp. olive oil

MEATBALLS

- 3½ Tbsp. olive oil
- 1 medium onion, finely diced
- 3 garlic cloves, sliced
- 1 tsp. finely chopped thyme
- 2½ tsp. kosher salt, divided
- ½ cup plain dry breadcrumbs
- ¼ cup whole milk
- 1 lb. ground pork
- 1 large egg, lightly beaten

TO FINISH

- 3 Tbsp. heavy cream
- Chopped fresh flat-leaf parsley and dill, for garnish

1 **Make the broth:** In a large saucepan spread pork and ham in a single layer; cook over medium-low, undisturbed, until browned on the bottom, about 7 minutes. Stir meat and continue cooking, stirring occasionally, until well browned, about 5 minutes. Add ½ cup water; scrape up browned bits from bottom of pan. Add chopped onion, chopped carrot, celery, garlic, thyme sprigs, bay leaves, peppercorns, coriander, and 2 quarts water. Bring to a boil. Cover and simmer over low 2 hours. Strain broth into a heatproof bowl; discard solids. Return broth to pan; bring to a boil, and cook until reduced to 1 quart. Skim any foam from surface. Season lightly with salt.

2 **Meanwhile, prepare the vegetables:** Combine mustard greens, sugar, and 1 teaspoon salt in a medium bowl. Massage greens until wilted. Let stand 1 hour.

3 Preheat oven to 400°F. Toss carrot pieces with 2 tablespoons oil and salt on a large parchment-lined baking sheet. Spread in an even layer, and roast until caramelized and tender, about 30 minutes.

4 **Make the meatballs:** In a medium skillet heat 3½ tablespoons oil until shimmering. Add diced onion, garlic cloves, chopped thyme, and ½ teaspoon salt. Cook over medium, stirring occasionally, until softened and browned, about 10 minutes. Cool completely.

5 In a large bowl stir together breadcrumbs and milk; let stand until absorbed, about 5 minutes. Add pork, egg, onion mixture, and remaining salt; stir well. Form mixture into 1½-inch meatballs and arrange on a parchment-lined baking sheet. Refrigerate until chilled, about 30 minutes.

6 Roast meatballs at 400°F until browned and cooked through, 20 to 25 minutes.

7 Bring broth to a simmer over medium. Add cream, meatballs, carrots, and mustard greens, and simmer until hot, about 5 minutes. Transfer to 4 bowls and garnish with chopped parsley and dill. —ANDREW AND ERIC DAYTON

WINE Plummy Merlot: 2014 Ridge Estate

SUPERGREEN GUMBO

Chef Andrea Reusing riffs on gumbo here, creating a hearty stew that's dense with spinach and mustard greens.

ACTIVE 45 MIN; TOTAL 2 HR; SERVES 6 TO 8

- 4 thick-cut slices of bacon, chopped
- 1 medium white onion, finely chopped
- 1 medium carrot, finely chopped
- 1 celery rib, finely chopped
- 3 dried chiles de árbol, finely crushed
  Kosher salt
- 4 oz. smoked ham, finely chopped
- 1 medium leek, white and light green parts only, halved lengthwise and thinly sliced crosswise
- 3 large garlic cloves, minced
- ½ cup dry white wine
- 2 qt. chicken stock or low-sodium broth
- 3 bay leaves
- 10 oz. leaf spinach, thick stems trimmed
- 1 lb. mustard greens, stems discarded
- 1 (15-oz.) can navy beans, rinsed and drained
  Black pepper
  Steamed jasmine rice and chile vinegar (see Note), for serving

1 In a large saucepan cook bacon over medium, stirring occasionally, until fat is rendered and bacon is not yet crisp, about 5 minutes. Add onion, carrot, celery, chiles, and a generous pinch of salt. Cook, stirring occasionally, until vegetables are softened and just starting to brown, about 10 minutes. Add ham, leek, and garlic. Cook, stirring occasionally, until fragrant, about 3 minutes. Stir in wine and simmer until reduced by half, 2 to 3 minutes.

2 Add stock and bay leaves to saucepan. Bring to a boil over high, then simmer over medium-low until vegetables and ham are tender, about 20 minutes. Remove from heat and let cool to room temperature; discard bay leaves.

3 Add spinach and mustard greens to saucepan. Stir until wilted slightly. In batches, puree greens in a blender to a chunky puree. Return gumbo to saucepan and bring to a simmer. Cook, stirring occasionally, until greens are tender, about 5 minutes. Stir in beans and season with salt and pepper. Ladle gumbo into bowls and serve with steamed rice and chile vinegar. — ANDREA REUSING

MAKE AHEAD The gumbo can be refrigerated up to 3 days. Reheat gently before serving.

NOTE Chile vinegar (also called hot pepper vinegar or pepper sauce) is a staple on Southern tables.

92 FOOD & WINE ONE POT MEALS

SALMOREJO

Salmorejo is a classic soup made primarily with tomatoes and bread. It's best with a splash of sherry vinegar, but Andalusian tomatoes pack a good hit of acidity, so vinegar is often omitted in Spain. Salmorejo is also frequently made with pan de telera, a type of hard roll, which thickens the soup. Anything from ciabatta to rustic white is good here.

ACTIVE 15 MIN; TOTAL 45 MIN; SERVES 4

- 2½ lb. vine-ripened tomatoes, cored and chopped
- ½ lb. rustic white bread, crust removed, bread cubed (2½ cups)
- 2 garlic cloves
- 1 tsp. sherry vinegar
- ¼ cup extra-virgin olive oil, plus more for serving
- Kosher salt
- 2 hard-boiled eggs, peeled and chopped
- ½ cup chopped serrano ham

1 In a blender puree tomatoes, bread, garlic, sherry vinegar, and ½ cup water until very smooth, about 1 minute. With blender running, drizzle in ¼ cup olive oil until incorporated. Season with salt. Cover and refrigerate until soup is chilled, at least 30 minutes.

2 Divide soup among 4 bowls. Garnish with chopped eggs and ham, drizzle with olive oil and serve. —JOSÉ ANDRÉS

MAKE AHEAD The soup can be refrigerated for up to 2 days.

WINE Brisk fino sherry: NV González Byass Tio Pepe

BUTTERNUT SQUASH SOUP

Adding collard greens, bell pepper, corn, and carrot to rustic butternut squash soup is chef Mary Ellen Diaz's clever way of making soup even more healthy. Together these vegetables deliver vitamins A and C as well as fiber and powerful antioxidants.

ACTIVE 45 MIN; TOTAL 1 HR 30 MIN; SERVES 6

- 6 cups low-sodium chicken broth
- 1 (2-lb.) butternut squash quartered, seeded, peeled, and cut into 2-inch pieces
- 5 thyme sprigs
- 2 garlic cloves, halved
- 2 medium leeks, white and pale green parts only, cut into 2-inch pieces
- 1 celery rib, cut into 2-inch pieces
- 1 Tbsp. vegetable oil
- 2 thick slices of bacon, cut crosswise ½ inch thick
- 2 packed cups coarsely chopped collards or kale
- 1 (15-oz.) can pinto or roman beans, drained and rinsed
- 1 medium carrot, finely diced
- 1 red bell pepper, finely diced
- 1 cup corn kernels
- Salt and freshly ground black pepper

1 In a large heavy pot combine broth, squash, thyme, garlic, leeks, and celery. Bring to a boil. Cover and simmer over low 45 minutes.

2 In a medium skillet heat vegetable oil over medium-high. Add bacon and cook, turning once, until crisp, about 7 minutes.

3 Discard thyme sprigs from soup. Working in batches, carefully puree soup in a blender. Return soup to pot. Add bacon, collards, pinto beans, carrot, bell pepper, and corn; bring to a boil. Reduce heat. Simmer over medium-low, stirring occasionally, until vegetables are tender, about 7 minutes. Season soup with salt and pepper, serve warm. —MARY ELLEN DIAZ

MAKE AHEAD The soup can be refrigerated overnight. Reheat gently.

HOMINY STEW WITH BACON

Chef JJ Johnson makes hominy the star in this humble, delicious stew. The maize kernels absorb flavor as they simmer while retaining a slight chew. Aromatics sauté in the rendered fat from crispy bacon, which is later used a garnish for each serving.

ACTIVE 25 MIN; TOTAL 1 HR 20 MIN; SERVES 6

8 oz. bacon, cut into ½-inch pieces

2 onions, chopped

5 garlic cloves, finely chopped

3 poblano chiles, seeded and cut into ½-inch pieces

1 jalapeño, seeded and finely chopped

Salt and freshly ground black pepper

2 (15-oz.) cans hominy, rinsed and drained

1 (14.5-oz.) can whole peeled tomatoes, crushed by hand, juice reserved

4 cups chicken stock or low-sodium chicken broth

3 Tbsp. lime juice

¼ cup chopped fresh cilantro

1 tsp. finely grated lime zest

1 Cook bacon in a large enameled cast-iron Dutch oven or heavy pot over medium, stirring occasionally, until crisp, about 10 minutes. Using a slotted spoon, transfer bacon to a paper-towel-lined plate to drain.

2 Add onions, garlic, poblanos, and jalapeño to pot; season with salt and pepper. Cook over medium, stirring occasionally, until softened, about 12 minutes. Stir in hominy, tomatoes and their juice, chicken stock, and lime juice, simmer over medium-low, covered, 20 minutes.

3 Uncover and cook over medium, stirring occasionally, until liquid is reduced slightly and thickened, 10 to 15 minutes. Stir in cilantro and lime zest; season with salt and pepper. Garnish with bacon and serve. —JOSEPH JOHNSON

TOMATO SOUP WITH IBÉRICO HAM

This soup calls for no broth or water; tomatoes form the entire base. Crispy ham and fresh mint offset the acidic sweetness of the tomatoes. If you cannot find rosa de Barbastro tomatoes, substitute the juiciest, ripest tomatoes at the market.

ACTIVE 30 MIN; TOTAL 1 HR 20 MIN; SERVES 6

¼ cup extra-virgin olive oil, plus more for serving

2 (1½-oz.) pkg. jamón Ibérico (such as Cinco Jotas), finely chopped

3 medium carrots, chopped

1 large yellow onion, chopped

1 medium leek, white and light green parts chopped

7 garlic cloves, finely chopped

6½ lb. rosa de Barbastro tomatoes or other juicy beefsteak-style tomatoes, chopped

¼ cup loosely packed fresh mint leaves, finely chopped, plus more fresh mint leaves, for garnish

4 tsp. kosher salt

1 tsp. ground cumin

¼ tsp. black pepper

Fig jam or fresh figs, for serving

1 Combine oil and ham in a large Dutch oven; cook over medium, stirring often, until fat is rendered, about 6 minutes. Remove ham with a slotted spoon.

2 Increase heat to medium-high. Add carrots, onion, leek, and garlic to Dutch oven; cook, stirring occasionally, until vegetables are tender but not browned, 6 to 8 minutes. Add chopped tomatoes, chopped mint, salt, cumin, and pepper. Cook, stirring occasionally, until tomatoes have released their liquid and are completely broken down, 45 to 50 minutes.

3 Working in batches, transfer soup to a blender. Secure lid on blender, and remove center piece to allow steam to escape. Place a clean towel over opening. Process until very smooth, about 1 minute. Pour soup through a fine wire-mesh strainer into a bowl; discard solids. Serve hot, sprinkled with reserved ham and mint leaves. Drizzle with oil and top with fig jam or fresh figs. —LUIS MIGUEL LÓPEZ DOMÍNGUEZ AND ADELA LÓPEZ DOMÍNGUEZ

WINE Substantial Spanish rosado: 2018 Bodegas Muga

POTATO, LEEK, AND BROCCOLI SOUP
WITH PANCETTA CRUMBS

During its first year, when Essex Farm harvested 10,000 pounds of potatoes in just one day, Kristin Kimball was inspired to make potato-leek soup. If you have a blender and good chicken broth, she swears it's one of the easiest soups to make. This version has a fabulous topping of supercrispy sourdough and pancetta crumbs mixed with sage and rosemary.

TOTAL 35 MIN; SERVES 12

- 1½ sticks unsalted butter
- 6 small leeks (about 1¾ lb.), white and light green parts only, thinly sliced (4 cups)
- 4 lb. large Yukon Gold potatoes, peeled and thinly sliced
- 1 bunch broccoli florets coarsely chopped, stems peeled and sliced
- 4 cups chicken stock or low-sodium broth
- 2 cups half-and-half or heavy cream
- Salt and freshly ground white pepper
- 1 (12-oz.) loaf sourdough bread, crusts removed and bread cut into 1-inch cubes
- ¼ cup canola oil
- 2 oz. thinly sliced pancetta, finely chopped (¼ cup)
- 2 Tbsp. chopped fresh sage
- 1 Tbsp. chopped fresh rosemary

1 Melt 1 stick butter in an extra-large pot. Add leeks, potatoes, and broccoli; cook over high 10 minutes, stirring frequently. Add stock and 6 cups water, cover and bring to a boil. Simmer over medium until vegetables are tender, about 10 minutes. Working in batches, puree soup in a blender until smooth. Return soup to pot; stir in half-and-half. Season soup with salt and white pepper. Keep warm.

2 Meanwhile, pulse bread cubes in a food processor until coarse crumbs form. In a large skillet melt remaining 4 tablespoons butter in the oil. Add pancetta, sage, rosemary, and bread crumbs. Cook over medium-high, stirring frequently, until bread crumbs and pancetta are browned and crisp, about 10 minutes. Drain on paper towels.

3 Ladle soup into bowls, garnish with pancetta crumbs and serve. —KRISTIN KIMBALL

MAKE AHEAD The soup and crumbs can be refrigerated separately up to 3 days. Recrisp the crumbs before serving.

WINE A fragrant, medium-bodied Italian white, such as an Arneis

CHICKPEA AND SWISS CHARD CHILI

This smoky, rich chili is one of my go-to weeknight dinners, and for good reason. It's a one-pot dish that has 10 ingredients (not including salt and pepper) and comes together in just 30 minutes. Plus, you can make it a day or two in advance because it reheats beautifully.

TOTAL 30 MIN; SERVES 6

6 slices bacon, chopped

1 large onion, chopped

1 large carrot, cut into ½-inch pieces

2 garlic cloves, thinly sliced

Salt

Black pepper

1 (28-oz.) can crushed tomatoes

2 cups chicken stock or low-sodium broth

2 (15-oz.) cans chickpeas, rinsed

1 lb. Swiss chard, leaves and stems chopped

3 chipotles in adobo, minced

Shredded Monterey Jack cheese, for serving

Cook bacon in a large saucepan over medium-high, stirring occasionally, until fat is rendered, about 7 minutes. Add onion, carrot, garlic, and a generous pinch each of salt and pepper. Cook, stirring occasionally, until softened, 8 to 10 minutes. Add tomatoes, stock, chickpeas, Swiss chard, and chipotles; bring to a boil. Simmer over medium-low just until chili is thickened and Swiss chard is wilted and tender, about 8 minutes. Serve in bowls topped with shredded cheese.

—JUSTIN CHAPPLE

MAKE AHEAD The chili can be refrigerated overnight. Reheat gently before serving.

BUTTERNUT SQUASH SOUP
WITH BACON AND CRÈME FRAÎCHE

Roasting butternut squash with honey and a bit of salt intensifies the natural sweetness of squash and caramelizes the honey. Take time browning the onions; cooking them low and slow deepens the foundational flavor of this hearty soup.

ACTIVE 1 HR 10 MIN; TOTAL 2 HR 45 MIN; SERVES 8 TO 10

1 large (3-lb.) butternut squash, halved and seeded

1 Tbsp. honey

1¼ tsp. kosher salt, divided, plus more to taste

½ cup salted butter (4 oz.)

2 medium-size yellow onions, chopped

11 garlic cloves, smashed

2 medium carrots, chopped

2 Tbsp. chopped fresh sage

8 cups lower-sodium chicken broth, or as needed, divided

½ tsp. Hungarian sweet paprika, plus more for garnish

½ tsp. black pepper

¼ tsp. ground nutmeg

½ cup crème fraîche or sour cream

6 thick-cut bacon slices, cooked and cut into ½-inch strips

3 Tbsp. chopped fresh flat-leaf parsley

1 Preheat oven to 375°F. Using a paring knife, score cut sides of squash in a crosshatch pattern. Arrange squash halves, cut-sides up, on a rimmed baking sheet lined with parchment paper. Brush cut sides of squash with honey; sprinkle with ½ teaspoon salt. Roast in preheated oven until tender when pierced with a paring knife, about 1 hour and 30 minutes. Let cool 20 minutes. Using a spoon, scrape squash flesh into a medium bowl. Discard peels.

2 Meanwhile, melt butter in a medium Dutch oven over medium until sizzling. Add onions and garlic; cook, stirring occasionally, until softened and translucent, about 12 minutes. Reduce heat to low and cook, stirring occasionally, until very tender and light golden brown, about 25 minutes. Add carrots and sage; cook, stirring occasionally, 5 minutes.

3 Stir in cooked squash and 6 cups broth. Bring to a boil over high. Cover, reduce heat to low and simmer until carrots are tender, about 30 minutes.

4 Ladle soup, in 3 batches, into a blender. Secure lid on blender; remove center piece to allow steam to escape. Place a kitchen towel over opening. Process until velvety smooth, about 30 seconds per batch. (Alternatively, puree soup in Dutch oven using an immersion blender until smooth.) Return pureed soup to Dutch oven over medium, and stir in paprika, pepper, nutmeg, and remaining ¾ teaspoon salt. Stir in remaining 2 cups chicken broth, ½ cup at a time, until desired consistency is reached. Season with salt to taste. Cook, stirring often, until heated through, about 4 minutes.

5 Divide soup evenly among bowls. Top each with a spoonful of crème fraîche, and sprinkle each serving with bacon, parsley, and paprika. —CLARE CARVER

MAKE AHEAD Soup may be stored in an airtight container in refrigerator up to 4 days.

WINE Tart, lightly spicy rosé: 2019 Big Table Farm Pinot Gris

POULTRY

CHICKEN WITH CHARRED-ROSEMARY VINAIGRETTE (P. 115)

BRISKET-BRAISED CHICKEN

Heaped with sliced onions and flavored with red wine, paprika, and honey, the chicken is falling-off-the-bone tender with a deeply craveable sweet-savory sauce.

ACTIVE 50 MIN; TOTAL 2 HR; SERVES 4 TO 6

¼ cup vegetable oil, divided

3½ lb. bone-in, skin-on chicken thighs and drumsticks, trimmed and patted dry

1 Tbsp. plus 1 tsp. kosher salt, divided

½ tsp. black pepper

2 large yellow onions, thinly sliced

4 garlic cloves, thinly sliced

2 Tbsp. tomato paste

2 tsp. Hungarian sweet paprika

1 tsp. onion powder

½ cup (4 oz.) dry red wine

2 Tbsp. apple cider vinegar

1 (14½-oz.) can diced tomatoes

1 cup chicken broth

¼ cup honey

2 fresh or dried bay leaves

1 Heat 2 tablespoons oil in a large Dutch oven over medium until shimmering. Sprinkle chicken with 1 tablespoon salt and the pepper. Working in 3 batches, arrange chicken pieces, skin-sides down, in Dutch oven; cook until browned on both sides, 4 to 5 minutes per side. Set aside. Wipe pan clean; add remaining 2 tablespoons oil.

2 Add onions and garlic to Dutch oven; cook over medium, stirring occasionally, until lightly browned, about 8 minutes. Stir in tomato paste, paprika, and onion powder; cook 30 seconds. Add wine and vinegar; cook, stirring constantly and scraping up browned bits, until mixture thickens, about 1 minute.

3 Stir in tomatoes, broth, honey, bay leaves, and remaining 1 teaspoon salt. Nestle chicken into mixture; bring to a boil over medium-high. Cover and reduce heat to low; simmer until chicken easily pulls away from bone, about 50 minutes, partially submerging chicken in mixture after 20 minutes.

4 Uncover Dutch oven; increase heat to medium-low. Simmer, gently stirring occasionally, until liquid has slightly thickened, about 15 minutes. Discard bay leaves. Transfer chicken to plates; spoon sauce over chicken. — LEAH KOENIG

MAKE AHEAD Chicken can be braised up to 2 days ahead and stored in an airtight container in refrigerator.

ROSEMARY-ROASTED CHICKEN
WITH ARTICHOKES AND POTATOES

Chicken and aromatic rosemary have long been a perfect pair. Added in stages, hardy rosemary sprigs infuse this spatchcocked chicken with herbal, piney flavor from start to finish. Add baby potatoes, shallots, and tangy marinated artichokes to the sheet pan to turn this roast chicken into a one-pan meal that's elegant enough for a dinner party and quick enough for a weeknight.

ACTIVE 25 MIN; TOTAL 1 HR 10 MIN; SERVES 4

- 2 **small lemons (about 6 oz.)**
- 1 **(4-lb.) whole chicken, neck and giblets removed, chicken patted dry**
- ¼ **cup extra-virgin olive oil, divided**
- 1 **Tbsp. plus 1½ tsp. kosher salt, divided**
- 1½ **tsp. smoked paprika**
- 2 **tsp. black pepper, divided**
- 1 **lb. baby potatoes**
- 4 **large shallots (about 8 oz.), halved lengthwise**
- 12 **(4- to 6-inch) fresh rosemary sprigs, divided**
- 1 **(12- to 14-oz.) jar marinated artichoke hearts, drained, halved lengthwise if whole**

1 Preheat oven to 450°F. Grate zest from lemons to measure 1 tablespoon. Slice grated lemons into thin rounds. Set zest and slices aside. Using poultry shears, cut along each side of chicken backbone; remove bone and reserve for stock, if desired. Flip chicken breast-side up; press on breastbone to flatten chicken. Tuck wing tips under; rub chicken all over with 2 tablespoons oil. Sprinkle all over with lemon zest, 1 tablespoon salt, smoked paprika, and 1½ teaspoons pepper. Place chicken, skin side up, on a rimmed baking sheet lined with aluminum foil.

2 Place potatoes, shallots, lemon slices, 8 rosemary sprigs, remaining 2 tablespoons oil, remaining 1½ teaspoons salt, and remaining ½ teaspoon pepper in a large bowl; toss to coat. Scatter potato mixture in an even layer around chicken on baking sheet.

3 Roast in preheated oven until a thermometer inserted in thickest portion of meat registers 140°F, 30 to 40 minutes. Scatter artichokes and remaining 4 rosemary sprigs around chicken. Return to oven; roast at 450°F until potatoes are tender and a thermometer inserted in thickest portion of meat registers 155°F, 5 to 10 minutes. Remove from oven; let rest 10 minutes. (Chicken temperature will continue to rise to 165°F.) Carve chicken. Toss vegetables with juices on baking sheet; serve with chicken. —JUSTIN CHAPPLE

WINE Fairly robust California rosé: 2019 Clif Family Winery Rosé of Grenache

CHICKEN SCARPARIELLO WITH PICKLED PEPPERS

Scarpariello is a classic Italian-American dish that's easy to pull off at home with jarred pickled peppers and sweet Italian sausage. This one-pot meal requires no chopping and features ingredients found just about anywhere.

ACTIVE 20 MIN; TOTAL 45 MIN; SERVES 4

4 (4-oz.) bone-in, skin-on chicken thighs

1 tsp. kosher salt

½ tsp. black pepper

2 Tbsp. extra-virgin olive oil

4 (4-oz.) sweet Italian sausages

½ cup dry white wine

6 small garlic cloves, gently smashed

3 oregano sprigs

2 cups lower-sodium chicken broth

2 cups mixed jarred pickled peppers (such as peperoncini, Peppadews, and sweet cherry peppers)

1 Tbsp. fresh oregano leaves

Crusty bread, for serving

1 Sprinkle chicken evenly with salt and pepper. Heat oil in a large, deep skillet over medium-high. Add chicken, skin-sides down, and sausages; cook until browned on all sides, about 10 minutes, flipping halfway through cook time. Transfer chicken and sausages to a plate; carefully pour out and discard excess drippings from skillet. (Do not wipe skillet clean.)

2 Add wine, garlic, and oregano sprigs to skillet; cook over medium-high, scraping up any browned bits from bottom of skillet, until wine is nearly evaporated, about 2 minutes.

3 Add broth to skillet; bring to a boil over high. Carefully nestle chicken and sausages in broth mixture; reduce heat to low and simmer, covered, until chicken is tender and a thermometer inserted in thickest portion of thigh registers 165°F, about 25 minutes.

4 Stir pickled peppers into skillet mixture; cover and cook over low until hot, about 5 minutes. Sprinkle evenly with oregano leaves; serve with crusty bread.
—JUSTIN CHAPPLE

WINE Medium-bodied, earthy Chianti Classico: 2015 Rocca delle Macìe

MEXICAN CHICKEN POZOLE VERDE

There are many variations on pozole, a traditional hominy-based Mexican stew closely associated with the Pacific-Coast state of Guerrero. Anya von Bremzen's version, a green pozole, derives much of its flavor from tangy ingredients like tomatillos, cilantro, and green chiles.

ACTIVE 45 MIN; TOTAL 1 HR 15 MIN; SERVES 6 TO 8

- 7 **cups chicken stock or low-sodium broth**
- 4 **bone-in chicken breast halves, with skin**
- 1 **lb. tomatillos, husked and halved**
- 1 **small onion, quartered**
- 2 **poblano chiles, seeded and quartered**
- 2 **jalapeños, seeded and quartered**
- 4 **large garlic cloves, smashed**
- ½ **cup chopped fresh cilantro**
- 1 **Tbsp. fresh oregano leaves**
  Salt and freshly ground black pepper
- 1 **Tbsp. vegetable oil**
- 3 **(15-oz.) cans of hominy, drained**
  Finely shredded iceberg lettuce, sliced radishes, chopped onion, diced avocado, sour cream, tortilla chips, and lime wedges, for serving

1 In a large, enameled cast-iron casserole bring chicken stock and 2 cups water to a boil. Add chicken breasts, skin-side down, cover and simmer over very low heat until tender and cooked through, about 25 minutes. Transfer chicken breasts to a plate; shred meat; discard bones and skin. Skim and reserve any fat from cooking liquid.

2 Meanwhile, in a blender combine halved tomatillos with onion quarters, poblanos, jalapeños, garlic, cilantro, and oregano. Pulse until coarsely chopped. With the machine running add 1 cup cooking liquid and puree until smooth. Season with salt and pepper.

3 Heat vegetable oil in a large deep skillet until shimmering. Add tomatillo puree and cook over medium, stirring occasionally, until sauce turns a deep green, about 12 minutes.

4 Pour sauce into cooking liquid in casserole. Add hominy and bring to a simmer over medium. Add shredded chicken to the stew, season with salt and pepper and cook just until heated through. Serve pozole in deep bowls with lettuce, radishes, onion, avocado, sour cream, tortilla chips, and lime wedges. — ANYA VON BREMZEN

MAKE AHEAD The pozole verde can be prepared through Step 3 and refrigerated, covered, overnight.

WINE A rich, but unoaked white wine, such as a smooth Alsace Pinot Gris

PERFECT SLOW COOKER CHICKEN BREASTS

Cookbook author Sarah DiGregorio slowly simmers chicken breasts in seasoned olive oil until they're wonderfully juicy and flavorful. She uses that delicious oil to make a silky aioli, to serve alongside the chicken. The duo makes for a spectacular light meal with a salad. It could also be turned into a tender sandwich.

ACTIVE 30 MIN; TOTAL 2 HR 30 MIN; SERVES 4

5 cups cold water

¼ cup fine salt

¼ cup granulated sugar

1 lemon, scrubbed and quartered, plus 2½ Tbsp. fresh lemon juice, divided

4 (7-oz.) skinless, boneless chicken breast halves

3 cups extra-virgin olive oil

3 garlic cloves

2 fresh bay leaves

2 fresh thyme sprigs

1 fresh rosemary sprig

½ tsp. whole black peppercorns

Kosher salt

2 large egg yolks

Crusty bread and green salad, for serving

1 In a large bowl whisk water with fine salt and sugar until dissolved. Squeeze and add 2 lemon quarters to bowl. Add chicken; cover with plastic wrap and refrigerate at least 1 hour or up to 6 hours.

2 Meanwhile, add olive oil to a 6-quart slow cooker. Add garlic, bay leaves, thyme, rosemary, black peppercorns, 1½ teaspoons kosher salt, and remaining 2 lemon quarters. Cover and cook on low until a thermometer inserted in oil registers 200°F, about 1 hour. (The oil can be kept in the slow cooker on low up to 6 hours.)

3 Remove chicken from the brine and pat dry; transfer to a plate. Discard brine. Using tongs, carefully lower chicken into the warm oil. Cover and cook on low until a thermometer inserted in chicken registers 155°F, about 40 minutes. Using a slotted spoon, transfer chicken and garlic to a plate. Cover with foil and keep warm. Discard lemon quarters and herbs. Using a ladle, transfer 1 cup infused oil to a measuring cup (do not use the peppercorns) and let cool just until warm, 15 minutes. Reserve remaining oil for another use.

4 In a blender puree the egg yolks, lemon juice, 1 cooked garlic clove, and ½ teaspoon kosher salt until smooth, about 30 seconds. With the machine on, gradually add the 1 cup of cooled oil until creamy, about 1 minute. Season the aïoli with kosher salt.

5 Slice chicken and serve with aïoli, bread, and salad. —SARAH DIGREGORIO

MAKE AHEAD The chicken and aïoli can be refrigerated overnight.

WINE Citrusy Chilean Chardonnay: 2014 Montes Alpha

QUICK SKILLET-ROASTED CHICKEN
WITH SPRING VEGETABLES

Tender vegetables simmer in a mixture of chicken drippings and butter in this simple, speedy dish. The attached drumette gives these airline chicken breasts more flavor; bone-in, skin-on chicken thighs make a good substitute.

ACTIVE 40 MIN; TOTAL 55 MIN; SERVES 4

- 4 **(10-oz.) skin-on airline chicken breasts**
- 1½ **tsp. kosher salt, divided, plus more to taste**
- ¾ **tsp. black pepper, divided**
- 1 **Tbsp. olive oil**
- 6 **small carrots, sliced diagonally into 1-inch pieces (about 1½ cups)**
- 8 **oz. fresh oyster mushrooms, halved**
- 6 **small hakurei turnips or radishes, trimmed and quartered (about 1 cup)**
- 3 **Tbsp. unsalted butter, cut into pieces, divided**
- 6 **fresh rosemary and thyme sprigs, divided**
- 2 **spring onions, or 4 scallions, cut into 2-inch pieces (about 1 cup)**
- ¼ **cup (2 oz.) rosé wine**
- ½ **cup unsalted chicken stock**
- 2 **Tbsp. chopped fresh flat-leaf parsley**

1 Preheat oven to 425°F. Sprinkle chicken evenly with 1¼ teaspoons salt and ½ teaspoon pepper. Heat oil in a 12-inch ovenproof skillet over medium. Cook chicken, skin side down, until skin is golden brown and crispy, 15 to 18 minutes. Transfer to a plate. Reserve drippings in skillet.

2 Increase heat to high. Add carrots, mushrooms, turnips, 1 tablespoon butter, 3 herb sprigs, remaining ¼ teaspoon salt, and remaining ¼ teaspoon pepper; stir to combine. Cook, stirring occasionally, until browned, about 6 minutes. Add onions and chicken, skin side up. Transfer skillet to preheated oven. Roast until a thermometer inserted in thickest portion of chicken registers 160°F, 18 to 20 minutes. Using a slotted spoon, divide chicken and vegetables among 4 plates; reserve drippings in skillet.

3 Return skillet to heat over high. Add rosé and remaining 3 herb sprigs; cook, undisturbed, 2 minutes. Add stock, and bring to a simmer over high. Simmer until reduced by one-third, 2 to 3 minutes. Stir in parsley and remaining 2 tablespoons butter; season to taste with salt. Pour sauce over chicken and vegetables.
—LIZ MERVOSH

WINE Creamy, lightly peppery rosé: 2020 Mas de Gourgonnier Les Baux de Provence

POULTRY

SKILLET CHICKEN AND CHORIZO PAELLA

While Spanish paella is traditionally made in its namesake pan, this cast-iron variation is a welcome alternative. It can go straight from stove to table. This recipe builds layers of flavors as you saute aromatics in the same pan used to sear the chorizo and chicken. From delicately floral saffron to smoky paprika and a bright lemony finish, this one-pan meal has it all.

ACTIVE 55 MIN; TOTAL 1 HR; SERVES 6

½ tsp. saffron threads

3¼ cups lower-sodium chicken broth, divided

1 Tbsp. olive oil

6 oz. dry-cured Spanish chorizo, cut into ¼-inch-thick slices

1 lb. boneless, skinless chicken thighs, cut into 1½-inch pieces

½ tsp. black pepper

1½ tsp. kosher salt, divided

¾ cup chopped yellow onion

1 small red bell pepper, finely chopped

4 small garlic cloves, minced

½ tsp. smoked paprika

1 (14½-oz.) can diced tomatoes, undrained

1½ cups uncooked short-grain white rice (such as Spanish bomba or Italian arborio)

1 cup thawed frozen sweet peas

Chopped fresh flat-leaf parsley

Lemon wedges

1 Stir together saffron and ¼ cup of the broth in a small bowl. Let stand at room temperature at least 15 minutes or up to 1 hour.

2 Meanwhile, heat oil in a 12-inch cast-iron skillet over medium-high. Add chorizo; cook, stirring occasionally, until lightly browned, about 2 minutes. Using a slotted spoon, transfer chorizo to a plate lined with paper towels; reserve drippings in skillet. Add chicken, pepper, and 1 teaspoon of the salt to skillet; cook over medium-high, stirring occasionally, until lightly browned but not fully cooked, about 7 minutes. Using a slotted spoon, transfer chicken to plate with chorizo. Do not wipe skillet clean.

3 Add onion and bell pepper to skillet; cook over medium-high, stirring occasionally, until tender, about 5 minutes. Stir in garlic and smoked paprika; cook, stirring constantly, until fragrant, about 1 minute. Stir in tomatoes and rice; cook, stirring constantly, until liquid is almost fully absorbed, about 2 minutes. Carefully stir in saffron mixture, remaining 3 cups broth, and ½ teaspoon salt; bring to a simmer over medium-high.

4 Return chorizo and chicken to skillet, stirring lightly to partially cover with rice; sprinkle mixture with peas (do not stir peas in). Cook, uncovered and undisturbed, over medium-low, rotating skillet occasionally to evenly distribute heat, until chicken and rice are tender and liquid is almost fully absorbed, about 20 minutes. Remove from heat; cover and let stand at room temperature until liquid is fully absorbed, about 5 minutes. Garnish with parsley and lemon wedges.
— MELISSA GRAY

CHICKEN WITH CHARRED-ROSEMARY VINAIGRETTE

PHOTO P. 103

To amp up oven-roasted chicken with artichokes, Food & Wine's *Justin Chapple drizzles the dish with a bright and mildly smoky charred-rosemary vinaigrette. The vinaigrette is inspired by chef John Manion of El Che Bar in Chicago.*

TOTAL 45 MIN; SERVES 4

- 4 (4-inch) fresh rosemary sprigs
- 3 Tbsp. Champagne vinegar
- 1 Tbsp. Dijon mustard
- ¼ cup plus 1 Tbsp. extra-virgin olive oil
  Kosher salt and black pepper
- 6 skin-on, bone-in chicken thighs
- 1 (10-oz.) pkg. frozen artichoke heart quarters, thawed
- 1 pint cherry tomatoes
- ½ cup drained capers

1 Preheat oven to 375°F. Roast 2 rosemary sprigs directly on oven rack until charred, about 5 minutes. Leave oven on. Strip needles off stem, then finely crush; discard stems. In a small bowl whisk rosemary with vinegar, mustard, and ¼ cup olive oil. Season with salt and pepper. Set vinaigrette aside.

2 Heat remaining 1 tablespoon oil in a large, deep ovenproof skillet. Season chicken with salt and pepper. Cook, skin-side down, over medium-high, turning once, until well browned, 12 minutes. Transfer to a plate.

3 Pour off all but 2 tablespoons fat from skillet. Stir in artichokes, tomatoes, capers, and remaining rosemary sprigs. Top with chicken; roast until a thermometer inserted in chicken registers 165°F, about 15 minutes. Drizzle with vinaigrette; serve with vinaigrette. —JUSTIN CHAPPLE

WINE Herbal Grüner Veltliner: 2015 Loimer Lois

CHICKEN FRICASSEE STIR-FRY

"Once you understand the basics of stir-frying, you don't have to limit yourself to Asian flavors," cookbook author Grace Young says. Here, she uses white wine in place of rice wine, garlic instead of ginger, and cream to enrich the sauce.

TOTAL 25 MIN; SERVES 4

- 1 lb. boneless, skinless chicken breasts, cut crosswise into ¼-inch-thick slices
- 1 Tbsp. minced fresh garlic
- 3 Tbsp. (1½ oz.) dry white wine, divided
- 5½ tsp. cornstarch, divided
- 1 tsp. kosher salt, divided, plus more to taste
- ¼ tsp. black pepper
- 2 Tbsp. plus 1 tsp. grapeseed or safflower oil, divided
- ½ cup chicken broth
- 2 Tbsp. heavy cream
- 1 (12-oz.) bunch asparagus, cut into 2-inch pieces (about 2 cups)
- 1 cup thinly sliced carrots
- 4 fresh thyme sprigs
- 3 medium scallions, thinly sliced
- 1 Tbsp. chopped fresh flat-leaf parsley

1 Combine chicken, garlic, 1 tablespoon wine, 1½ teaspoons cornstarch, ½ teaspoon salt, and pepper in a medium bowl; toss to coat. Add 1 teaspoon oil and toss until chicken is lightly coated; set aside. Whisk together broth, cream, remaining 2 tablespoons wine, and remaining 4 teaspoons cornstarch in a small bowl until cornstarch is completely dissolved; set aside.

2 Heat a 14-inch flat-bottomed wok or a 12-inch skillet over high until a drop of water evaporates within 1 to 2 seconds of contact. Swirl in 1 tablespoon oil. Add chicken; spread in a single layer. Cook, undisturbed, until chicken begins to sear, 1 minute. Cook, stir-frying, until chicken is no longer pink but not cooked through, about 1 minute.

3 Swirl remaining 1 tablespoon oil into wok. Add asparagus, carrots, thyme sprigs, and remaining ½ teaspoon salt; cook, stir-frying constantly, until asparagus turns bright green, 1 minute to 1 minute and 30 seconds. Whisk broth mixture, then pour into wok; stir-fry until well combined, about 30 seconds. Cover wok with a baking sheet and cook until sauce comes to a full boil and starts to thicken, about 1 minute. Uncover; add scallions and parsley. Stir-fry until chicken is cooked through and sauce is thickened, 30 seconds to 1 minute. Discard thyme sprigs. Season with salt to taste. —GRACE YOUNG

WINE Creamy, citrusy Chardonnay: 2019 Chateau Ste. Michelle Columbia Valley

CAPE MALAY CHICKEN CURRY

Served over creamy mielie pap, this mild chicken curry gets gentle heat from grassy jalapeño and spicy ginger. Considered a South African staple, this recipe's roots can be traced back to the Indonesian and Southeast Asian homelands of the enslaved Cape Malay people who were brought to the country centuries ago.

ACTIVE 40 MIN; TOTAL 1 HR; SERVES 6

- 1 (2-inch) cinnamon stick
- 2 tsp. fennel seeds
- 1 (3½- to 4½-lb.) whole chicken, cut into 10 bone-in pieces
- 1 Tbsp. plus 2½ tsp. kosher salt, divided, plus more to taste
- 2 Tbsp. neutral oil (such as grapeseed)
- 2 medium-size yellow onions, cut into ½-inch-thick slices (about 5 cups)
- 2 medium jalapeños, halved lengthwise, seeded, and thinly sliced (about ⅓ cup)
- 2 Tbsp. grated peeled fresh ginger
- 2 Tbsp. curry powder
- 3 medium garlic cloves, finely chopped
- 1 (15-oz.) can diced tomatoes, undrained
- ¼ cup mango chutney or apricot preserves
- 2 fresh or dried bay leaves
- 1½ Tbsp. fresh lime juice
  Mielie Pap (recipe follows)
  Chopped fresh cilantro, for garnish

1 Heat cinnamon stick and fennel seeds in a small skillet over medium-low, stirring often, until lightly toasted and fragrant, 1 to 2 minutes. Transfer to a spice grinder; process until very finely ground, about 45 seconds. Set aside.

2 Sprinkle chicken pieces all over with 1 tablespoon salt. Heat oil in a large Dutch oven over medium-high. Working in 2 batches, cook chicken until browned on all sides, 8 to 12 minutes per batch. Transfer chicken to a plate.

3 Reduce heat under Dutch oven to medium. Add onions and ½ teaspoon salt; cook, stirring occasionally and scraping bottom of Dutch oven to loosen any browned bits, until onions are softened, 10 to 12 minutes. Stir in jalapeños, ginger, curry powder, garlic, and ground cinnamon mixture. Cook, stirring often, until fragrant, about 2 minutes.

4 Stir undrained tomatoes into curry mixture; cook, stirring occasionally, until liquid reduces and forms a thick paste, 3 to 4 minutes. Stir in 1 cup water, chutney, bay leaves, and remaining 2 teaspoons salt. Nestle chicken pieces into mixture. Bring to a boil over medium. Reduce heat to low; cover and cook until a thermometer inserted in thickest portion of chicken thighs registers 165°F, 20 to 25 minutes.

5 Stir lime juice into curry mixture; season with salt to taste. Discard bay leaves. Ladle curry over mielie pap; garnish with cilantro. —MARIA SINSKEY

MAKE AHEAD Chicken curry may be stored in an airtight container in refrigerator up to 3 days.

WINE Fresh, citrusy South African white: 2019 Radley & Finch Viking Point Sauvignon Blanc

MIELIE PAP (CORNMEAL PORRIDGE)

Mielie pap is a South African cornmeal porridge with thick, creamy consistency. Its mild flavor is the ideal base for spicy, flavorful dishes like Cape Malay Chicken Curry.

ACTIVE 35 MIN; TOTAL 40 MIN; SERVES 6

- ½ cup unsalted butter (4 oz.), divided
- 1½ cups uncooked stone-ground white polenta (about 7 oz.)
- 1 Tbsp. kosher salt, plus more to taste

1 Bring 6 cups water and 6 tablespoons butter to a boil in a large saucepan over medium-high. Gradually add polenta, whisking constantly. Reduce heat to low; cook, whisking constantly, until mixture thickens slightly, about 3 minutes.

2 Continue cooking, uncovered, whisking occasionally and scraping bottom of pan, until polenta is tender and thickened, about 30 minutes. Whisk in salt, and add more to taste. Transfer mielie pap to a serving bowl; top with remaining 2 tablespoons butter. Serve immediately. —MARIA SINSKEY

HUNTER'S SAUSAGE-AND-SAUERKRAUT STEW

Polish hunter's stew typically has at least three meats—from wild game to pork ribs and sausages to veal. In his version, chef Andrew Zimmern adds lightly smoked bacon, chicken thighs, and kielbasa.

ACTIVE 30 MIN; TOTAL 1 HR 15 MIN; SERVES 4 TO 6

2 red bell peppers

4 tomatoes

1 lb. boneless, skinless chicken thighs

   Kosher salt and freshly ground black pepper

2 Tbsp. unsalted butter

4 oz. diced bacon

1 yellow onion, diced

3 cups fresh chanterelle or button mushrooms, sliced

1 fennel bulb, halved and thinly sliced

1 leek, thinly sliced

¼ cup sliced garlic

¼ cup sweet paprika

1½ lb. Polish kielbasa, cut into ¼-inch slices

½ cup chopped fresh dill

¼ cup chopped fresh flat-leaf parsley

2 cups red wine

4 cups chicken stock

4 cups fresh sauerkraut with juices

1 Preheat broiler. Place bell peppers on a small baking sheet, and roast under broiler or directly over a gas flame, turning frequently, until skins are blackened, about 5 minutes. Transfer to a medium heatproof bowl, and cover tightly with plastic wrap. Let stand until peppers are cool enough to handle, about 10 minutes. Remove and discard skins, stems, and seeds; place in a blender. Add tomatoes; process until smooth.

2 Season chicken with salt and pepper. Melt butter in a large Dutch oven over medium-high. Add chicken thighs and cook until browned, about 4 minutes per side. Transfer chicken to a plate.

3 Add bacon to Dutch oven; cook, stirring, until bacon begins to render, about 2 minutes. Add onion and mushrooms; cook, stirring occasionally, until onion begins to turn golden, about 5 minutes. Stir in fennel, leek, garlic, and paprika, cook 2 minutes. Add kielbasa, dill, and parsley. Cook, stirring, until sausage is heated through, 3 to 4 minutes.

4 Return chicken to Dutch oven. Add wine, bring to a boil, and cook until liquid is reduced by half, about 5 minutes. Add pepper mixture and bring to a simmer. Add stock and sauerkraut; stir to combine. Bring to a simmer, reduce heat, and simmer gently until vegetables are tender and chicken shreds with a fork, about 45 minutes. Season to taste with salt. —ANDREW ZIMMERN

WINE Spicy Slovenian Pinot Noir: 2010 Movia Modri

POULET MAFÉ

For chef Pierre Thiam, poulet mafé is the ultimate comfort food. His advice: "Be patient when cooking mafé. Let the stew simmer slowly until the oil rises to the surface." Creamy peanut butter adds body and nuttiness to this savory chicken dish, balancing the aromatic ginger, garlic, and tomato paste.

ACTIVE 50 MIN; TOTAL 2 HR, PLUS 3 HR MARINATION; SERVES 4 TO 6

3 medium garlic cloves, finely chopped

1 Tbsp. peeled and finely chopped fresh ginger

Pinch of kosher salt, plus more to taste

Pinch of black pepper

1 lb. bone-in chicken thighs, skin removed

1 lb. chicken drumsticks, skin removed

3 Tbsp. vegetable oil

1 small yellow onion, chopped

1 (6-oz.) can tomato paste

¼ cup fish sauce (such as Red Boat)

1 cup unsweetened creamy peanut butter (such as Smucker's Natural Creamy Peanut Butter), well stirred

8 oz. green cabbage, cored and cut into 2-inch wedges

3 medium carrots, cut into 2-inch-long pieces

2 medium Yukon Gold potatoes, peeled and cut into 1½-inch pieces

1 medium-size sweet potato, peeled and cut into 1½-inch pieces

Sliced fresh Scotch bonnet chiles, to taste (optional)

Cooked white rice, for serving

1 Stir together garlic, ginger, salt, and black pepper in a large bowl. Add chicken; press garlic mixture into chicken pieces. Cover with plastic wrap; refrigerate at least 3 hours or up to 12 hours.

2 Heat oil in a large Dutch oven over medium-high until oil shimmers. Add onion; cook, stirring often, until onion starts to become translucent, about 3 minutes. Stir in tomato paste and fish sauce. Cook, stirring constantly, until combined and tomato paste caramelizes and turns a few shades darker, 6 to 8 minutes. Add 7 cups water, scraping up any browned bits from bottom of Dutch oven. Add chicken and any remaining garlic mixture in bowl to Dutch oven. Bring to a boil over high. Reduce heat to medium-low.

3 Place peanut butter in a medium-size heatproof bowl; stir in 1½ cups liquid from Dutch oven, ¼ cup at a time, until peanut butter is thinned out and mixture is creamy. Add to mixture in Dutch oven; bring to a vigorous simmer over medium-low. Simmer, undisturbed, 20 minutes.

4 Stir cabbage and carrots into mixture in Dutch oven; return to a vigorous simmer over medium-low. Simmer, undisturbed, 10 minutes.

5 Stir potato and sweet potato pieces into mixture in Dutch oven; return to a vigorous simmer over medium-low. Simmer, undisturbed, until chicken and vegetables are tender and oil has separated from thickened sauce, 30 to 35 minutes. Remove from heat; stir in Scotch bonnet chiles, if using, and season with salt to taste. Serve over rice. —PIERRE THIAM

MAKE AHEAD Poulet mafé can be made up to 3 days ahead and stored in an airtight container in refrigerator. Reheat gently before serving.

WINE Generous, spicy red: 2017 Bila-Haut Côtes du Roussillon Rouge

CHICKEN AND PORK PAELLA

In this delicious adaptation of a classic Spanish recipe, rice, artichoke hearts, and romano beans are combined with chicken and pork ribs for a hearty and satisfying dish—laced with alluring flavors of saffron, garlic, and smoky pimentón.

ACTIVE 1 HR; TOTAL 1 HR 45 MIN; SERVES 6 TO 8

1 lb. skinless, boneless chicken thighs, cut into 1½-inch pieces

1 lb. boneless country-style pork ribs, cut into 1½-inch pieces

¼ cup plus 1 Tbsp. extra-virgin olive oil

2 Tbsp. finely grated garlic

2 tsp. pimentón de la Vera (smoked sweet Spanish paprika)

Kosher salt and black pepper

Large pinch of saffron, finely ground in a mortar

¼ cup boiling water

2 large tomatoes, halved crosswise

1 (9-oz). pkg. frozen artichoke hearts, thawed

¼ lb. romano beans, cut into 2-inch lengths

8 scallions, cut into 1-inch lengths

6 cups chicken stock or low-sodium broth

2 cups Bomba rice

1 large rosemary sprig

1 roasted red bell pepper—quartered lengthwise, seeded, and cut crosswise into small strips

1 cup thawed frozen peas

1 In a large bowl mix the chicken and pork with 1 tablespoon each olive oil and garlic, and 1 teaspoon pimentón. Season generously with salt and pepper; mix well. Let stand at room temperature 30 minutes.

2 Meanwhile, preheat oven to 425°F. In a small heatproof bowl combine saffron and boiling water; let cool completely. Grate tomato halves on the large holes of a box grater set in a bowl until only the skins remain; discard skins.

3 In a 15-inch paella pan or large enameled cast-iron casserole, heat 2 tablespoons of the olive oil over high until shimmering. Add half the chicken-pork mixture and cook, stirring occasionally, until well browned but not cooked through, about 6 minutes. Transfer to a plate. Repeat with another 1 tablespoon olive oil and remaining chicken-pork mixture.

4 Add the artichokes, romano beans, remaining 1 tablespoon olive oil and a generous pinch each of salt and pepper to the pan; cook, stirring occasionally, until lightly browned, about 3 minutes. Push mixture to one side of pan and reduce heat to medium. Add the remaining 1 tablespoon of garlic and 1 teaspoon of pimentón to the opposite side of the pan; cook until fragrant, about 2 minutes. Add grated tomatoes and scallions. Cook, stirring frequently, until vegetables are deeply colored and coated in a thick sauce, about 5 minutes. Stir in chicken-pork mixture, 4 cups of the stock and the brewed saffron. Bring to a boil over high, then scatter the rice evenly on top, shaking the pan to evenly distribute it. Simmer over medium-high, shaking pan occasionally, until slightly reduced, about 5 minutes. Add rosemary sprig and remaining 2 cups of stock; season with salt and pepper.

5 Transfer paella to oven; bake until the rice is tender and liquid is absorbed, about 15 minutes. Scatter roasted red pepper and peas on top; bake 3 minutes more. Serve hot. —ANYA VON BREMZEN

WINE Berry-rich Monastrell from Alicante: 2014 Enrique Mendoza La Tremenda

FOOD & WINE ONE POT MEALS **125**

FETTUCCINE WITH WHITE CHICKEN RAGÙ

This creamy chicken ragù is easy to make and boasts remarkable depth thanks to the flavors of an Italian-style sofrito made with onions, carrots, celery, and parsley.

ACTIVE 50 MIN; TOTAL 1 HR 45 MIN; SERVES 6

2 Tbsp. olive oil

4 oz. pancetta or guanciale, finely chopped

2 medium garlic cloves

2 lb. bone-in, skin-on chicken thighs

1 tsp. sea salt, plus more to taste

½ tsp. black pepper, plus more to taste

1½ cups Sofrito (recipe follows)

6 Tbsp. dry white wine

2 cups organic chicken stock

2 leek leaves (from 1 leek) or 2 scallions

2 fresh rosemary sprigs

2 fresh thyme sprigs

1 fresh bay leaf

½ cup heavy cream or half-and-half

1 cup frozen sweet peas, thawed

12 oz. uncooked dried fettuccine or 16 oz. fresh fettuccine

1½ oz. Parmesan cheese, grated (about ⅓ cup)

1½ Tbsp. unsalted butter

1 tsp. lemon zest

2 Tbsp. chopped fresh flat-leaf parsley

1 Heat oil in a large Dutch oven over medium. Add pancetta; cook, stirring often, until fat has rendered, about 5 minutes. Using a slotted spoon, transfer pancetta to a plate, reserving drippings in Dutch oven. Add garlic to Dutch oven; increase heat to medium-high. Sprinkle chicken all over with salt and pepper. Working in batches, if needed, add chicken, skin-sides down, to Dutch oven. Cook until golden brown on both sides, about 6 minutes. Transfer chicken thighs to a plate.

2 Reserve garlic and 2 tablespoons drippings in Dutch oven; discard remaining drippings. Add sofrito and wine; bring to a simmer over medium. Cook, stirring and scraping up browned bits, until mixture is reduced by half, about 3 minutes. Return chicken to Dutch oven in a single layer; add stock, ensuring chicken is barely covered. Bring mixture to a simmer over medium. Bundle together leek leaves, rosemary sprigs, thyme sprigs, and bay leaf; secure with kitchen twine and add to Dutch oven. Reduce heat to medium-low; cover and cook until chicken is tender, 45 minutes to 1 hour. Remove Dutch oven from heat.

3 Transfer chicken to a cutting board; partially cover Dutch oven. Let chicken and sauce stand 10 minutes. Skim and discard fat from sauce; remove and discard garlic cloves and leek-herb bundle. Stir reserved pancetta into sauce. Remove and discard skin and bones from chicken; finely shred meat.

4 Stir cream into sauce. Cook over medium-high, stirring occasionally, until sauce is reduced by nearly half and has slightly thickened, 8 to 12 minutes. Stir peas and shredded chicken into sauce; cook until peas are just tender, about 2 minutes. Season with salt and pepper to taste. Remove from heat; cover to keep warm.

5 Cook pasta according to package directions; drain reserving ½ cup cooking liquid. Add pasta, Parmesan, butter, and lemon zest to sauce. Stir to combine, adding splashes of reserved cooking liquid as needed to form a creamy sauce. Sprinkle with parsley. Serve in large bowls. —SILVIA BALDINI

WINE Tart, medium-bodied Barbera d'Asti: 2016 Marchesi di Gresy

SOFRITO

ACTIVE 25 MIN; TOTAL 40 MIN; MAKES 4 CUPS

¼ cup extra-virgin olive oil

1 large onion, finely chopped

8 large garlic cloves, minced

4 green bell peppers, chopped

2 jalapeños, seeded and minced

Large pinch cayenne pepper

2 medium tomatoes, seeded and chopped, or 1 (28-oz.) can peeled tomatoes, drained and chopped

Salt and black pepper

½ cup chopped fresh cilantro

Heat olive oil in a large skillet. Add onion and cook over low until softened, about 4 minutes. Add garlic, bell peppers, jalapeños, and cayenne pepper. Cook, stirring occasionally, until vegetables are softened, about 20 minutes. Add tomatoes and cook over medium-high, stirring frequently, until juices have evaporated, about 7 minutes. Season with salt and black pepper. Stir in cilantro. —LINDA JAPNGIE

CHICKEN-BARLEY SOUP
WITH HERBS AND EGG NOODLES

No need to settle for just one type of soup when you can have two. Here, chicken-noodle meets mushroom-barley, in an incredibly delightful and soothing pot of soup.

ACTIVE 45 MIN; TOTAL 2 HR 30 MIN; SERVES 8

2 Tbsp. extra-virgin olive oil

3 lb. skin-on, bone-in chicken legs

Kosher salt and black pepper

2 leeks, white and light green parts only, thinly sliced

2 celery ribs, thinly sliced, plus chopped light green leaves for garnish

8 oz. mixed mushrooms, such as small white button and oyster, halved

3 garlic cloves, finely chopped

3 fresh thyme sprigs

4 qt. chicken stock or low-sodium broth

1¼ cups pearled barley

8 oz. egg noodles

1 Tbsp. fresh lemon juice

Chopped fresh flat-leaf parsley and tarragon, for garnish

1 Heat olive oil in a large enameled cast-iron casserole. Season chicken with salt and pepper; cook over medium, turning, until golden, about 8 minutes. Transfer to a large plate. Add leeks and sliced celery to casserole and cook, stirring occasionally, until softened, about 5 minutes. Add mushrooms and garlic; cook, stirring occasionally, until garlic is fragrant, about 2 minutes. Add thyme sprigs, stock, chicken, and 2 quarts of water; bring to a simmer. Cook, partially covered, 30 minutes. Stir in barley and cook until barley is tender and chicken is cooked through, about 1 hour. Transfer chicken to a baking sheet; when cool enough to handle, discard skin and shred meat.

2 Discard thyme sprigs. Add egg noodles to casserole and cook until al dente. Stir in shredded chicken and lemon juice; season with salt and pepper. Serve soup garnished with chopped parsley, tarragon, and celery leaves. —KAY CHUN

MAKE AHEAD The soup can be refrigerated up to 2 days.

MISO CHICKEN RAMEN

Sometimes a ramen fix is just the right dish, and this quick and easy version from Food & Wine's Justin Chapple hits the spot. The addition of white miso and runny eggs are key to making it feel more special than standard chicken noodle soup.

TOTAL 30 MIN; SERVES 2

1 qt. chicken stock or low-sodium broth

3 Tbsp. white miso

1 Tbsp. soy sauce

½ lb. shredded cooked chicken (about 2 cups)

2 large eggs

2 (3-oz.) pkg. ramen noodles, seasoning packets discarded

Shredded carrot, thinly sliced scallion and sriracha, for serving

1 Combine stock, miso, and soy sauce in a medium saucepan; bring to a boil over high, whisking to dissolve miso. Add chicken; simmer over medium 2 minutes. Keep warm over low heat.

2 Set up a small ice bath. Fill another medium saucepan with water and bring to a boil. Add eggs and simmer over medium for 7 minutes. Using a slotted spoon, transfer eggs to ice bath to cool. Carefully peel eggs and cut in half lengthwise.

3 Meanwhile, return broth to a boil. Add ramen and cook just until softened, about 3 minutes. Drain well and transfer to 2 large bowls. Ladle broth and chicken over noodles then top with eggs. Serve with shredded carrot, thinly sliced scallion, and sriracha. —JUSTIN CHAPPLE

MEXICAN CHICKEN SOUP

In chef and author Jane Coxwell's take on tortilla soup that she makes with tomatoes, toasted flour tortillas stand in for corn tortillas.

ACTIVE 30 MIN; TOTAL 1 HR 40 MIN; SERVES 4 TO 6

- 1 (3½-lb.) chicken
- 3 medium tomatoes, cored and quartered
- 1 medium carrot, sliced ½ inch thick
- 1 small red onion, cut into 1-inch pieces
- 2 garlic cloves, crushed
- ½ tsp. ground coriander
- ½ tsp. ground cumin
- 1 small cinnamon stick
- ½ cup chopped fresh cilantro, plus more for garnish
- Salt and black pepper
- 2 small flour tortillas, halved
- 6 Tbsp. fresh lime juice

1 Combine chicken, tomatoes, carrot, onion, garlic, coriander, cumin, cinnamon, ½ cup of cilantro, and 10 cups water in a large saucepan. Add a generous pinch each of salt and pepper; bring to a boil. Simmer, partially covered, over medium-low 30 minutes, skimming as necessary. Discard cinnamon stick; continue simmering until chicken is cooked through, 30 minutes longer.

2 Meanwhile, in a large skillet toast tortillas over medium, turning once, until crisp in spots, 3 minutes. Cut tortillas into thin strips.

3 Transfer chicken to a plate and let cool slightly. Shred meat; discard skin and bones. Return chicken to saucepan and reheat soup. Stir in lime juice and season with salt and pepper. Ladle soup into bowls. Garnish with tortilla strips and cilantro. —JANE COXWELL

CHICKEN TORTELLINI SOUP WITH KALE

Fresh ingredients team up with store-bought shortcuts to get this comforting dinner on the table in just over 30 minutes. Cheese tortellini needs only a 5-minute dip in simmering broth to cook up perfectly. Be sure to drain the juice from the tomatoes, then crush the whole tomatoes with your hands before adding them to sauce.

ACTIVE: 35 MIN; TOTAL: 35 MIN; SERVES 8

6 Tbsp. olive oil, divided

1 lb. boneless, skinless chicken thighs

½ tsp. black pepper

2½ tsp. kosher salt, divided

2 cups chopped yellow onion (from 1 large onion)

1 cup chopped celery (from 2 stalks)

5 garlic cloves, chopped (about 2 Tbsp.)

¼ cup fresh basil leaves, plus more for garnish

½ cup dry white wine

1 Tbsp. tomato paste

4 cups unsalted chicken stock

1 (28-oz.) can whole peeled tomatoes, drained

4 cups stemmed and thinly sliced lacinato kale (from 1 bunch)

1 (8-oz.) pkg. refrigerated cheese tortellini

2 oz. Parmesan cheese, grated (about ½ cup)

1 Heat 2 tablespoons oil in a large Dutch oven over high. Sprinkle chicken with pepper and 1 teaspoon salt; cook until browned, 2 to 3 minutes per side. Remove chicken; let rest 5 minutes. Cut chicken into cubes; set aside.

2 Reduce heat to medium-high. Add onion and celery, and cook, stirring occasionally, until tender, 3 to 4 minutes. Add garlic and basil; cook, stirring often, 2 minutes. Add wine and tomato paste; bring to a boil and reduce until liquid has almost evaporated, 3 to 4 minutes. Stir in stock. Add tomatoes, using your hands to crush tomatoes over pot as you add them. Bring to a boil. Add chicken, kale, tortellini, remaining ¼ cup oil, and remaining 1½ teaspoons salt. Simmer until tortellini are al dente, about 5 minutes.

3 Ladle soup into bowls. Top with Parmesan and additional basil. — ROBIN BASHINSKY

CHICKEN POT PIE SOUP
WITH PUFF PASTRY CROUTONS

This creamy, soul-warming soup captures everything there is to love about chicken pot pie: Aromatic vegetables, a rich, silky broth seasoned with tarragon and cream sherry, and plenty of tender chicken. Topped with puff pastry croutons, the soup is heavenly.

ACTIVE 1 HR 10 MIN; TOTAL 1 HR 50 MIN; SERVINGS: 6

All-purpose flour

1 sheet of frozen puff pastry, such as Pepperidge Farm, defrosted (see note)

1 extra-large egg beaten with 1 Tbsp. heavy cream, for egg wash

3 chicken breasts, skin-on, bone-in (2½ to 3 lb. total)

Olive oil

Kosher salt and freshly ground black pepper

6 Tbsp. (¾ stick) unsalted butter

5 cups chopped leeks, white and light green parts (3 leeks)

4 cups chopped fennel, tops and cores removed (2 bulbs)

3 cups (½-inch) diced scrubbed carrots

1 Tbsp. minced garlic (3 cloves)

1 Tbsp. chopped fresh tarragon leaves

¼ cup Wondra flour

¾ cup cream sherry, divided

7 cups good chicken stock, preferably homemade

1 (2 × 3-inch) piece of Italian Parmesan cheese rind

1 (10-oz.) box frozen peas

1 cup frozen whole pearl onions

¼ cup minced fresh flat-leaf parsley

1 Preheat oven to 350°F. Line a sheet pan with parchment paper. Lightly dust a cutting board and rolling pin with all-purpose flour. Unfold puff pastry on the board, dust lightly with all-purpose flour, and lightly roll pastry just to smooth out folds. With a star-shape or fluted round cookie cutter, cut 12 stars or rounds of pastry and place them on prepared pan. Brush tops with egg wash, sprinkle with salt and pepper, and refrigerate until ready to bake.

2 Place chicken on a sheet pan, skin-side up. Rub skin with olive oil and season generously with salt and pepper. Roast 30 to 35 minutes, until a thermometer inserted in breast registers 130°F to 140°F. Set aside until cool enough to handle, about 15 minutes. Remove and discard skin and bones; cut chicken in 1-inch dice. Increase oven temperature to 400°F.

3 Meanwhile, melt butter in a medium-size heavy-bottom pot or Dutch oven over medium. Add leeks, fennel, and carrots; cook over medium-high 10 to 15 minutes, stirring occasionally, until leeks are tender but not browned.

4 Stir in garlic and tarragon; cook, stirring often, 1 minute. Sprinkle Wondra flour on vegetables; cook, stirring constantly, 2 minutes. Add ½ cup sherry, the chicken stock, 4 teaspoons salt, 1½ teaspoons pepper, and Parmesan rind. Bring to a boil over medium-high; reduce heat to low. Simmer, partially covered, 20 minutes.

5 Meanwhile, bake puff pastry until puffed and golden brown, 8 to 10 minutes.

6 Add chicken, peas, and onions to vegetables and broth in pot. Return to a simmer over medium. Cook, uncovered, 5 minutes. Remove from heat. Remove Parmesan rind and add remaining ¼ cup sherry and the parsley. Serve in large shallow bowls , topped with croutons. — INA GARTEN

MAKE AHEAD Roll and cut pastry cutouts then refrigerate; bake just before serving soup. To prep leeks, cut off and discard dark green leaves at a 45-degree angle. Chop white and light green parts, wash well in a bowl of water, and spin dry in a salad spinner (wet leeks will steam rather than sauté).

NOTE Defrost puff pastry overnight in the refrigerator. The pastry should be very cold when baked.

STRACCIATELLA

Stracciatella is the Italian version of egg drop soup. This tasty recipe from chef Hugh Acheson includes shredded chicken, spinach, basil, peas, grated Parmigiano-Reggiano, and eggs.

TOTAL 30 MIN; SERVES 4

- 6 cups Basic Chicken Stock (recipe follows) or good-quality store-bought stock
- 2 large eggs
- ¼ cup finely grated Parmigiano-Reggiano cheese
- 2 cups shredded rotisserie chicken
- 1 cup frozen peas
- 2 cups leaf spinach (about 2 oz.), thinly sliced
- 1 cup fresh basil leaves, thinly sliced
- Kosher salt and pepper

In a medium pot bring chicken stock to a simmer over medium. In a small bowl, whisk together eggs and cheese. Slowly add egg mixture to hot stock, stirring constantly, just until eggs are set, about 1 minute. Stir in chicken and peas; simmer until heated through, about 2 minutes. Add spinach and basil; cook just until wilted, about 1 minute. Season with salt and pepper. —HUGH ACHESON

BASIC CHICKEN STOCK

Making chicken stock is so easy that you might never use store-bought again.

ACTIVE 30 MIN; TOTAL 8 HR 30 MIN; MAKES 3 QTS

- 1 (3½- to 4-lb.) chicken, quartered
- 2 medium white onions, quartered
- 3 large carrots, scrubbed and cut into 2-inch pieces
- 3 celery ribs with leaves, cut into 2-inch pieces
- 2 garlic cloves
- 2 fresh parsley sprigs
- 2 fresh thyme sprigs
- 2 bay leaves
- 1 tsp. coriander seeds
- 6 black peppercorns
- Kosher salt

1 In a large stockpot combine 4 quarts of water with all the ingredients except salt. Simmer, partially covered, over very low heat, 8 hours; skim surface of stock as necessary.

2 Strain stock into a large bowl then season with salt; discard solids. Let stock cool, then refrigerate. Skim fat from surface of stock before using. —HA

MAKE AHEAD Stock can be refrigerated up to 5 days or frozen up to 1 month.

CHICKEN-ORZO SOUP WITH 10 VEGETABLES

Any combination of vegetables will work in this nutritious soup from chef Hugh Acheson. If including 10 vegetables isn't a priority, you can also cut some and double up on others.

TOTAL 45 MIN; SERVES 4

2 Tbsp. extra-virgin olive oil

1 medium carrot, halved lengthwise and thinly sliced crosswise

1 small turnip, finely diced

½ small sweet onion, finely chopped

½ small fennel bulb, cored and finely diced

1 celery rib, thinly sliced

2 garlic cloves, minced

Kosher salt and black pepper

¼ lb. green or yellow beans, cut into ¼-inch pieces

6 cups Basic Chicken Stock (recipe p. 131) or good-quality store-bought stock

¼ cup cherry tomatoes, quartered

½ cup frozen peas

¾ cup orzo, boiled and drained

2 oz. arugula (about 2 cups packed), thinly sliced

½ cup fresh basil leaves, thinly sliced

1 Heat olive oil in a medium-size heavy saucepan or enameled cast-iron pot over medium. Add carrot, turnip, onion, fennel, celery, garlic, and a generous pinch of salt. Cook, stirring occasionally, until vegetables begin to soften, about 6 minutes. Stir in green beans and cook 1 minute. Add stock and bring to a simmer. Add cherry tomatoes and peas. Simmer soup, partially covered, over medium-low until vegetables are tender, about 15 minutes. Season with salt and pepper.

2 Divide orzo, arugula, and basil among 4 bowls; ladle hot soup on top.
—HUGH ACHESON

MAKE AHEAD The soup can be prepared through Step 1; refrigerated overnight. Gently reheat and continue with Step 2.

DRUNKEN CHICKEN SOUP

Justin Chapple developed this recipe for whole-bottle cooking. Inspired by Chinese drunken chicken, his drunken chicken soup has an entire bottle of wine. For this soup, use a wine for drinking to yield a more balanced broth.

ACTIVE 30 MIN; TOTAL 2 HR; SERVES 6

1 (750-ml) bottle Shaoxing wine or dry sherry (not cooking wine)

4 oz. fresh ginger, peeled and sliced (about ¾ cup)

3 Tbsp. granulated sugar

6 whole scallions

2 Tbsp. plus ½ tsp. kosher salt, divided

1 (3½-lb.) whole chicken

1 lb. kohlrabi, peeled and cut into 1-inch pieces

4 oz. shiitake mushrooms, stemmed and cut into 1-inch pieces (2 cups)

3 baby bok choy, trimmed and sliced (about 4 cups)

2 Tbsp. toasted sesame oil

1 cup thinly sliced scallions

Ground Szechuan peppercorns, for serving (optional)

1 Stir together 8 cups water, wine, ginger, sugar, whole scallions, and ½ teaspoon salt in a large Dutch oven. Remove giblets from chicken; reserve for another use, if desired. Add chicken to Dutch oven. Bring mixture to a boil over medium-high. Reduce heat to low, cover, and simmer until a meat thermometer inserted in thickest portion of thigh registers 165°F, about 1 hour and 30 minutes, skimming foam from surface.

2 Transfer chicken to a work surface; cool slightly. Remove and discard ginger and whole scallions, and add kohlrabi and mushrooms. Cover; cook over medium-low until kohlrabi is tender, about 30 minutes.

3 Meanwhile, remove and discard skin from chicken; pull meat off bones. Discard bones. Shred meat into bite-size pieces.

4 Stir shredded chicken, bok choy, and sesame oil into soup. Cover and cook until chicken is heated through and bok choy is crisp-tender, about 10 minutes. Stir in sliced scallions and remaining 2 tablespoons salt. Ladle soup into bowls and serve with Szechuan peppercorns, if using. —JUSTIN CHAPPLE

WINE Dry amontillado sherry: Lustau Los Arcos

SOTO AYAM

The fragrant soup of juicy chicken and delicate vermicelli noodles is topped with cabbage and sprouts for texture and crunch. The spice paste, bloomed in oil alongside fresh lemongrass and lime leaves, layers a mildly earthy, warming flavor into the broth.

ACTIVE 35 MIN; TOTAL 1 HR 30 MIN; SERVES 6 TO 8

SPICE PASTE

- 1 cup chopped shallots
- 1 Tbsp. ground turmeric
- 2 tsp. cumin seeds
- 6 macadamia nuts
- 4 medium garlic cloves
- 1 (3-inch) piece fresh ginger, peeled and roughly chopped
- 1 (2-inch) piece fresh galangal, peeled and sliced
- 2 Tbsp. grapeseed oil

SOUP

- 1 lemongrass stalk, trimmed
- ¼ cup grapeseed oil
- 3 fresh makrut lime leaves
- 2 fresh or 4 dried bay leaves
- 4 cups unsalted chicken broth
- 1 Tbsp. kosher salt, plus more to taste
- 1 tsp. freshly ground black pepper
- 1 (3½-lb.) whole chicken
- 2 cups well-shaken and stirred coconut milk
- 1 (8.8-oz.) pkg. rice vermicelli noodles, prepared according to pkg. directions
- 1 cup fresh bean sprouts
- 1 cup thinly sliced napa cabbage
- 4 hard-boiled eggs, peeled and quartered
- 1 (8-oz.) tomato, chopped (about 1¼ cups)
- ¼ cup thinly sliced scallions
- ¼ cup fried shallots (such as Maesri)
- 2 limes, cut into wedges

1 **Make the spice paste:** Combine shallots, turmeric, cumin, macadamia nuts, garlic, ginger, and galangal in bowl of a food processor. Pulse until mixture is finely chopped and forms a paste, about 15 pulses. Add grapeseed oil; pulse until loosened and completely combined, about 5 pulses. Set aside.

2 **Make the soup:** Bruise lemongrass using flat side of a knife. Heat grapeseed oil in a large stockpot over medium. Add lime leaves, bay leaves, and bruised lemongrass; cook, stirring constantly, until fragrant, about 30 seconds. Add spice paste; cook, stirring often, until mixture starts to darken and thicken, about 5 minutes. Add 8 cups water, broth, salt, and pepper; bring to a boil over high. Add whole chicken to broth mixture, adding water as needed to cover chicken. Reduce heat to medium-low; simmer until a thermometer inserted in thickest portion of chicken registers 155°F, about 30 minutes.

3 Add coconut milk to chicken mixture in pot. Bring to a boil over medium; boil until slightly thickened, about 5 minutes. Remove from heat and carefully transfer chicken to a plate. Remove and discard lime leaves, bay leaves, and lemongrass from broth; season broth with salt to taste. Cover and keep broth warm. Let chicken stand until cool enough to handle, about 15 minutes. Remove and discard skin and bones from chicken; pull and shred meat into large pieces.

4 Divide noodles evenly among bowls; top with bean sprouts, cabbage, and chicken. Ladle warm broth into bowls; top evenly with eggs, tomato, scallions, and fried shallots. Serve with lime wedges. —DIANA AND MAYLIA WIDJOJO

WINE Lemony, zesty Sauvignon Blanc: 2019 Blackbird Vineyards Dissonance

NOTE Look for lemongrass, galangal, and makrut lime leaves at Asian grocery stores.

SOUPY RICE WITH CHICKEN AND VEGETABLES

Asopao de pollo, Puerto Rican chicken-and-rice stew, is one of New York chef JJ Johnson's childhood favorites—a recipe that he calls soupy rice with chicken and vegetables. Just like his grandmother did, Johnson stirs briny pimiento-stuffed olives into the finished dish.

ACTIVE 30 MIN; TOTAL 1 HR; SERVES 10

- 5 Tbsp. olive oil, divided
- 2 lbs. skinless, boneless chicken thighs
- 1 tsp. adobo seasoning

  Salt and freshly ground black pepper
- 2 red bell peppers, thinly sliced
- 1 onion, finely chopped
- 4 garlic cloves, finely chopped
- 2 Tbsp. tomato paste
- 4 cups chicken stock or low-sodium chicken broth
- 2 (14.5-oz.) cans diced tomatoes
- 1 bay leaf
- ¼ tsp. crushed red pepper
- 1½ cups medium-grain rice
- 1 cup thawed frozen peas
- 1 cup small pimiento-stuffed olives
- ¼ cup chopped fresh cilantro

1 Heat 3 tablespoons olive oil in a large enameled cast-iron Dutch oven or heavy pot. Season chicken with adobo and black pepper. Brown chicken in 3 batches over medium-high, 6 to 8 minutes per batch, turning each halfway through. Transfer browned chicken thighs to a plate.

2 Heat remaining 2 tablespoons oil in the same pot. Add bell peppers, onion, and garlic to pot; cook over medium, stirring occasionally, until softened, about 6 minutes. Stir in tomato paste and cook until it turns brick red, about 1 minute. Add chicken stock, tomatoes and their juice, 2 cups water, bay leaf, and crushed red pepper. Bring to a simmer.

3 Return chicken to pot, stir in rice: cook, covered, over medium-low until rice is tender, about 20 minutes. Season with salt and black pepper. Stir in peas and olives; let stand until heated through, about 1 minute. Sprinkle with cilantro before serving. —JOSEPH JOHNSON

CREAMY PIQUILLO PEPPER AND CHICKPEA SOUP WITH CHICKEN

The trick to this speedy soup is ingredients that have lots of built-in flavor, like hummus and jarred piquillo peppers.

ACTIVE 10 MIN; TOTAL 20 MIN; SERVES 2

1 cup drained piquillo peppers (8 oz.), plus ¼ cup cut into thin strips

¾ cup hummus (7 oz.)

2 cups chicken or beef stock

½ cup cooked white rice

1 cup shredded rotisserie chicken

Salt

Freshly ground black pepper

2 Tbsp. chopped fresh flat-leaf parsley

Olive oil, for serving

Hot sauce, for serving

Combine whole piquillos, hummus, and stock in a blender or food processor; blend until smooth. Transfer soup to a medium saucepan. Add rice and chicken, and season with salt and pepper. Bring to a boil over medium-high; cook until heated through. Ladle soup into bowls and garnish with parsley, piquillo strips, olive oil, and hot sauce. — GRACE PARISI

CALDO DE POLLO

Barely covering the chicken legs with water, along with a few aromatics, quickly produces a flavorful and rich chicken stock that's lightly spiced with jalapeños and sweet tomatoes. For a spicier broth use a paring knife to cut small incisions in each chile before adding them to the vegetables.

ACTIVE 40 MIN; TOTAL 1 HR 45 MIN; SERVES 6

4 (10-oz.) chicken leg quarters

1 Tbsp. cumin seeds

4 garlic cloves, smashed

1 Tbsp. plus ½ tsp. kosher salt, divided, plus more to taste

3 carrots, peeled and cut into 1-inch pieces

½ lb. yellow or red baby new potatoes (about 5 potatoes), quartered

1 medium-size yellow onion, cut into ½-inch pieces (about 1½ cups)

3 celery stalks, cut into ½-inch pieces (about 1 cup)

1 cup uncooked pearled barley

1 (14½-oz.) can stewed tomatoes

1 (10-oz.) can diced tomatoes and green chiles (such as Ro*Tel)

2 jalapeños, stemmed

1 Combine chicken leg quarters, 5 cups water, cumin, garlic, and 1 tablespoon salt in a large saucepan. Bring to a boil over high. Reduce heat to low; cover and gently simmer 25 minutes.

2 Stir in carrots, potatoes, onion, celery, barley, stewed tomatoes, diced tomatoes and green chiles, and jalapeños. Increase heat to medium and bring to a simmer. Reduce heat to low; cover and gently simmer, stirring occasionally, until vegetables and barley are tender and chicken is falling off the bone, about 40 minutes. Remove chicken meat from bones; discard bones. Stir chicken and remaining ½ teaspoon salt into soup. Add additional salt to taste. —JOHN PAUL BRAMMER

MAKE AHEAD Prepare the soup, omitting barley. Prepared soup can be stored in an airtight container in refrigerator up to 3 days. Stir in cooked barley when ready to serve.

WINE Planeta Chardonnay

CURRIED CARROT AND APPLE SOUP

This velvety soup has a wonderful balance of sweetness, spice and tang. The secret ingredient: gingersnap cookies.

ACTIVE 30 MIN; TOTAL 1 HR; SERVES 12

- 4 Tbsp. unsalted butter
- 1 medium onion, chopped
- 1 medium leek, halved lengthwise and thinly sliced crosswise
- 1 medium fennel bulb, cored and chopped
- Salt and black pepper
- 2 lb. carrots, cut into ¼-inch rounds
- 1¼ lb. celery root, peeled and chopped
- 1 Granny Smith apple—peeled, cored and chopped
- 7 gingersnap cookies
- 1 Tbsp. Madras curry powder
- 2 garlic cloves, crushed
- 1 tsp. finely grated peeled fresh ginger
- 2 fresh thyme sprigs
- 2 qt. chicken stock
- 1 cup sour cream
- 1 tsp. apple cider vinegar
- Toasted pumpkin seeds and chopped fresh mint and cilantro, for garnish

1 Melt butter in a large saucepan. Add onion, leek, fennel, and a generous pinch each of salt and pepper. Cook over medium-high, stirring occasionally, until softened and just starting to brown, about 9 minutes. Add carrots, celery root, apple, gingersnaps, curry powder, garlic, ginger, and thyme sprigs. Cook, stirring, until the carrots and celery root soften slightly, 10 minutes. Add stock; bring to a boil. Simmer over medium, stirring, until vegetables are tender, 25 minutes. Discard thyme sprigs.

2 Working in batches, puree soup, along with sour cream and vinegar in a blender with until smooth. Reheat soup if necessary and season with salt and pepper. Ladle soup into bowls; top with toasted pumpkin seeds, chopped mint, and cilantro. —TAMALPAIS STAR ROTH-MCCORMICK AND MARK SLAWSON

MAKE AHEAD The soup can be refrigerated overnight. Reheat gently before serving.

WINE Ripe California Chardonnay: 2012 Copain Tous Ensemble

CHICKPEA-VEGETABLE STEW

"The dish is rich in texture and full of healthy goodness," chef Cathal Armstrong says about this hearty vegetable stew. Armstrong adds heft to the coconut milk broth with quick-cooking fingerling potatoes, and subtle heat with harissa, a Tunisian chile paste.

TOTAL 35 MIN; SERVES 4

- 2 Tbsp. extra-virgin olive oil
- 1 cup frozen pearl onions (about 4 oz.), thawed and halved
- 1 red bell pepper, diced
- ½ lb. fingerling potatoes, halved lengthwise
- 2 garlic cloves, minced
- 1 Tbsp. finely chopped peeled fresh ginger
- 1 Tbsp. harissa
- 3 cups chicken stock or low-sodium broth
- 1 (15-oz.) can chickpeas, drained and rinsed
- ¾ cup unsweetened coconut milk
- 2 Tbsp. fresh lemon juice
  Kosher salt and pepper
- 1 Tbsp. minced cilantro
  Toasted bread, for serving

1 Heat olive oil in a large saucepan. Add onions and bell pepper; cook over medium-high, stirring, until browned, about 5 minutes. Add potatoes, garlic, ginger, and harissa; cook, stirring, until the harissa darkens, about 2 minutes. Add stock and chickpeas; bring to a boil. Cover and simmer over medium-low until potatoes are tender, 12 to 14 minutes.

2 Add coconut milk and bring to a simmer. Stir in lemon juice and season with salt and pepper. Sprinkle stew with cilantro and serve with toasted bread.
—CATHAL ARMSTRONG

WINE Juicy, unoaked Spanish white: 2013 Zestos Blanco

VEGETABLE HOT-AND-SOUR SOUP

This Vegetable Hot-and-Sour Soup offers extraordinary depth of flavor from ginger, soy sauce, and sesame oil and layers of texture from lily buds, mushrooms, and bamboo shoots. Dried lily buds—also called tiger lily buds or golden needles—are nutritious and slightly sweet.

ACTIVE 25 MIN; TOTAL 50 MIN; SERVES 4

40 dried lily buds (about ½ oz.) (see Note)

¼ cup small dried tree ear mushrooms (see Note) or dried shiitake mushroom caps

5 cups unsalted chicken stock or canned low-sodium broth

½ cup drained canned bamboo shoots, rinsed and julienned

2 tsp. minced peeled fresh ginger

½ tsp. kosher salt

3 Tbsp. red wine vinegar

1 tsp. crushed red pepper

3 Tbsp. cornstarch

1 large egg

1 large egg white

4 oz. firm tofu, drained and cut into ⅓-inch cubes

2½ Tbsp. soy sauce

1 tsp. toasted sesame oil

2 Tbsp. thinly sliced scallions (from 1 medium scallion)

1 Place lily buds and mushrooms in a small bowl and add very hot water to cover by 1 inch. Let soak until softened, about 30 minutes. Drain and rinse thoroughly. Trim and discard tough ends from buds, then cut in half crosswise. Coarsely chop mushrooms.

2 Stir together lily buds, mushrooms, chicken stock, bamboo shoots, ginger, and salt in a large nonreactive saucepan over high. Cover and bring to a boil. Reduce heat to medium; simmer 10 minutes. Stir in vinegar and red pepper; increase heat to medium-high and boil 2 minutes.

3 Whisk together cornstarch and 3 tablespoons water in a small bowl. Whisk cornstarch mixture into chicken stock mixture in a slow, steady stream; cook 1 minute. Beat together egg and egg white in a medium bowl. Pour egg mixture into chicken stock mixture in a slow, steady stream, stirring gently. Stir in tofu, soy sauce, and sesame oil; cook, stirring occasionally, until warmed, about 2 minutes. Sprinkle with scallions before serving. —EILEEN YIN-FEI LO

NOTE Find dried lily buds and dried tree ear mushrooms at Asian markets.

SUMMER VEGETABLE SOUP

This soup can be prepared in stages, which is nice when you make it for guests.
The broth and vegetables can be kept separately and combined just before serving.

ACTIVE 30 MIN; TOTAL 1 HR; SERVES 4 TO 6

3 Tbsp. extra-virgin olive oil or schmaltz

2 Tbsp. minced garlic

1 large onion, finely chopped

Kosher salt and pepper

2 qt. chicken stock, preferably homemade

1 Tbsp. finely grated peeled fresh turmeric

¼ lb. green beans, trimmed and cut into 1-inch lengths

½ cup peas, thawed if frozen

½ cup lima beans, thawed if frozen, peeled

½ cup fresh corn kernels (from 1 ear)

1 cup cherry tomatoes, halved

1 Tbsp. fresh lime juice

¾ cup mixed finely chopped dill, fresh flat-leaf parsley, and chives

1 Heat 2 tablespoons olive oil in a large saucepan. Add garlic and cook over medium, stirring, until lightly browned, about 2 minutes. Add onion and a generous pinch of salt. Cook, stirring occasionally, until softened, about 5 minutes. Add stock and turmeric; bring to a boil. Simmer over medium-low until reduced to 6 cups, 25 to 30 minutes.

2 Meanwhile, set up an ice bath. Blanch green beans in a medium saucepan of salted boiling water, until crisp-tender, about 3 minutes. Using a slotted spoon, transfer beans to ice bath. Add peas and lima beans to saucepan and blanch until crisp-tender, about 1 minute. Drain well and transfer to ice bath. Drain beans and peas. Wipe out saucepan.

3 Heat remaining 1 tablespoon oil in the saucepan. Add corn and cook over medium, stirring, until crisp-tender, about 3 minutes.

4 Stir green beans, peas, lima beans, corn, tomatoes, and lime juice into broth; season with salt and pepper. Stir in mixed herbs. —ERIN O'SHEA

FRENCH ONION SOUP
WITH ROASTED POBLANO

TOTAL 2 HR 45 MIN; SERVES 6

French onion soups can lean quite beefy. Chef Carlos Gaytán though, makes his version with a base of chicken broth that allows allium flavors to truly shine. Poblano chiles add a mild, vegetal heat and slight charred flavor. To ensure even caramelization, keep onions in an even layer while they cook.

½ cup unsalted butter (4 oz.), cut into pieces

5 large Spanish onions, sliced (about 17 cups)

6 fresh or dried bay leaves

2 (7-inch) fresh thyme sprigs

1 tsp. kosher salt, plus more to taste

1 tsp. black pepper

3 medium-size fresh poblano chiles

⅓ cup balsamic vinegar

1½ Tbsp. all-purpose flour

2 qt. lower-sodium chicken broth

12 (½-inch-thick) baguette slices, toasted

8 oz. Gruyère cheese, shredded (about 2 cups)

Microgreens or fresh cilantro, for garnish (optional)

1 Melt butter in a large Dutch oven over medium until sizzling. Add onions, bay leaves, thyme sprigs, salt, and pepper; stir to coat onions in butter mixture. Cover and cook, stirring occasionally, until onions are translucent and have cooked down to about half their original volume, 20 to 25 minutes. Uncover and cook, stirring occasionally, until most liquid has evaporated and onions begin to stick to bottom of Dutch oven, 35 to 40 minutes. Cook, stirring often with a wooden spoon to scrape up any browned bits, adding splashes of water to deglaze the bottom of the pan, until onions are jammy and deeply browned, about 40 minutes.

2 While onions cook, roast poblano chiles, 1 at a time, over a medium gas flame, turning with tongs occasionally, until blackened all over, 10 to 12 minutes. Place charred chiles in a small bowl and cover with plastic wrap. Let steam 10 minutes. Rub charred skin off chiles; discard skins. Cut chiles in half; remove and discard seeds. Slice chile halves into thin strips; set aside.

3 Preheat oven to 400°F. Stir balsamic vinegar into onion mixture. Reduce heat to medium-low; cook, stirring often, until onions have absorbed vinegar and look dry, about 5 minutes. While onions cook, remove and discard bay leaves and thyme sprigs. Dust onion mixture with flour, and cook, stirring often, 10 minutes, adding about 2 tablespoons water at a time as needed to scrape up any browned bits. Stir in chicken broth and bring to a vigorous simmer over medium-high. Reduce heat to medium-low and simmer, stirring occasionally, to allow flavors to meld, about 10 minutes. Turn off heat; stir in roasted poblano strips. Season with salt to taste.

4 Divide soup evenly among 6 ovenproof bowls. Place bowls on a large rimmed baking sheet. Top each bowl with 2 baguette slices and ⅓ cup cheese. Bake in preheated oven until cheese is melted, about 8 minutes. Garnish with microgreens or cilantro, if desired. —CARLOS GAYTÁN

MAKE AHEAD Soup can be made up to 3 days ahead and stored in an airtight container in refrigerator.

WINE Medium-bodied, red-fruited Pinot Noir: 2018 Brooks Willamette Valley

TURKEY CHILI SOUP WITH HOMINY

Determined to strike a balance between a soup and a stew, award-winning cookbook author Grace Parisi started with the basic recipe and added tomato paste and flour to thicken the broth, then gave it a kick of flavor with cumin, chile powder, and chipotle powder.

TOTAL 35 MIN; SERVES 4

2 Tbsp. extra-virgin olive oil

1 medium onion, finely chopped

2 garlic cloves, minced

1 lb. ground turkey

1½ Tbsp. ancho chile powder

2 tsp. ground cumin

½ tsp. chipotle powder

Salt

2 Tbsp. all-purpose flour

1 Tbsp. tomato paste

3 cups beef stock or low-sodium broth

1 (15-oz.) can hominy, drained and rinsed

Shredded cheddar, chopped fresh cilantro, sour cream, and tortilla chips, for serving

1 Heat olive oil in a medium saucepan until shimmering. Add onion and garlic; cook over high, stirring, until barely softened, about 3 minutes. Add turkey, ancho powder, cumin, and chipotle powder; season with salt. Cook, breaking up turkey with a wooden spoon, until liquid has evaporated and turkey is lightly browned, about 5 minutes.

2 Stir in flour and tomato paste. Add stock and hominy; simmer over medium, stirring occasionally, until thickened slightly, about 15 minutes. Ladle soup into bowls. Serve with cheddar, cilantro, sour cream, and tortilla chips. — GRACE PARISI

WINE Pair with a cassis-flavored, smoky Merlot like Havens Napa Valley

BLACK-BEAN TURKEY CHILI

"In this industry, you often don't eat when you need to," says chef and restaurateur Ronnie Killen. "What helped me lose weight was eating at the right times." He recommends having real meals with lean proteins, like this turkey chili.

TOTAL 1 HR 30 MIN; SERVES 4

2 Tbsp. extra-virgin olive oil

1 lb. ground turkey breast

Salt and freshly ground black pepper

3 garlic cloves, minced

1 medium onion, finely chopped

2 Tbsp. ancho chile powder

1 Tbsp. New Mexico chile powder

1 tsp. ground cumin

1 (14-oz.) can chopped tomatoes

1 (15-oz.) can tomato sauce

1 (15-oz.) can black beans, drained and rinsed

4 corn tortillas

Low-fat sour cream, for serving

1 Heat oil in a large saucepan. Add turkey; season with salt and pepper. Cook over medium, breaking up meat, until cooked, about 4 minutes. Add garlic, onion, chile powders, and cumin. Cook, stirring, until fragrant, 5 minutes. Stir in tomatoes, tomato sauce, and 1 cup water; bring to a simmer. Cook over low, stirring occasionally, until thickened, 45 minutes. Add beans and simmer 15 minutes.

2 Meanwhile, grill tortillas in a grill pan or on a grill over medium until soft, 30 seconds per side; wrap in a towel.

3 Season chili with salt and pepper; serve with grilled tortillas and sour cream.
— RONNIE KILLEN

MAKE AHEAD The chili can be refrigerated up to 3 days. Reheat gently.

WINE Juicy, not-too-tannic Montepulciano is a good fit for tomatoey dishes

SEAFOOD

PROVENÇAL FISH STEW (P. 176)

GINGER CRISPY RICE WITH SALMON AND BOK CHOY

Grains of jasmine rice take on a toasty, crispy crust in this perfect pot of rice topped with salmon, bok choy, and corn. To achieve the crust at the bottom of the pot, use a squeeze bottle to drizzle oil around the edge of the pot, or apply it precisely with a spoon.

ACTIVE 25 MIN; TOTAL 2 HR 10 MIN; SERVES 2

1 cup uncooked jasmine rice (6½ oz.) (such as Three Ladies Thai Hom Mali Rice)

½ tsp. kosher salt

1⅓ cups cold water

1 Tbsp. toasted sesame oil

2 (2-oz.) pieces boneless, skinless salmon belly (about ½-inch thick)

3 oz. baby bok choy, yu choy, or broccoli florets (about 1½ cups)

¼ cup fresh or frozen yellow corn kernels

2 scallions

Ginger-Scallion Sauce (recipe follows)

Mirin-Soy Sauce (recipe follows)

1 Rinse rice in a strainer until water runs clear. Shake rice dry in strainer. Stir together rice, salt, and cold water in a 1-quart Chinese clay pot. Let stand at room temperature 1 hour.

2 Heat rice mixture, uncovered and undisturbed, on a gas stovetop over medium-high until water along edges of clay pot begins to simmer in spots, 8 to 10 minutes. Continue simmering, uncovered and undisturbed, over medium-high until water is completely absorbed and rice makes a faint crackling sound, 5 to 6 minutes. Drizzle sesame oil evenly around inner edges of pot. Reduce heat to low; cover and cook just until rice is tender, about 10 minutes.

3 Working quickly, turn off heat, uncover, and arrange salmon belly, baby bok choy, and corn in an even layer on rice. Increase heat to medium-high. Cook, covered, until rice smells nutty and makes a constant crackling sound, 4 to 5 minutes. Turn off heat and let stand, covered, 15 minutes. Slice green parts of scallions to equal 3 tablespoons; sprinkle scallions over salmon, baby bok choy, and corn. (Reserve remaining scallion for another use.) Serve with Ginger-Scallion Sauce and Mirin-Soy Sauce. —MARY-FRANCES HECK AND PAIGE GRANDJEAN

WINE Apple-scented, complex Chenin Blanc: 2017 Habit Santa Ynez Valley

GINGER-SCALLION SAUCE

ACTIVE 10 MIN; TOTAL 1 HR 10 MIN; MAKES 1¼ CUPS

⅔ cup thinly sliced peeled fresh ginger

1¼ cups thinly sliced scallions, white and light green parts only

2 tsp. kosher salt

½ cup peanut oil

1 Process ginger in a food processor until very finely chopped, about 30 seconds, stopping to scrape sides of bowl as needed. Add scallions and salt; pulse until scallions are finely chopped, about 10 pulses, stopping to scrape sides of bowl as needed. Transfer to a medium-size heatproof bowl.

2 Heat peanut oil in a small saucepan over high until hot but not smoking, about 4 minutes. Carefully pour hot oil over ginger mixture (it will bubble up). Stir to combine. Let cool to room temperature, about 1 hour. —MH AND PG

MAKE AHEAD Sauce can be kept covered in the refrigerator up to 1 week. Let stand at room temperature before serving.

MIRIN-SOY SAUCE

ACTIVE 20 MIN; TOTAL 35 MIN; MAKES ¾ CUP

½ cup soy sauce

½ cup mirin

¼ cup granulated sugar

Bring soy sauce, mirin, and sugar to a simmer in a small saucepan over medium-low. Cook, stirring occasionally to dissolve sugar, until sauce coats the back of a spoon and is reduced to about ¾ cup, 6 to 8 minutes. Remove from heat. Let cool to room temperature, about 15 minutes. —MH AND PG

SHALLOW-POACHED SALMON
WITH LEEK BEURRE BLANC

Shallow poaching under a cartouche, a circle of parchment paper, yields tender fish in minutes. This method works with any mild fish, such as flounder, rockfish, or grouper. If any fillets are of uneven thickness (such as tapered portions near the tail), fold the thin portion underneath to achieve an even ¾-inch thickness.

ACTIVE 30 MIN; TOTAL 35 MIN; SERVES 4

4 (6-oz.) skinless salmon fillets

1½ tsp. fine sea salt, plus more to taste

¾ tsp. black pepper

2 Tbsp. extra-virgin olive oil

6 Tbsp. unsalted butter (3 oz.), divided

1 lemon, thinly sliced crosswise

½ cup thinly sliced leeks or shallots

6 fresh thyme sprigs, plus additional thyme leaves for garnish

½ cup (4 oz.) dry white wine

1 cup halved cherry tomatoes

Salad and cooked rice, for serving

1. Preheat oven to 500°F. Sprinkle fillets evenly with salt and pepper. Fold a 12-inch square of parchment paper in half from bottom to top to create a rectangle; fold left side over to form a square. Fold bottom right corner up to top left corner to form a triangle. Set the bottom left point of the parchment triangle in the center of a 12-inch ovenproof skillet. Mark where the outer edge of the parchment meets the bottom edge of the skillet; trim parchment along the mark in an arc shape to mimic the curve of the skillet. Snip ½ inch from the folded point of the triangle. Unfold cartouche, and set aside.

2. Heat oil and 2 tablespoons butter in a 12-inch ovenproof skillet over medium-high until butter is melted. Add lemon slices; cook until lemon flesh is bubbling, about 1 minute. Flip lemon slices. Add leeks to skillet; stir to coat. Cook, stirring occasionally, until leeks are wilted, about 5 minutes. Add thyme sprigs to skillet; top with salmon fillets. Add wine to skillet, and top mixture with parchment cartouche. Bring to a simmer over medium-high. Carefully transfer skillet to preheated oven. Roast until fish is opaque and flaky, about 6 minutes.

3. Carefully remove skillet from oven. Remove cartouche; transfer fillets to a warm platter, and re-cover with cartouche. Return skillet to heat over medium; bring pan juices to a light simmer. Add tomatoes and remaining ¼ cup butter; cook, stirring constantly, until butter is melted and sauce is creamy, about 2 minutes. If desired, add salt to taste. Remove from heat.

4. Discard parchment cartouche; divide salad and rice among 4 plates; top rice with fillets. Spoon sauce over fillets; garnish with thyme leaves. Serve immediately.
—MARY-FRANCES HECK

WINE Lemon-citrusy, unoaked Chardonnay: 2018 Sterling Vineyards Carneros Unoaked

CLASSIC CEVICHE

This knockout ceviche is the result of a delicate balance of heat, salt, acidity, freshness, and crunch. Although it's widely believed that soaking raw fish in an acidic liquid "cooks" the seafood, it actually just denatures the protein. As with any seafood recipe, it's essential to use the freshest, most sustainably sourced fish and shellfish you can get your hands on, both for flavor and the sake of food safety.

ACTIVE 15 MIN; TOTAL 45 MIN; SERVES 4

- 1 lb. ½-inch-cubed skinless red snapper fillet (from 1 [2-lb.] skin-on red snapper fillet)
- 1 cup lime juice (from 8 large limes)
- ¾ cup ¾-inch-diced plum tomato
- 4 medium radishes, cut into ¼-inch-thick half-moons (about ½ cup)
- ¼ cup fresh orange juice
- 1 tsp. finely chopped serrano chile or 2 tsp. finely chopped jalapeño
- 1 tsp. sea salt, plus more to taste
- ⅓ cup loosely packed fresh cilantro leaves
- 2 Tbsp. salted roasted pepitas
  Plantain chips, for serving

1 Place fish in a medium-size nonreactive bowl. Add lime juice; gently fold to combine, ensuring fish is covered with juice. Cover and chill until fish is opaque and firm, about 30 minutes.

2 Drain and discard liquid. Gently fold in tomato, radishes, orange juice, chile, and salt. Top with cilantro and pepitas, and, if desired, sprinkle with salt to taste. Serve immediately with plantain chips. — SANDRA GUTIERREZ

WINE Tart Chilean Sauvignon Blanc: 2017 Ventisquero Reserva

CILANTRO-LIME SHRIMP SCAMPI

Although "scampi" are technically langoustines, in the United States the term has come to describe the famous dish of shrimp cooked with butter, garlic, and white wine. Here, cilantro, lime, and tequila offer a bold twist on the classic.

TOTAL 20 MIN; SERVES 4

¼ cup unsalted butter

¼ cup extra-virgin olive oil

¼ cup finely chopped fresh cilantro stems plus ½ cup chopped fresh cilantro leaves, divided

4 large garlic cloves, finely chopped

1 crushed chile de árbol or ½ tsp. crushed red pepper

3 Tbsp. (1½ oz.) tequila blanco

1½ lb. peeled and deveined raw large shrimp, tail-on

1 tsp. kosher salt, plus more to taste

¾ tsp. black pepper

3 Tbsp. fresh lime juice

Torn baguette, for serving

1 Heat butter and oil in a large skillet over medium-high, stirring often, until butter is melted. Add cilantro stems, garlic, and chile. Cook, stirring constantly, until very fragrant, 1 to 2 minutes. Remove skillet from heat, and turn off heat.

2 Carefully add tequila to skillet. Return to heat over medium-high; cook, stirring occasionally, until liquid has evaporated, about 1 minute. Add shrimp, salt, and black pepper; cook, stirring occasionally, until shrimp are opaque and cooked through, 4 to 5 minutes. Remove from heat. Stir in lime juice and cilantro leaves. Season with salt to taste. Serve immediately with torn baguette. —JUSTIN CHAPPLE

WINE Lime-scented, dry Australian Riesling: 2019 Jim Barry Watervale

**BUTTERY CAST-IRON SHRIMP
WITH WINTER SALAD**

BUTTERY CAST-IRON SHRIMP
WITH WINTER SALAD

Shrimp are seared and glazed in chipotle-honey butter in this warm seasonal salad from chef JJ Johnson. He serves the shrimp over gently sautéed radicchio and endive, which mellows their bitter edge while keeping their color and delicate crunch.

TOTAL 25 MIN; SERVES 6

¼ cup unsalted butter, at room temperature

1 Tbsp. honey

1 chipotle in adobo with sauce, minced

Salt and freshly ground black pepper

2 lb. raw large shrimp, peeled and deveined

4 oz. frisée, coarsely chopped (about 4 cups)

4 oz. radicchio and/or escarole, coarsely chopped (about 4 cups)

1 endive, cored, leaves halved crosswise

1 cup coarsely chopped fresh flat-leaf parsley

1 In a small bowl stir together butter, honey, chipotle, and ½ teaspoon salt until smooth.

2 Melt 1 tablespoon chipotle-butter in a large cast-iron skillet. Season shrimp with salt and pepper. Add half the shrimp to skillet; cook over medium-high until opaque, turning once, about 4 minutes. Transfer shrimp to a plate. Repeat with 1 tablespoon chipotle-butter and remaining shrimp.

3 In the same skillet melt remaining chipotle-butter. Add frisée, radicchio, endive, and parsley; cook, tossing with tongs, until greens are wilted, 1 to 2 minutes. Remove skillet from heat; top greens with reserved shrimp and any pooled juices before serving. —JOSEPH JOHNSON

SHRIMP BOIL

Eating a shrimp boil is fun and messy, with each person shelling his or her own shrimp at the table. We've given this Southern tradition a double dose of cloves and bay leaves, adding whole spices to ground spices in Old Bay Seasoning. The result is a deliciously spicy mound of shrimp, potatoes, and onion.

TOTAL 40 MIN; SERVES 4

6 cloves garlic (peeled)

½ lemon (cut into 4 wedges)

¼ cup Old Bay Seasoning

10 cloves

2 bay leaves

2 tsp. salt

½ tsp. Tabasco sauce

1 lb. boiling potatoes (about 3 quartered)

1 onion (cut through the root end into 8 wedges)

1½ lb. large shrimp

1 Bring 4 quarts water, garlic, lemon, Old Bay Seasoning, cloves, bay leaves, salt, and Tabasco sauce to a boil in a large pot. Reduce heat and simmer 10 minutes.

2 Add potatoes and onion; simmer until both are tender, about 15 minutes.

3 Add shrimp to pot and return to a boil. Simmer just until shrimp are done, about 1 minute. Using a slotted spoon, transfer shrimp, onion, and potatoes onto a large deep platter or into individual shallow bowls. Ladle some broth over all.

WINE Verdicchio, an Italian white wine

SHRIMP AND CORN CHOWDER

Grated plantain in this coastal Ecuadoran soup gives the dish wonderfully light and creamy body.

ACTIVE 1 HR; TOTAL 2 HR; SERVES 6

- 2 lb. peeled and deveined raw medium shrimp
- 2 scallions, minced
- 2 Tbsp. fresh lime juice
- 6 garlic cloves, minced and divided
- 1 tsp. kosher salt, plus more to taste
- 2 cups fresh or thawed frozen corn kernels
- 2 cups whole milk
- 2 Tbsp. Annatto Oil (recipe follows)
- 1 large red onion, finely chopped
- 1 large red bell pepper, finely chopped
- 1 tsp. ground cumin
- 3 plum tomatoes, peeled, seeded, and finely chopped
- 6 cups fish or chicken stock or canned low-sodium broth
- 1 green plantain, peeled and coarsely grated
- 2 Tbsp. fresh cilantro
- ¼ tsp. cayenne pepper
- Tangy Corn Salsa (recipe follows)

1 Toss together shrimp, scallions, lime juice, two-thirds of the minced garlic, and 1 teaspoon salt in a large shallow glass or stainless-steel bowl. Cover with plastic wrap and chill 1 hour or up to 3 hours.

2 Puree corn and milk in a food processor until smooth. Pour puree through a coarse strainer, pressing on solids to extract as much liquid as possible. Discard solids.

3 Heat annatto oil in a large saucepan or enameled cast-iron casserole over medium. Add remaining garlic, onion, bell pepper, and cumin. Cook, stirring often, until vegetables are slightly softened, about 5 minutes. Stir in tomatoes, and cook 2 minutes. Add corn milk, stock, plantain, cilantro, and cayenne; bring to a boil. Simmer over medium-low until very flavorful, about 20 minutes.

4 Ladle chowder into bowls and top with Tangy Corn Salsa. —MARICEL PRESILLA

ANNATTO OIL

ACTIVE 5 MIN; TOTAL 25 MIN; MAKES ABOUT 1 CUP

- 1 cup corn oil
- ¼ cup annatto seeds

Combine oil and annatto seeds in a small saucepan; bring to a simmer over low. Remove from heat, cover, and let cool completely. Strain oil into a jar; discard solids. —MP

TANGY CORN SALSA

ACTIVE 10 MIN; TOTAL 1 HR 30 MIN; MAKES ABOUT 1½ CUPS

- Kosher salt
- 1 cup fresh or thawed frozen corn kernels
- 3 plum tomatoes, peeled, seeded, and finely chopped
- 2 scallions, minced
- 2 Tbsp. coarsely chopped fresh cilantro
- 2½ Tbsp. fresh lime juice
- Freshly ground black pepper

1 Bring a small saucepan of salted water to a boil; add corn. Cook just until tender, about 3 minutes for fresh or 1 minute for frozen. Drain and let cool; pat dry.

2 Toss together corn, tomatoes, scallions, cilantro, and lime juice in a small bowl. Season with salt and pepper; let stand at least 1 hour before serving. —MP.

SHRIMP-AND-YUCA DUMPLINGS SOUP

Hannah Black and Carla Perez-Gallardo, of Lil Deb's Oasis, developed this light and tropical take on Italian wedding soup—savory broth, collard greens, and tender shrimp-and-yuca dumplings.

ACTIVE 2 HR 25 MIN; TOTAL 2 HR 45 MIN; SERVES 4 TO 6

1 lb. yuca, peeled and cut into 1-inch pieces

1½ lb. shrimp shells (about 11 cups)

3 Tbsp. olive oil

4½ tsp. kosher salt, divided

2 large (11-oz.) red bell peppers

4 garlic cloves, peeled

¾ cup dry white wine

1 large bunch fresh cilantro

1 large bunch scallions

1 (1-lb.) large yellow onion, chopped

1 (5-oz.) large carrot, peeled and chopped

16 cups water

½ lb. peeled and deveined raw large shrimp, cut into ¼-inch pieces

1 large egg

1 tsp. lime zest

¼ cup (2 oz.) unsalted butter

2 cups thinly sliced stemmed collard greens (from 1 bunch)

Chile oil, for serving

Lime wedges, for serving

1 Preheat oven to 500°F. Place yuca in a medium saucepan, and add water to cover. Bring to a boil over high; reduce heat to medium-high, and boil until centers are translucent when cut into, about 50 minutes. Drain yuca, and spread in an even layer on a plate; let stand at room temperature until cool, 8 to 10 minutes.

2 Meanwhile, toss together shrimp shells, olive oil, and 1 teaspoon salt on a large rimmed baking sheet; spread in an even layer. Roast in preheated oven until shells turn red and begin to caramelize, about 30 minutes, stirring every 10 minutes.

3 Roast bell peppers over a gas flame or under a broiler heated to high, turning with tongs until skins are blackened all over, 10 to 12 minutes. Place in a bowl, and cover with plastic wrap. Let stand at room temperature until cool enough to handle, about 15 minutes.

4 Meanwhile, smash garlic on a cutting board; sprinkle with 1 teaspoon salt. Using flat side of a large knife, drag knife back and forth over garlic to form a paste.

5 Peel charred skin off bell peppers; discard skin and seeds. Coarsely chop peppers. Combine peppers and garlic paste in blender, and process until smooth, about 40 seconds, stopping to scrape down sides as needed. Set bell pepper paste aside.

6 Add white wine to baking sheet with shrimp shells. Using a metal spatula, scrape up shells and browned bits.

7 Chop cilantro stems and leaves to equal 1 cup; chop scallions to equal ½ cup. Combine chopped cilantro, chopped scallions, shrimp shells, onion, and carrot in a medium stockpot. Add 16 cups water, and bring to a boil over high. Reduce heat to low, and simmer until broth has a shrimpy aroma, about 40 minutes. Pour mixture through a fine wire-mesh strainer into a large stockpot; discard solids. Set broth aside.

8 Press yuca, in batches, through a ricer into a medium bowl. Chop cilantro leaves to equal 3 tablespoons, and thinly slice scallions to equal ⅓ cup. Combine chopped cilantro leaves, sliced scallions, yuca, raw shrimp, egg, lime zest, 2 tablespoons bell pepper paste, and 1½ teaspoons salt in a bowl. Turn mixture out onto a work surface, and knead until combined. Shape into 36 (½-ounce) balls; arrange balls on a baking sheet. Refrigerate until thoroughly chilled and set, about 30 minutes.

9 Bring shrimp broth to a simmer over medium-high. Whisk in butter, ¾ cup bell pepper paste (reserve remaining paste for another use), and remaining 1 teaspoon salt. Stir in collard greens. Add dumplings, and cook, maintaining a simmer, until dumplings are cooked through, about 4 minutes.

10 Thinly slice 1 scallion, and chop remaining cilantro. Ladle soup into bowls. Garnish each bowl with 1 teaspoon thinly sliced scallion, 1 teaspoon chopped cilantro, and a drizzle of chile oil. Serve with lime wedges. —CARLA PEREZ-GALLARDO

CAROLINA FISH, SHRIMP, AND OKRA STEW
WITH BLACK RICE

Chef and cookbook author Alexander Smalls builds rich flavor into this low-country stew with a quick homemade stock using shrimp shells. Worcestershire adds a hit of umami, while fresh okra thickens the broth.

ACTIVE 40 MIN; TOTAL 1 HR 10 MIN; SERVES 6 TO 8

- 1 lb. raw medium shrimp, peeled and deveined, shells reserved
- 1½ lb. skinless catfish or cod fillets (halve fillets lengthwise if large), cut crosswise into 1-inch strips
- 1 tsp. kosher salt, plus more to taste
- 2 Tbsp. olive oil, plus more for drizzling
- 2 Tbsp. all-purpose flour
- 1 large white onion, chopped
- 1 large red bell pepper, chopped
- 2 medium celery stalks, chopped
- 3 medium garlic cloves, chopped
- 1 (15-oz.) can diced tomatoes, undrained
- 8 oz. fresh okra, stemmed, cut crosswise into ½-inch pieces, or 2 cups frozen sliced okra
- 2 Tbsp. Worcestershire sauce
- 2 tsp. chopped fresh thyme
- 2 fresh or dried bay leaves
- 2 tsp. Creole seasoning
- ½ tsp. black pepper, plus more to taste
- Cooked black rice (such as Nature's Earthly Choice), for serving
- Thinly sliced scallions, for garnish

1 Combine shrimp shells and 3 cups water in a medium saucepan. Bring to a simmer over medium. Remove from heat and let stand 15 minutes. Pour mixture through a fine wire-mesh strainer into a bowl; discard solids. Set stock aside. Toss together catfish pieces and salt in a large bowl. Cover and chill until ready to use, up to 1 hour.

2 Heat oil in a large Dutch oven over medium. Add flour; cook, whisking constantly, until smooth and lightly browned, about 1 minute. Add onion, bell pepper, celery, and garlic. Cook, stirring often and scraping bottom of Dutch oven to prevent scorching, until softened, 8 to 10 minutes. Stir in shrimp stock, tomatoes with juices, okra, Worcestershire, thyme, bay leaves, Creole seasoning, and black pepper. Bring to a simmer over medium-high. Reduce heat to medium-low; cover and simmer until okra is almost tender, about 15 minutes.

3 Stir in catfish and shrimp; reduce heat to low. Cover and cook until catfish and shrimp are cooked through, 5 to 8 minutes. Remove and discard bay leaves. Season to taste with salt and pepper. Serve with black rice; garnish servings with scallions and drizzle with olive oil. —ALEXANDER SMALLS

WINE Berry-scented, lightly spicy California rosé: 2018 McBride Sisters Collection Black Girl Magic Rosé

NOTE Black rice is available at Whole Foods or amazon.com.

SEAFOOD PAELLA

ACTIVE 45 MIN; TOTAL 1 HR 15 MIN; SERVES 6 TO 8

- 4 cups chicken stock or low-sodium broth
- 2 cups fish stock or clam broth
- ¼ tsp. saffron threads, crumbled
- ¼ cup extra-virgin olive oil
- ½ cup finely chopped onion
- 3 garlic cloves, minced
- ½ tsp. smoked paprika
- 2¼ cups Bomba or arborio rice
- 1 (12-oz.) pkg. cooked chorizo, sausages halved lengthwise and crosswise
- 8 large head-on shrimp
- 1 lb. littleneck clams and cockles, scrubbed
- ½ lb. mussels, scrubbed
- ¼ cup thawed frozen peas
- Chopped fresh flat-leaf parsley, for garnish

1 Combine chicken stock, fish stock, and crumbled saffron in a medium saucepan; bring to a simmer over medium-high.

2 Meanwhile, heat olive oil in a 15-inch paella pan or large enameled cast-iron casserole. Add onion and cook over medium, stirring occasionally, until softened, about 5 minutes. Add garlic and paprika; cook until fragrant, about 2 minutes. Add rice and cook, stirring, until it is evenly coated in oil, 1 minute. Add hot broth and stir rice once to evenly spread it in pan. Cook over medium, without stirring, rotating pan for even cooking, until half the liquid is absorbed, about 15 minutes. Reduce heat to low.

3 Nestle chorizo and shrimp into the rice. Add clams, cockles, and mussels (hinge-side down) and cook, turning shrimp halfway through, until shrimp and shellfish are cooked through and all the liquid is absorbed, about 20 minutes. Scatter peas on top and let stand 5 minutes. Garnish with parsley. —KAY CHUN

FISHERMAN'S-STYLE SEAFOOD STEW

Chef Fabio Trabocchi of Casa Luca in Washington, D.C., says the key to this brodetto-inspired recipe is to cook the fish and shellfish in stages. Crusty ciabatta toasts not only complement the one-dish meal, they soak up every bit of tasty cooking juices.

ACTIVE 25 MIN; TOTAL 40 MIN; SERVES 4 TO 6

- 6 (1-inch-thick) ciabatta slices
- ¼ cup extra-virgin olive oil, plus more for brushing and drizzling
- 5 garlic cloves, divided
- 1 cup finely chopped onion
- ½ cup dry white wine
- 1 (32-oz.) jar tomato sauce
- 2 Tbsp. white wine vinegar
- 1 lb. mussels, scrubbed
- 12 littleneck clams, scrubbed
- 12 oz. cod fillets, cut into 2-inch pieces
- 12 oz. skin-on snapper fillets, cut into 2-inch pieces
- 10 oz. raw large shrimp, peeled and deveined
- 2 tsp. kosher salt
- 6 oz. cleaned squid, bodies cut into ½-inch-thick rings
- 3 Tbsp. chopped fresh flat-leaf parsley

1 Preheat broiler to high with oven rack 4 inches from heat. Brush bread with olive oil, and place it on a baking sheet. Broil until golden brown, 3 to 4 minutes, flipping halfway through. Rub toast with 1 garlic clove and keep warm.

2 Thinly slice remaining 4 garlic cloves. Heat ¼ cup oil over medium-high in a large Dutch oven. Add onion and sliced garlic; cook, stirring occasionally, until translucent, about 5 minutes. Add wine; boil until reduced by half, about 2 minutes. Add tomato sauce and vinegar; bring to a simmer. Add mussels and clams; cover and cook until mussels open, about 5 minutes. Remove mussels with a slotted spoon and place in a large bowl. (Discard any that do not open.) Cover pot and cook until clams open, 3 to 4 minutes. Remove clams with a slotted spoon; place in bowl with mussels.

3 Season cod, snapper, and shrimp with salt. Add to pot, cover, and reduce heat to medium; simmer 6 minutes. Add squid, cover, and cook until fish are just cooked through, about 2 minutes. Stir in parsley, mussels, and clams. Remove from heat. Cover and let stand until shellfish are heated through, about 2 minutes. Serve in shallow bowls with a drizzle of olive oil and garlic toast. —FABIO TRABOCCHI

PROVENÇAL FISH STEW

PHOTO P. 155

Clare de Boer and Jess Shadbolt, of King in New York City, distill the essence of the dish by serving buttery lobsters, briny clams and mussels along with mild, flaky white fish in a fresh tomato sauce made from concentrated aromatics—like fennel seeds and chile flakes—plus a generous glug of wine. The result is bright and fresh, with simmered-all-day flavor achieved in under an hour.

ACTIVE 35 MIN; TOTAL 55 MIN; SERVES 4

AÏOLI

- 1 Tbsp. fresh lemon juice
- 1 small garlic clove
  Pinch of saffron threads
- ¾ tsp. flaky sea salt (such as Maldon), divided
- 1 large pasteurized egg yolk
- ⅔ cup mild-tasting extra-virgin olive oil

STEW

- 3 garlic cloves, thinly sliced
- 2 tsp. crushed fennel seeds
- ⅛ tsp. crushed red pepper
- 5 Tbsp. olive oil, divided
- 3¼ tsp. flaky sea salt, divided
- ¾ tsp. black pepper, divided
- 2 lb. ripe tomatoes, roughly chopped (about 5 cups)
- 1 cup dry white wine
  Pinch of saffron threads
- 2 (1¼-lb.) live lobsters
- 1 (1-lb.) skin-on red snapper fillet or any skin-on flaky white fish fillet, cut into 8 pieces
- 1 lb. littleneck clams (about 12 clams), scrubbed and thoroughly rinsed
- 1 lb. mussels (about 32 mussels), scrubbed and debearded

ADDITIONAL INGREDIENTS

- Crusty bread, toasted
- Leafy green salad (optional)

1 Make the aïoli: Using a mortar and pestle, mash together lemon juice, garlic, saffron, and ¼ teaspoon salt until smooth and combined. Scrape mixture into a medium bowl; whisk in egg yolk. (Alternatively, using the flat side of a knife, mash garlic and ¼ teaspoon salt on a cutting board to form a paste. Transfer to a medium bowl; whisk in lemon juice, saffron, and egg yolk.) Slowly drizzle in olive oil, whisking constantly, until emulsified. Whisk in remaining ½ teaspoon salt; cover and refrigerate up to 1 day.

2 Make the stew: Stir together garlic, fennel seeds, red pepper, 2 tablespoons oil, ¾ teaspoon salt, and ⅛ teaspoon black pepper in a large Dutch oven. Cook over medium, stirring occasionally, until garlic begins to sizzle, about 3 minutes. Stir in tomatoes, wine, and saffron; bring to a simmer. Reduce heat to medium-low; cook, stirring occasionally, until sauce is slightly reduced, 12 to 15 minutes. Stir in 1 teaspoon salt and ⅛ teaspoon black pepper. Transfer tomato mixture to a bowl. Wipe Dutch oven clean.

3 Place a damp paper towel on a work surface. Top with a rimmed baking sheet; line with another damp paper towel. Fit a cutting board inside baking sheet. Place 1 lobster on cutting board and straighten its tail. With the blade of a chef's knife over the head, pierce lobster straight down through the midline of the carapace (where head connects to body) until knife tip reaches cutting board. Using a lever motion, cut lobster head in half. Rotate lobster 180 degrees and cut lengthwise through the midline, through body and tail, to separate lobster into 2 halves. Remove and discard stomach sac from head, intestinal tract, and tomalley. If desired, using back of knife, crack claws on inner side and loosen shells. Remove and discard rubber bands, if necessary. Repeat procedure with remaining lobster.

4 Sprinkle cut sides of lobsters with ½ teaspoon salt and ¼ teaspoon black pepper. Sprinkle snapper pieces with remaining 1 teaspoon salt and remaining ¼ teaspoon black pepper. Heat 1 tablespoon oil in Dutch oven over medium. Add 2 lobster halves, cut sides down, making sure claws are in contact with bottom of Dutch oven. Cook until meat is lightly browned, about 2 minutes. Flip and cook until claws are bright red, 1 to 3 minutes. Remove from Dutch oven. Add 1 tablespoon oil to Dutch oven, and repeat with remaining 2 lobster halves. Remove from Dutch oven. Add remaining 1 tablespoon oil to Dutch oven. Place snapper pieces in Dutch oven, skin-sides down. Top with lobster halves, shell-sides down. Add clams and mussels. Pour tomato mixture over seafood. Bring to a simmer over medium. Reduce heat to medium-low, cover, and cook until clams and mussels open and lobster claws are cooked through, 10 to 12 minutes. Discard any clams and mussels that do not open.

5 Serve stew immediately on warm plates or a platter with toasted bread spread with aïoli and, if desired, leafy green salad. —CLARE DE BOER AND JESS SHADBOLT

GOCHUJANG CIOPPINO

Food & Wine's *Justin Chapple makes his zippy cioppino with shrimp, squid, mussels, and cod, then, to give it a lively Korean twist, he also includes tofu and gochujang.*

TOTAL 40 MIN; SERVES 4

¼ cup extra-virgin olive oil

1 onion, finely chopped

6 garlic cloves, thinly sliced

2 scallions, thinly sliced, plus more for garnish

1 (15-oz.) can whole peeled tomatoes, crushed by hand

½ cup dry white wine

3 Tbsp. gochujang (Korean red pepper paste)

1 (8-oz.) bottle clam juice

½ lb. shelled and deveined large shrimp

½ lb. cleaned squid, bodies thinly sliced and tentacles halved

½ lb. mussels, scrubbed

½ lb. cod, cut into 1-inch pieces

½ lb. firm tofu, cut into 1-inch pieces

Rice crackers or steamed rice, for serving

1 Heat oil in a large cast-iron casserole. Add onion, garlic, and 2 sliced scallions; cook over medium, stirring occasionally, until softened, 7 minutes. Stir in tomatoes, wine, and gochujang. Cook, stirring, just until tomatoes start to break down, about 5 minutes.

2 Add clam juice and bring to a boil. Nestle seafood and tofu into the broth. Cover and cook over medium until the mussels open and the other seafood is opaque, about 7 minutes. Ladle cioppino into shallow bowls; garnish with scallion. Serve with rice crackers or steamed rice. —JUSTIN CHAPPLE

FROGMORE STEW WITH OLD BAY AÏOLI

Taste how Chef Joe Kindred's deeply flavorful fish stock sets this recipe apart from a traditional low-country boil. Pile some of the seafood into a shallow bowl and ladle the strained cooking liquid over the top for a more refined stew, or save the golden stock to make the best seafood chowder of your life the next day.

ACTIVE 2 HR; TOTAL 2 HR 30 MIN; SERVES 8 TO 10

- 1 cup extra-virgin olive oil
- 6 celery ribs, coarsely chopped, plus light green leaves for garnish
- 2 large carrots, coarsely chopped
- 1½ bulbs garlic (26 cloves), crushed
- 1 large fennel bulb, chopped
- 1 large white onion, chopped
- Kosher salt and pepper
- 1 small bunch fresh thyme
- 2 Tbsp. fennel seeds
- 1 (28-oz.) can whole peeled San Marzano tomatoes
- 4 qt. chicken stock or low-sodium broth
- 2 (12-oz.) bottles lager or pilsner
- 1 (5-lb.) whole snapper, filleted and skinned, fillets cut into thirds and head and bones reserved (see Note)
- 2 Tbsp. Old Bay Seasoning
- 1¾ lb. small new potatoes
- 40 littleneck clams (3½ lb.)
- 1 lb. Spanish chorizo, sliced ¼ inch thick
- 4 ears corn, shucked, cut into thirds
- 8 live large blue crabs (see Note)
- 40 extra-large shell-on shrimp (2 lb.)
- Fresh cilantro and parsley leaves, for garnish
- Old Bay Aioli (recipe follows), lemon wedges, hot sauce, and melted salted butter, for serving

1 In a large pot heat olive oil. Add celery, carrots, garlic, chopped fennel, and onion; season with salt. Cook over medium-high, stirring occasionally, until very tender, 20 minutes. Add thyme and fennel seeds. Cook, stirring, until fragrant, 2 minutes. Add tomatoes and their juices. Cook over medium-high, breaking up tomatoes with a wooden spoon and stirring occasionally, until tomato liquid is reduced, about 10 minutes. Stir in stock, beer, fish head and bones, Old Bay, and 8 cups water. Bring to a boil; reduce to medium and simmer 30 minutes.

2 Strain fish stock through a fine-mesh sieve set over an extra-large pot, pressing on solids; discard solids. Season generously with salt. Bring stock to a boil over high, add potatoes and cook until barely tender, 15 to 17 minutes. Add clams and chorizo, cover and cook 2 minutes. Add corn, cover and cook 4 minutes. Season fish fillets with salt and pepper and add to the stew. Cover and cook 2 minutes. Add crabs, cover and cook 3 minutes. Finally, add shrimp, cover and cook until all seafood is cooked through and potatoes and corn are tender, about 5 minutes.

3 Using a slotted spoon, transfer seafood, potatoes, and corn to 2 large platters. Alternatively, spread seafood on a paper-lined table. Garnish with celery leaves, cilantro leaves, and parsley leaves. Serve immediately with Old Bay Aioli, lemon wedges, hot sauce, and melted butter. Reserve the fish stock for another use. —JOE KINDRED

NOTE Ask your fishmonger to do this. If you can't get a 5-pound snapper, use 2 small snappers. As an alternative to live blue crabs, use 2 pounds frozen cooked king crab legs and add with the shrimp in Step 2. Also, if making this recipe in a large turkey fryer pot, add the perforated insert after fish stock has finished simmering, and skip the straining process.

BEER Malty, full-flavored ale: The Duck-Rabbit Amber Ale

OLD BAY AÏOLI

TOTAL 5 MIN; MAKES 1½ CUPS

- 2 Tbsp. fresh lemon juice
- 1 large egg yolk
- 1 garlic clove
- 1¼ tsp. Old Bay Seasoning
- 1 cup canola oil
- Kosher salt

In a food processor pulse lemon juice, egg yolk, garlic, Old Bay and ¼ cup cold water until garlic is finely chopped. With machine running, slowly drizzle in oil until emulsified, about 2 minutes. Season with salt. Transfer to a bowl. —JK

MAKE AHEAD The aioli can be refrigerated up to 1 week.

FRENCH SEAFOOD BISQUE WITH BAGUETTE

The freshest seafood—preferably sourced from local fishmongers—is the highlight of this velvety-smooth bisque. Cooking each type as directed preserves its delicate flavor and texture. This resourceful recipe uses every last bit of the briny haul to yield a rich seafood stock that enhances the thick, soppable soup.

TOTAL 1 HR 30 MIN; SERVES 4

1 small yellow onion, halved, divided

3 small celery stalks, divided

1 fresh or dried bay leaf

¼ tsp. black pepper

1¼ tsp. kosher salt, divided, plus more to taste

8 oz. unpeeled raw extra-large shrimp

4 oz. Prince Edward Island (PEI) mussels, scrubbed and debearded

4 oz. bay scallops, side muscles removed and reserved

3 oz. cleaned small squid tubes and tentacles, tubes cut into ¼-inch rings, tentacles left whole

¼ cup olive oil or unsalted butter

3 medium carrots, roughly chopped (about ½ cup)

2 Tbsp. tomato paste

1 Tbsp. chopped fresh flat-leaf parsley, plus more for garnish

1 tsp. roughly chopped fresh thyme

¾ tsp. smoked paprika

¼ tsp. crushed red pepper, or more to taste

3 medium garlic cloves, smashed

½ cup heavy cream

Baguette, for serving

1 Cut 1 onion half into 4 wedges, leaving root end attached. Cut 1 celery stalk in half crosswise; set remaining onion and celery aside. Combine onion wedges, celery halves, 5 cups water, bay leaf, black pepper, and ¼ teaspoon salt in a large saucepan. Bring to a boil over medium-high. Fill a medium bowl with ice water; set aside.

2 Add shrimp to boiling water mixture in saucepan; cook until opaque and cooked through, 2 to 3 minutes. Using a slotted spoon, transfer shrimp to prepared ice bath. Add mussels to saucepan; cook until mussels open, 2 to 3 minutes. Transfer mussels to ice bath, discarding any mussels that did not open. Add scallops and squid to saucepan; cook until scallops and squid rings turn opaque, about 1 minute. Using a slotted spoon, transfer scallops and squid to ice bath. Reserve water mixture in saucepan.

3 Remove shrimp and mussels from ice water; drain in a colander. Peel shrimp and shuck mussels, reserving some mussels in shells for garnish, if desired. Reserve shrimp and mussel shells. Add reserved shells and reserved scallop side muscles to water mixture in saucepan; bring to a boil over medium-high. Reduce heat to medium-low; simmer, stirring occasionally, until liquid reduces to about 3 cups, 20 to 25 minutes. Meanwhile, remove remaining seafood from ice bath; pat dry, and set aside.

4 Remove saucepan with seafood stock from heat; pour mixture through a fine wire-mesh strainer into a large heatproof bowl; discard solids. Set strained stock aside. Wipe saucepan clean.

5 Roughly chop remaining onion half and remaining 2 celery stalks, keeping them separate. Add oil to cleaned saucepan; heat over medium. Add onion; cook, stirring often, until softened, 2 to 3 minutes. Add celery and carrots; cook, stirring often, until slightly softened but not browning, 4 to 6 minutes. Add tomato paste, parsley, thyme, paprika, crushed red pepper, garlic, and remaining 1 teaspoon salt. Cook, stirring constantly, until mixture is fragrant and vegetables are well coated in tomato mixture, 1 to 2 minutes. Stir in reserved seafood stock; cook over medium, stirring occasionally, until flavors meld and mixture reduces to about 3 cups, 10 to 15 minutes.

6 Set aside 4 cooked shrimp and ¼ cup mixed mussels, scallops, and squid for garnish. Add heavy cream and remaining cooked seafood to stock in saucepan. Reduce heat to low; cook, stirring occasionally, until seafood is heated through, 8 to 10 minutes.

7 Transfer seafood mixture to a blender. Secure lid on blender and remove center piece to allow steam to escape. Place a clean towel over opening. Process until smooth, about 1 minute, adding water, 2 tablespoons at a time, if needed to thin bisque to desired consistency. Season with salt to taste.

8 Divide bisque evenly among bowls; garnish with reserved seafood and additional parsley. Serve with baguette. —JAMILA ROBINSON

LOBSTER BISQUE

Lobster shells from the tail, claws, knuckles, and legs are flavorful and, when very gently simmered in water, yield a clean-tasting, briny stock. Seasoned with mirepoix, sherry, and herbs, this classic bisque is thickened with fragrant jasmine rice. Serve it hot or cold for a knockout lunch or simple supper.

ACTIVE 45 MIN; TOTAL 1 HR 45 MIN; SERVES 8

12 cups 2-inch pieces lobster tail, claw, knuckle, and leg shells or 6 (1½-lb.) lobsters, carapaces discarded

½ cup (4 oz.) unsalted butter

1 large yellow onion, chopped (about 2 cups)

2 celery stalks, chopped

¼ cup tomato paste

½ cup amontillado sherry

¾ cup uncooked jasmine rice

2 Tbsp. fresh thyme leaves

2 bay leaves

1 tsp. black pepper

2¼ tsp. kosher salt, divided, plus more to taste

2 Tbsp. fresh lemon juice, plus more to taste

⅛ tsp. cayenne pepper, plus more to taste

1½ cups heavy cream, divided

3 Tbsp. chopped fresh chives

1 In a large stockpot combine lobster shells and 12 cups water. Bring to a boil over medium-high. Reduce heat to low and gently simmer 45 minutes. Pour stock through a fine wire-mesh strainer into a large bowl; discard shells.

2 Melt butter in the same stockpot over medium. Add onion and celery and cook, stirring occasionally, until very soft and translucent, about 15 minutes. Stir in tomato paste and cook, stirring often, until brick red in color, about 2 minutes. Add sherry; increase heat to high, and bring to a boil. Stir in rice, thyme, bay leaves, black pepper, and 2 teaspoons salt. Add lobster stock and bring to a simmer. Reduce heat to medium-low; simmer until rice is very soft, about 25 minutes. Remove and discard bay leaves. Remove from heat and let stand 15 minutes.

3 Place one-third of mixture in a blender. Remove center piece of blender lid (to allow steam to escape); secure lid on blender, and place a clean towel over opening in lid. Process until very smooth, about 1 minute. Transfer bisque to a large saucepan. Repeat procedure twice with remaining bisque.

4 If serving bisque hot, reheat over medium-low, stirring, until hot. If serving bisque cold, chill until cold.

5 When ready to serve, stir lemon juice, cayenne, and 1 cup cream into bisque.

6 Place remaining ½ cup cream in a chilled bowl and whisk until soft peaks form. Stir remaining ¼ teaspoon salt into whipped cream.

7 Season bisque with salt, lemon juice, and cayenne to taste. Divide bisque among 8 bowls; top servings with whipped cream and chives. —MARY-FRANCES HECK

MAKE AHEAD Bisque may be made through Step 3 up to 2 days ahead. Keep chilled until ready to serve.

SLOW-COOKER SEAFOOD AND CHICKEN GUMBO

Although gumbo isn't a classic slow-cooker recipe, chef Grant Achatz swears by the method and convenience. His version is packed with spicy andouille sausage, okra, shrimp, and crab. "Given the many regional variations, I think it's fair to say that you should put whatever you want to eat in your gumbo," Achatz says.

ACTIVE 30 MIN; TOTAL 4 HR 30 MIN; SERVES 8

5 oregano sprigs

5 thyme sprigs

1½ sticks unsalted butter

1½ cups all-purpose flour

½ lb. andouille sausage, cut into 1-inch pieces

16 cipollini onions, peeled

6 garlic cloves, minced

1 leek, white and light green parts only, chopped

1 red bell pepper, diced

1 green bell pepper, diced

3 celery ribs, sliced

3 carrots, cut into ½-inch-thick rounds

2 Tbsp. smoked paprika

1 lb. okra, thickly sliced

2 tsp. kosher salt, plus more for seasoning

4 bay leaves

2 qt. chicken stock or low-sodium broth

½ cup long-grain rice

1 lb. boneless, skinless chicken thighs, cut into 1½-inch pieces

16 shelled and deveined jumbo shrimp

8 snow crab legs

Chopped fresh flat-leaf parsley and hot sauce, for serving

1 Using kitchen twine, tie the oregano and thyme sprigs into a bundle. Turn a 6- to 6½-quart slow cooker to high and set the timer for 4 hours. Add butter and cover cooker until butter melts. Stir in flour and mix with a wooden spoon until well incorporated and a paste forms. Add herbs and the next 13 ingredients, up to and including the stock; stir. Cover and cook 3 hours.

2 Stir in rice and chicken, cover and cook for 45 minutes. Add shrimp and crab; cover and cook 15 minutes longer.

3 Discard herb bundle and bay leaves; season with salt. Garnish gumbo with parsley. Serve in bowls with hot sauce, and provide shell crackers for breaking the crab legs. —GRANT ACHATZ

BEER Crisp, hoppy ale: Shipyard Brewing Co. Export Ale

CURRY-COCONUT CLAM CHOWDER, PAPI-STYLE

One of Roy Choi's early chef jobs was at an L.A. country club where he made New England clam chowder every Friday. This Asian-inflected version includes green curry paste, coconut milk, and plenty of lime juice.

TOTAL 45 MIN; SERVES 6

1 small baking potato, peeled and cut into ½-inch dice

4 oz. pancetta or bacon, finely chopped

1 Tbsp. minced fennel

2 garlic cloves, thinly sliced

2 Tbsp. Thai green curry paste

½ cup dry white wine

1 (13-oz.) can unsweetened coconut milk

¼ cup fresh lime juice

2 dozen Manila or littleneck clams

3 cups chopped clams with their juices

Kosher salt

Freshly ground black pepper

Fresh cilantro sprigs, for garnish

Fresh Thai basil and rau ram (Vietnamese coriander), for garnish

1 Cook potato in a medium saucepan of salted boiling water just until tender, about 5 minutes. Drain.

2 In a large saucepan cook pancetta over medium, stirring occasionally, until light golden, 7 to 8 minutes. Add fennel, garlic, and green curry paste. Cook, stirring, until fragrant, 1 minute. Add wine and simmer until reduced by half, about 2 minutes. Add coconut milk and lime juice and return to a simmer. Add potato, Manila clams, and chopped clams and juices. Cover and cook until Manila clams open, 5 to 7 minutes. Discard any clams that do not open. Season chowder with salt and pepper. Garnish with cilantro, basil, and rau ram; serve warm. — ROY CHOI

WINE Zesty, herb-scented Sauvignon Blanc: 2012 Brander Santa Ynez Valley

NEW ENGLAND CLAM CHOWDER

With only ½ cup of heavy cream, this quick version of classic New England clam chowder is light and healthy.

ACTIVE 1 HR; TOTAL 1 HR; SERVES 4

2 Tbsp. unsalted butter

2 garlic cloves, minced

1 cup finely chopped yellow onion

½ cup finely chopped celery, plus celery leaves for garnish

1 lb. baking potatoes, peeled and cut into 1-inch pieces

3 Tbsp. all-purpose flour

2 cups low-sodium chicken broth

2 (8 oz.) jars clam broth

½ cup whole milk

½ cup heavy cream

1 bay leaf

3 (6.5 oz.) cans chopped clams

Kosher salt and black pepper

1 Tbsp. chopped fresh flat-leaf parsley

Crusty bread, for serving

1 Melt butter in a large saucepan. Add garlic, onion, and chopped celery. Cook over medium, stirring occasionally, until softened, about 5 minutes. Add potatoes and flour and cook for 2 minutes, stirring to coat potatoes. Add broths, milk, cream, and bay leaf; bring to a boil. Simmer, partially covered, over medium-low until potatoes are tender, about 20 minutes.

2 Stir in clams and season with salt and pepper; simmer 2 minutes. Stir in parsley. Serve hot in bowls with crusty bread. Garnish with celery leaves. —KAY CHUN

MAKE AHEAD The soup can be refrigerated overnight and reheated before serving.

CREAMY CLAM AND WHITE BEAN CHOWDER

White beans substitute for the usual potatoes in this chowder, made with sweet butternut squash, briny littleneck clams, and smoky bacon. Rancho Gordo cellini beans give the soup a buttery richness, although Great Northern beans are terrific as well.

ACTIVE 1 HR; TOTAL 1 HR 50 MIN; SERVES 8

1¼ cups dried cellini or Great Northern beans, rinsed and picked over, then soaked for 2 hours

Kosher salt

1¼ lb. butternut squash, peeled and cut into ½-inch dice (2 cups)

1 Tbsp. extra-virgin olive oil

Freshly ground pepper

3 dozen littleneck clams, scrubbed

6 thick slices of bacon (4 oz.), cut crosswise into ¼-inch strips

2 Tbsp. unsalted butter

1 medium onion, cut into ½-inch dice

3 large celery ribs, cut into ½-inch dice

¼ tsp. crushed red pepper

4 large garlic cloves, minced

1⅓ cups dry white wine

1 cup heavy cream

Garlic bread, for serving

1 In a saucepan cover the beans with 2 inches of water and bring to a boil. Simmer over medium-low, stirring occasionally, until tender, about 1½ hours. Add water as needed to keep the beans covered by 2 inches. Season beans with salt and let stand 5 minutes. Drain beans, reserving 1½ cups cooking liquid.

2 Meanwhile, preheat oven to 375°F. On a rimmed baking sheet, toss squash with oil; season with salt and pepper. Bake until browned, about 20 minutes.

3 Set a colander over a bowl. Cook clams, covered, in 2 tablespoons water in a skillet over medium-high, shaking skillet a few times, until clams open, about 5 minutes. Transfer opened clams to colander; discard any clams that do not open. Remove clams from shells. Strain and reserve 1 cup clam broth.

4 Cook bacon in a saucepan over medium-low, about 4 minutes. Stir in butter. Add onion, celery, and red pepper. Cover and cook, stirring, until softened, 8 minutes. Add garlic; cover and cook until fragrant, 4 minutes. Add wine and boil until reduced by two-thirds, about 6 minutes. Pour in reserved clam broth, reserved bean cooking liquid, and cream; simmer 10 minutes. Stir in beans, squash ,and clams; simmer just until heated through. Serve chowder in bowls with garlic bread alongside. — LAURENCE JOSSEL

WINE Full-bodied, buttery, oaky white wine: California Chardonnay

CHILLED AVOCADO SOUP WITH CRAB

At their San Antonio restaurant, Rico Torres and Diego Galicia serve this zesty, creamy cold soup as a refreshing beginning course to their Michoacán tasting menu. That region is the largest and most important avocado producer in Mexico, so this dish is a fitting start to the meal. The chilled soup, topped with fiery, crisp serranos and sweet crab, is a smooth contrast to a classic tomato gazpacho.

ACTIVE 30 MIN; TOTAL 1 HR 30 MIN; SERVES 4

3 large Hass avocados—halved, pitted, and peeled

2 cups cold vegetable stock, preferably homemade

¼ cup plus 1 Tbsp. fresh lime juice

½ cup heavy cream

Kosher salt

Canola oil, for frying

4 medium serrano chiles, thinly sliced crosswise with seeds

½ lb. jumbo lump crabmeat, picked over

Mexican crema and micro cilantro, for garnish

1 In a food processor combine avocados, stock, 1 cup water, and ¼ cup lime juice; puree until very smooth. With machine running, gradually add heavy cream. Strain through a fine-mesh sieve into a large bowl; season with salt. Cover and refrigerate until well chilled, about 1 hour.

2 Meanwhile, in a medium saucepan, heat ¼ inch canola oil until shimmering. Add serranos and fry over medium-high, stirring, until lightly browned and crisp, 1 to 2 minutes. Using a slotted spoon, transfer chips to paper towels to drain.

3 Gently toss crab with remaining 1 tablespoon lime juice in a medium bowl. Ladle chilled soup into bowls; top with crab and crispy serranos. Garnish with crema and cilantro. —RICO TORRES AND DIEGO GALICIA

MAKE AHEAD The avocado soup can be refrigerated overnight.

CHILLED ENGLISH PEA SOUP
WITH CRAB AND MEYER LEMON

This refreshing, verdant English pea and watercress soup is the ideal base for a zesty crab salad. Chef Sarah Heller of Napa's Radish Leaf Cuisine folds sweet Dungeness crab with Meyer lemon, crème fraîche, and a host of delicate spring herbs before mounding atop each serving of the soup. Any lump crabmeat or cooked, chilled shrimp would also work.

ACTIVE 45 MIN; TOTAL 2 HR 45 MIN; SERVES 6

- 2 Tbsp. olive oil, plus more for garnish
- 1 small sweet onion, diced
- 2 small celery stalks, diced
- 1 garlic clove, smashed
- 2 tsp. kosher salt, divided
- 3 cups whole milk, divided
- 4 lb. fresh English peas, shelled (about 5 cups or 30 oz. shelled peas)
- 2 bunches watercress (about 4 oz.), rinsed
- 1 tsp. ground white pepper
- ¼ cup crème fraîche
- 1 Tbsp. chopped fresh chives, plus more for garnish
- 1 Tbsp. chopped fresh dill
- 1 Tbsp. chopped fresh tarragon
- 1 tsp. Meyer lemon zest
- 3 Tbsp. fresh Meyer lemon juice, divided
- ½ lb. cooked Dungeness or other lump crabmeat
- Pea tendrils and freshly ground black pepper, for garnish (optional)

1 Heat oil in a large saucepan over low. Add onion, celery, garlic, and 1 teaspoon salt. Sauté until onions are translucent, 10 to 12 minutes. Add 2 cups milk; bring to a simmer, and cook until vegetables are tender, about 10 minutes. Remove from heat; let cool slightly.

2 While vegetables are cooking, prepare a large bowl of ice water and bring a large pot of water to a boil over high. Add peas to pot, return to a boil, and cook until peas are bright green and just tender, about 2 minutes. Remove peas with a slotted spoon and immediately plunge into ice water. Return water in pot to a boil, add watercress and cook until bright green and wilted, about 1 minute. Plunge watercress into ice water. Drain peas and watercress; set aside peas. Squeeze watercress to remove as much water as possible.

3 Combine peas, watercress, and remaining 1 cup milk in a blender. Process on high until smooth. Working in batches if necessary, add onion mixture to blender; process on high until smooth. Pour through a fine-mesh strainer into a bowl; discard solids. Season with remaining 1 teaspoon salt and white pepper. Cover and chill until ready to serve, at least 2 hours or up to 1 day.

4 Whisk together crème fraîche, 1 tablespoon chives, 1 tablespoon dill, tarragon, lemon zest, and 2 tablespoons lemon juice in a medium bowl. Gently fold in crab. Chill until ready to serve, at least 30 minutes or up to 2 hours.

5 Stir remaining 1 tablespoon lemon juice into soup. To serve, pour ¾ cup soup into each bowl; add one large dollop of crab salad in center of soup and drizzle with oil. Garnish with chives, and, if desired, with pea tendrils and black pepper.
—SARAH HELLER

ORZO AND CHICKPEAS
WITH TURMERIC-GINGER BROTH

*Coconut milk and fresh lime juice are natural flavor partners to ginger and turmeric.
In this recipe they form a restorative tea-based broth—deliciously studded with
chickpeas and pasta.*

ACTIVE 15 MIN; TOTAL 20 MIN; SERVES 2

- 4 single-serving turmeric-ginger tea bags (such as Rishi)
- ½ cup unsweetened coconut milk
- 3 Tbsp. fresh lime juice (from 2 limes), plus lime wedges, for serving
- ¾ tsp. kosher salt
- ½ tsp. fish sauce (such as Red Boat)
- 1 (15-oz.) can chickpeas, drained and rinsed
- 1 cup cooked orzo or other small pasta
- Toppings: Thinly sliced shallot, fresh cilantro sprigs, and sambal oelek or Asian chile-garlic sauce, for serving

1 Bring 3 cups water to a boil in a teapot or small saucepan over high; remove from heat. Add tea bags, coconut milk, and lime juice; cover and steep 5 minutes. Remove and discard tea bags; stir in salt and fish sauce. Bring just to a simmer over medium. Remove from heat.

2 Divide chickpeas and orzo evenly between 2 bowls. Pour hot tea mixture evenly into bowls; serve immediately with lime wedges and desired toppings.
—JUSTIN CHAPPLE

WINE Dry, lime-zesty California Riesling: 2016 Smith-Madrone Napa Valley

NOTE Look for Rishi turmeric-ginger tea at Asian markets.

MEATLESS

MISO-TOFU HOT POT WITH
RAMEN (P. 212)

LINGUINE WITH FRENCHED GREEN BEANS AND PARSLEY PESTO

In this classic recipe, Johanne Killeen employs starchy pasta water to thicken her fresh pesto into a sauce that clings to and flavors each strand of linguine. Thinly sliced green beans intertwine with the pasta, offering a refreshing crunch.

TOTAL 20 MIN; SERVES 6

- 8 oz. fresh green beans, trimmed and cut into very thin strips (about 3 cups)
- 8 oz. uncooked linguine
- 2 cups loosely packed fresh flat-leaf parsley leaves
- 10 large fresh basil leaves
- ½ cup light-tasting olive oil or extra-virgin olive oil
- 1 small garlic clove, trimmed
- ½ tsp. fine sea salt, plus more for salting water
- ⅛ tsp. cayenne pepper, or to taste
- 2 oz. pecorino Romano cheese, grated (about ½ cup), plus more for serving

1 Bring a large pot of salted water to a boil over medium-high. Add green beans, and cook just until tender, about 2 minutes and 30 seconds. Transfer beans to a colander; set aside. Return water to a boil over medium-high; add pasta. Cook, stirring often, until al dente, about 10 minutes. Reserve 1 cup cooking liquid; pour pasta and remaining cooking liquid into colander over beans (to warm the beans if they have begun to cool).

2 Combine parsley, basil, olive oil, garlic, salt, and cayenne in a food processor or blender; pulse until pureed but still slightly chunky, 8 to 10 times. Transfer to a warmed serving bowl. Stir in pecorino Romano; set aside.

3 Transfer pasta and beans to serving bowl with pesto; toss to combine. Add some of the reserved cooking liquid, 1 tablespoon at a time, to loosen pesto and ensure pesto evenly coats pasta. Serve immediately; pass extra pecorino Romano at the table. —JOHANNE KILLEEN

MAKE AHEAD Pesto can be made up to 3 days in advance and stored in an airtight container in refrigerator.

WINE Fresh, herbal Sauvignon Blanc: 2018 Alphonse Mellot La Moussière Sancerre

NOTE Regular green beans are thicker than French haricots verts, but haricots verts may be substituted.

MUSHROOM DUMPLINGS IN KATSUOBUSHI BROTH

Chef George Meza bathes plump, silky mushroom dumplings and slightly bitter bok choy in a clear, mineral-rich dashi broth for this elegant soup. A final drizzle of tamari and hot chile oil adds savory depth and heat, and a sprinkling of dill makes for a light, refreshing finish.

TOTAL 1 HR 40 MIN; SERVES 8

KOMBU BROTH

- 4 qt. filtered water
- 3 oz. kombu
- 3 oz. dried bonito flakes
- 2 Tbsp. tamari or soy sauce, plus more for serving

DUMPLINGS

- 7 Tbsp. grapeseed oil, divided
- 1¼ lb. fresh hen-of-the-woods or oyster mushrooms, cut into 1-inch pieces (about 10 cups)
- 1 medium yellow onion (about 10 oz.), thinly sliced
- 1 large garlic clove, finely chopped
- 1 bunch scallions (about 4¼ oz.), thinly sliced
- 1¾ tsp. kosher salt
- 1 tsp. toasted sesame oil
- ¼ tsp. black pepper
- 1 (12-oz.) pkg. square wonton wrappers

ADDITIONAL INGREDIENTS

- 1 (1½-lb.) head bok choy, sliced
- Chopped fresh dill, for serving
- Chile Oil, for serving (recipe follows) (optional)

1 **Make the kombu broth:** Combine 4 quarts water and kombu in a large pot. Heat over medium-high until water begins to steam and small bubbles form around kombu (do not boil), about 15 minutes. Remove from heat and stir in bonito flakes. Let steep 30 minutes. Pour mixture through a fine wire-mesh strainer into a bowl; discard solids. Stir in tamari, and keep broth warm.

2 **Make the dumplings:** Heat 3 tablespoons grapeseed oil in a large skillet over high. Add half the mushrooms; cook, without stirring, until mushrooms begin to brown, about 2 minutes. Stir mushrooms. Cook, without stirring, until well browned, about 3 minutes. Remove mushrooms from skillet, then repeat with 3 tablespoons grapeseed oil and remaining half of mushrooms. Remove mushrooms from skillet, and set aside. Heat remaining 1 tablespoon grapeseed oil in skillet over medium. Add onion and garlic, and cook, stirring often, until onion is very tender, about 20 minutes. Remove from heat.

3 Finely chop half the browned mushrooms; transfer to a medium bowl. Place remaining mushrooms in a food processor. Add onion mixture, and process until a paste forms, about 2 minutes. Transfer mixture to bowl with chopped mushrooms. Stir in scallions, salt, sesame oil, and pepper until combined.

4 Place 1 heaping teaspoon mushroom mixture in center of each of 48 wonton wrappers. Lightly brush edges of wrappers with water; fold 1 corner of each over to opposite corner and pinch edges together to seal. Set dumplings aside.

5 Bring a large saucepan filled with salted water to a boil over high. Add bok choy, and cook just until tender, about 2 minutes. Using a slotted spoon, remove bok choy from water. Add one-third of dumplings to bok choy cooking water and cook until dumplings are tender and float to surface, about 2 minutes. Remove from water; repeat twice with remaining dumplings.

6 To serve, place 6 dumplings and ¼ cup bok choy in each of 8 serving bowls. Top each with 1½ cups kombu broth. Garnish with fresh dill, and serve with tamari and, if desired, Chile Oil. —GEORGE MEZA

WINE Crisp, earthy white: 2016 Les Frères Couillaud Château de la Ragotière Muscadet de Sèvre et Maine sur lie

CHILE OIL

TOTAL 1 HR 10 MIN; MAKES ½ CUP

- ½ cup canola oil, divided
- 1 Tbsp. crushed red pepper
- ¼ tsp. kosher salt

Heat ¼ cup oil in a small saucepan over medium until shimmering, about 3 minutes. Remove from heat and stir in red pepper and salt. Let stand until fragrant, 1 to 2 minutes. Stir in remaining ¼ cup oil. Let cool completely, about 1 hour. Store in an airtight container at room temperature up to 5 days. —ABRA BERENS

ONE-POT WHITE WINE PASTA
WITH MUSHROOMS AND LEEKS

This creamy, savory pasta dish comes together in just one pot—no need to boil the pasta separately. A combination of sautéed mushrooms and gently sweet leeks combine with cream, lemon juice, and white wine to create the rich sauce. For a second choice of herbs, tarragon is a good stand-in for the dill.

ACTIVE 30 MIN; TOTAL 30 MIN; SERVES 6

- 3 Tbsp. extra-virgin olive oil
- 1 lb. cremini mushrooms, trimmed and sliced
- 2 Tbsp. unsalted butter
- 2 medium leeks, trimmed and thinly sliced (white and light green parts only), about 1½ cups)
- 4 medium garlic cloves, thinly sliced
- 2½ tsp. kosher salt, divided
- 1 lb. short pasta, such as penne, casarecce, or pipe rigate
- 1⅓ cups low-sodium vegetable broth
- ⅔ cup dry white wine
- ½ cup heavy whipping cream
- ½ cup grated Parmigiano-Reggiano cheese (about 2 oz.), plus more for serving
- 2 Tbsp. chopped fresh dill
- 2 Tbsp. chopped fresh flat-leaf parsley
- 1 tsp. grated lemon zest plus 1½ tsp. fresh juice (from 1 lemon)
- ½ tsp. black pepper

1 Heat oil in a large saucepan over medium-high. Add mushrooms and cook, stirring often, until all liquid has evaporated, about 12 minutes. Add butter, stirring until melted. Add leeks, garlic, and 1 teaspoon salt; cook, stirring often, until leeks are tender, 4 to 5 minutes.

2 Stir in pasta, 3 cups water, broth, wine, and remaining 1½ teaspoons salt. Increase heat to high and bring to a boil. Reduce heat to medium; simmer, stirring occasionally, until about 3 minutes short of al dente (check cook time on package). Stir in cream and simmer until sauce evenly coats pasta, about 3 minutes. Remove from heat. Stir in cheese, herbs, lemon zest and juice, and pepper. Divide pasta evenly among shallow bowls, and serve topped with cheese.

— ROBIN BASHINSKY

PEA TORTILLA WITH MINT AND YOGURT

A Spanish tortilla is like a frittata. Chef and author Francis Mallmann makes a lovely spring version with yogurt, fresh mint, and sweet peas, baked (preferably in a wood-fired oven) just until set. It's delicious served warm or at room temperature.

TOTAL 20 MIN; SERVES 10

4 Tbsp. unsalted butter

½ lb. frozen baby peas, thawed, drained, and patted dry

1½ cups plain Greek-style yogurt, divided

8 large eggs

½ cup coarsely chopped fresh mint

1 tsp. kosher salt

¼ tsp. freshly ground black pepper

1 Preheat broiler. Melt butter in a large ovenproof nonstick skillet. Add peas and cook over medium until warm, about 3 minutes.

2 Beat ½ cup yogurt, the eggs, mint, salt, and pepper in a large bowl until smooth. Pour egg mixture over peas; cook over medium-high until set on the bottom and around edges, about 4 minutes. Transfer skillet to oven. Broil 6 inches from heat until the top of tortilla is set and lightly golden in spots, about 3 minutes. Slide tortilla onto a plate, cut into wedges, and serve with remaining 1 cup yogurt.

—FRANCIS MALLMANN

WINE South American Sauvignon Blanc from Chile's Pacific Coast

SPAGHETTI WITH CACIO E PEPE BUTTER

Cacio e pepe is a Roman pasta dish prized for its simplicity. Our Mad Genius culinary director, Justin Chapple, puts a spin on the original with a black pepper and Pecorino Romano compound butter. Just boil the pasta, grate the chilled butter over the top, and dinner is done.

TOTAL 20 MIN; SERVES 4 TO 6

Kosher salt

1 lb. broccoli rabe, trimmed and chopped

1 lb. dried spaghetti

Cacio e Pepe Butter (recipe follows)

1 Cook broccoli rabe in a large pot of boiling salted water until crisp-tender, 2 to 3 minutes. Using a slotted spoon, transfer to a colander to drain. Add pasta to boiling water and cook until al dente. Reserve ½ cup cooking liquid; drain pasta.

2 In a serving bowl toss pasta with broccoli rabe. Grate some Cacio e Pepe Butter over pasta and toss vigorously to coat. Season with salt and toss again. Serve immediately. —JUSTIN CHAPPLE

WINE Earthy Italian white: 2016 Mastroberardino Falanghina del Sannio

CACIO E PEPE BUTTER

ACTIVE 10 MIN; TOTAL 30 MIN; MAKES ½ CUP

4 oz. softened unsalted butter

1 cup freshly grated Pecorino Romano cheese

2 Tbsp. freshly ground black pepper

1½ tsp. kosher salt

Mash butter with cheese, pepper, and salt. Roll butter in parchment; freeze until firm. Grate over pasta, popcorn, or steamed veggies. —JC

THIN SPAGHETTI WITH TOMATOES, KALAMATA OLIVES, FETA, AND MINT

For a weeknight when speed is key, whip up this one-pot pasta, inspired by Greek ingredients—cherry tomatoes, briny olives, salty feta cheese, and fresh mint and oregano. With very little effort, it's a satisfying meal on a summer evening.

ACTIVE 15 MIN; TOTAL 25 MIN; SERVES 4

- 1¼ lb. multicolor cherry or grape tomatoes
- 12 oz. uncooked thin spaghetti (spaghettini)
- 2½ cups chicken or vegetable stock
- 1½ tsp. kosher salt, divided
- ¼ tsp. crushed red pepper
- ¾ cup pitted Kalamata olives, gently smashed
- ¼ tsp. black pepper
- 4 oz. feta cheese, crumbled (1 cup)
- ¼ cup packed fresh mint leaves
- ¼ cup loosely packed fresh oregano leaves
- ¼ cup extra-virgin olive oil

1 Stir together tomatoes, pasta, stock, 2 cups water, 1 teaspoon salt, and crushed red pepper in a large saucepan; bring to a boil over medium-high. Cook, stirring occasionally, until pasta is slightly softened, about 5 minutes.

2 Crush tomatoes in saucepan using the back of a spoon. Cook over medium-high, stirring occasionally, until pasta is al dente and liquid thickens and reduces slightly, about 6 minutes. (If needed, add additional water, 1 tablespoon at a time, until sauce reaches desired consistency.)

3 Stir in olives, black pepper, and remaining ½ teaspoon salt. Divide pasta mixture evenly among 4 bowls. Sprinkle with feta, mint, and oregano; drizzle with oil.
—JUSTIN CHAPPLE

WINE Lemony, light-bodied Greek white: 2016 Argyros Estate Assyrtiko

PROVENÇAL EGGPLANT-TOMATO GRATIN

Frank Stitt, owner of Highlands Bar & Grill in Birmingham, Alabama, started his culinary education in Provence, France while working for the late great cookbook author Richard Olney. This gratin recipe—of beautifully arranged summer tomatoes and eggplant— was one served at a dinner party inspired by Olney's love of seasonal produce and exceptional wine.

ACTIVE 30 MIN; TOTAL 2 HR; SERVES 4 TO 6

- 6 small or medium eggplants (1½ lb.)
- 4 garlic cloves (1 crushed and 3 thinly sliced, slices divided)
- ⅓ cup plus 1 Tbsp. extra-virgin olive oil, divided
- 2 medium yellow onions, sliced (about 4 cups), divided
- 1 tsp. dried thyme
- 1 tsp. dried marjoram
- ¼ tsp. ground coriander
- 1½ tsp. kosher salt, divided
- 5 medium tomatoes, cored and cut into 6 slices each
- 1 tsp. freshly ground black pepper
- 6 button mushrooms, sliced
- ⅓ cup niçoise olives, pitted and crushed
- 5 fresh bay leaves
- ⅓ cup fresh basil leaves, torn

1 Preheat oven to 450° F.

2 Trim stems from eggplants. If using medium-size eggplant, cut in half lengthwise. Cut small or medium eggplant halves into 7 slices each, cutting to, but not through, stem end (eggplant should be able to be fanned out without falling apart).

3 Rub a 9- × 13-inch gratin dish with crushed garlic clove. Drizzle 1 tablespoon olive oil in bottom of dish, and rub to coat evenly. Place 2 cups onion slices, thyme, marjoram, coriander, and one-third of the sliced garlic in an even layer in prepared dish. Arrange eggplants on onion, and sprinkle with ¾ teaspoon salt. Place 1 tomato slice between each eggplant "fan blade." Sprinkle with pepper and remaining ¾ teaspoon salt. Top with remaining sliced garlic, remaining 2 cups onion slices, mushrooms, olives, and bay leaves. Drizzle with remaining ⅓ cup olive oil.

4 Cover dish tightly with aluminum foil. Bake in preheated oven 15 minutes. Reduce oven temperature to 375° F (do not remove dish), and continue cooking until eggplant is almost tender, about 1 hour and 10 minutes. Remove and discard foil; bake until juices are slightly reduced and eggplant is very tender, about 20 minutes longer. Garnish with torn basil. —FRANK STITT

NOTE Baked gratin also holds well covered and refrigerated overnight. Serve warm or at room temperature.

PINEAPPLE BLACK FRIED RICE

Black rice, also called forbidden rice, gives this dish from New York chef JJ Johnson its striking appearance. "Kids love fried rice," says Johnson. "And it's a perfect vehicle for sneaking in some fruits and veggies." This black rice is stir-fried with edamame, bean sprouts, and juicy diced pineapple.

TOTAL 20 MIN; SERVES 6

2 Tbsp. canola oil

1 onion, chopped

2 garlic cloves, finely chopped

1 bird chile, stemmed and thinly sliced

1 medium carrot, halved lengthwise and thinly sliced crosswise

1 cup stemmed and coarsely chopped mustard greens

3 cups cooked black rice (see Note)

1 cup bean sprouts

1 cup thawed frozen edamame

4 oz. cored pineapple, cut into ¼-inch pieces (about 1 cup)

3 Tbsp. soy sauce

2 scallions, thinly sliced

1 tsp. sweet chili sauce

1 Heat oil in a large cast-iron skillet over medium-high. Add onion and cook, stirring occasionally, until softened, about 6 minutes. Add garlic and chile. Cook, stirring, until fragrant, about 1 minute.

2 Increase heat to high. Add carrot and mustard greens; stir-fry until crisp-tender, 2 to 3 minutes. Stir in rice until hot, about 2 minutes. Add bean sprouts, edamame, pineapple, and soy sauce; stir-fry until bean sprouts are crisp-tender and pineapple and edamame are heated through, about 2 minutes. Fold in scallions and chili sauce. —JOSEPH JOHNSON

NOTE To cook black rice, in a medium saucepan, bring 1⅔ cups water and 1 cup black rice to a boil over medium. Simmer, covered, over medium-low until tender, about 20 minutes. Remove from heat; let stand 5 minutes. Transfer rice to a large rimmed baking sheet to cool completely.

GARDEN PAELLA

Bomba rice, a short-grain rice from Spain, is traditional in paella for the best texture. A carbon steel pan works well for evenly distributing heat while cooking this paella; you'll be less likely to encounter hot spots and burn the vegetables.

ACTIVE 30 MIN; TOTAL 1 HR 20 MIN; SERVES 6 TO 8

5 Tbsp. extra-virgin olive oil, divided

2 small zucchini, trimmed, quartered lengthwise, and cut into ½-inch-thick slices (about 2 cups)

1 small eggplant, cut into ½-inch pieces (about 2 cups)

5 tsp. kosher salt, divided

Pinch of saffron threads (about ⅛ tsp.)

1 small yellow onion, chopped (about 1¼ cups)

1 medium tomato, finely chopped (about 1 cup)

¼ cup finely chopped jarred roasted piquillo peppers (about 2 oz.)

1½ tsp. hot pimentón, or more to taste

2¼ cups uncooked Bomba rice (about 15 oz.)

½ cup dry white wine

¼ cup roughly chopped fresh flat-leaf parsley, plus more for garnish

Lemon wedges, for serving

1 Preheat oven to 400°F. Heat ¼ cup oil in a 15-inch carbon steel paella pan over medium-high. Add zucchini and eggplant. Sprinkle with 1½ teaspoons salt. Cook, stirring occasionally, until lightly browned and just starting to soften, 5 to 6 minutes. Transfer vegetables to a plate; set aside.

2 While zucchini mixture is cooking, microwave 2 tablespoons water in a small microwavable bowl on high until hot, about 30 seconds. Crumble saffron threads into hot water; let stand until ready to use, about 10 minutes.

3 Reduce heat under paella pan to medium-low. Add remaining 1 tablespoon oil to pan. Add onion and ½ teaspoon salt. Cook, stirring often, until onion is softened and lightly browned, about 5 minutes. Stir in tomato. Cook, stirring often, until tomato breaks down and begins to caramelize, 3 to 4 minutes.

4 Stir in piquillo peppers, pimentón, saffron mixture, and remaining 3 teaspoons salt until well combined. Add rice and cook, stirring constantly, until well coated and very lightly toasted, about 2 minutes. Stir in zucchini mixture, wine, parsley, and 3 cups water until combined. Spread mixture in an even layer. Transfer pan to preheated oven. Bake until liquid is absorbed, rice is tender, and top is lightly browned, 34 to 38 minutes.

5 Return pan to stovetop over medium-low. Cook, occasionally rotating pan over burner for even browning, until rice smells faintly nutty and you hear a constant crackling sound, 6 to 8 minutes. Remove from heat and let stand 15 minutes. Garnish with parsley and serve with lemon wedges. —MARIA SINSKEY

WINE Darkly fruity, earthy Tinta de Toro: 2018 Kiko Calvo Bigardo

NOTE Find high-quality Kashmiri saffron at kalustyans.com.

COCONUT CHICKPEAS WITH WINTER SQUASH

Starchy, slightly sweet plantains are a natural addition to winter squash. Here, New York chef JJ Johnson simmers both, along with canned chickpeas, in coconut milk that's steeped with aromatics. The result is creamy, fragrant, and so comforting.

ACTIVE 35 MIN; TOTAL 1 HR 10 MIN; SERVES 6 TO 8

3 Tbsp. olive oil

1 red onion, chopped

5 garlic cloves, finely chopped

1½ lb. butternut squash, peeled, seeded, and cut into 1-inch pieces

1 lb. delicata squash, halved, seeded, quartered, and cut into ½-inch-thick slices

1 large carrot, cut into ½-inch-thick slices

1 celery stalk, cut into ½-inch-thick slices

1 firm-ripe plantain, cut into ½-inch-thick slices

2 Tbsp. chopped cilantro

1 bird chile, stemmed and thinly sliced

1 tsp. ground cumin

Salt

1 (13.5-oz.) can well-stirred unsweetened coconut milk

2 long lime zest strips

2 (15.5-oz.) cans chickpeas, rinsed and drained

2 Tbsp. lime juice

½ cup cilantro leaves, for garnish

1 Heat oil in a large enameled cast-iron Dutch oven or heavy pot. Add onion and cook over medium, stirring occasionally, until softened, about 5 minutes. Add garlic and cook, stirring, until fragrant, about 1 minute. Add butternut squash, delicata squash, carrot, celery, plantain, chopped cilantro, chile, cumin, and 1 teaspoon salt. Cook, covered, until vegetables start to soften, about 10 minutes. Add coconut milk, lime zest strips, and 2 cups water; bring to a boil. Reduce heat to medium-low. Simmer, covered, until vegetables are tender, 20 to 25 minutes.

2 Add chickpeas and simmer until heated through, about 5 minutes. Season with salt. Stir in lime juice. Discard lime zest strips, and garnish with cilantro leaves before serving. —JOSEPH JOHNSON

MISO-TOFU HOT POT WITH RAMEN

PHOTO P. 193

A hot pot is the perfect excuse to set out ingredients and casually dine around the table. Although this recipe can be turned out at the stove, donabe hot pot is traditionally prepared on a portable burner at the table. We suggest cooking the tofu and vegetables first, then soak up the delicious broth with chewy ramen noodles as a second course.

TOTAL 40 MIN; SERVES 2

- 1 Tbsp. toasted sesame oil
- 1 garlic clove, grated
- 2 tsp. grated peeled fresh ginger
- 1 bunch scallions, white parts sliced, green parts thinly diagonally sliced, for garnish
- 2 tsp. chile bean sauce (toban djan) (such as Lee Kum Kee)
- ¼ cup junmai sake (such as Hakushika Junmai Yamadanishiki)
- 2 Tbsp. white miso
- 4 cups warm Shiitake Dashi (recipe follows), divided
- 1 Tbsp. soy sauce
- 5 large napa cabbage leaves, cut into 1½-inch pieces
- 3 oz. white beech mushrooms, trimmed and separated into clusters
- 2 medium carrots, peeled (using a julienne peeler, if desired) and thinly diagonally sliced
- 7 oz. firm silken tofu, drained and cut into 4 (½-inch-thick) slabs
- Coarsely ground toasted sesame seeds, chile oil, kurozu (Japanese black vinegar), and Quick-Pickled Shiitakes (recipe follows), for serving
- 5 oz. fresh or thawed frozen ramen noodles (such as Sun Noodle), cooked according to package directions

1 Heat sesame oil in a 3-quart classic-style donabe over medium. Add garlic, ginger, and white scallion pieces. Cook, stirring constantly, until softened and fragrant, about 2 minutes. Push mixture to 1 side of pot, and add chile bean sauce to empty side. Cook, stirring constantly, until fragrant, about 30 seconds. Stir in sake, incorporating garlic, ginger, and white scallion pieces; cook 1 minute. Whisk together miso and ¼ cup shiitake dashi in a small bowl until smooth; set aside. Stir soy sauce and remaining 3¾ cups shiitake dashi into pot. Cover and bring to a simmer over medium-low.

2 Uncover pot and stir in cabbage, mushrooms, and carrots. Add tofu. Cook, covered, until tofu is heated through and vegetables are crisp-tender, 4 to 5 minutes. Stir in miso mixture. Using a spider or slotted spoon, divide vegetables and tofu between 2 serving bowls (about 2 cups each). Ladle about 1 cup of broth into each bowl; reserve remaining broth in donabe. Garnish with ground sesame seeds, chile oil, kurozu, quick-pickled shiitakes, and green scallion pieces.

3 Reheat remaining broth (about 1½ cups) in donabe over medium-low until steaming. Add ramen to broth; let stand until heated through, and serve as second course. —MARY-FRANCES HECK AND PAIGE GRANDJEAN

BEER Silky, rich sake: Hakkaisan Honjozo

NOTE Source chile bean sauce, junmai sake, and kurozu at Japanese grocery stores.

SHIITAKE DASHI

A gentle steep is the best way to coax the sweet umami—without any bitter notes—from the kombu and shiitakes in this all-purpose dashi.

ACTIVE 25 MIN; TOTAL 1 HR 25 MIN; MAKES ABOUT 4 CUPS

1½ oz. dried shiitake mushroom caps (about 2½ cups, or 22 caps), rinsed well

1 oz. dried kombu (about 1 [9-inch] square, halved)

1 oz. dried smoked bonito flakes (katsuobushi) (about 3 cups) (optional)

1 Combine 6 cups water, shiitakes, and kombu in a 3-quart classic-style donabe. Let stand for 30 minutes.

2 Heat mixture, uncovered, over medium-low until steaming but not simmering (about 140°F), about 10 minutes. Cook 15 minutes, adjusting heat as needed to prevent simmering. Using a slotted spoon or spider, remove and discard kombu.

3 Stir in dried smoked bonito flakes, if using, and continue cooking over medium-low until flavors are infused, dashi has a light smoky flavor, and liquid has reduced to about 4 cups, 12 to 15 minutes. Remove from heat; pour through a fine wire-mesh strainer into a bowl, reserving shiitakes for quick-pickled shiitakes (recipe follows). —MH AND PG

MAKE AHEAD Dashi can be kept in an airtight container in refrigerator up to 3 days.

QUICK-PICKLED SHIITAKES

Hydrated shiitakes from making dashi are full of flavor and are a good choice for tossing with this mild soy-sherry pickling liquid. Serve with hot pot or as a condiment for soups or sandwiches.

ACTIVE 10 MIN; TOTAL 20 MIN; MAKES ABOUT 1½ CUPS

9 oz. rehydrated shiitake mushroom caps (from Shiitake Dashi) (about 2 cups), rinsed

2 Tbsp. granulated sugar

2 Tbsp. soy sauce

2 Tbsp. sherry vinegar

Slice mushroom caps into ⅛-inch-thick pieces. Whisk together sugar, soy sauce, and vinegar in a small bowl until sugar is dissolved. Add mushrooms, and toss to coat. Let stand 10 minutes. —MH AND PG

MAKE AHEAD Mushrooms can be kept in an airtight container in refrigerator up to 1 week.

LENTIL AND BEAN STEW WITH GREMOLATA

Lentils add a delicious earthy flavor to the stew, and their starchiness helps thicken the broth. Brown lentils work fine in this recipe, but we prefer French green lentils; they hold their shape better. Feel free to cook dried beans especially for this recipe, but any leftover or canned beans—rinsed and drained—will work well.

ACTIVE 25 MIN; TOTAL 55 MIN; SERVES 10

- 1 cup extra-virgin olive oil, divided
- 1 medium-size yellow onion, chopped (about 2 cups)
- 5 medium carrots, cut into ½-inch pieces (about 2 cups)
- 5 celery stalks, cut into ½-inch pieces (about 2 cups)
- 1 (15-oz.) can diced tomatoes, undrained
- 6 garlic cloves, finely chopped, divided
- 2 Tbsp. plus ½ tsp. kosher salt, divided, plus more to taste
- 2 tsp. black pepper, divided, plus more to taste
- 1½ cups dried French green lentils
- 2 bay leaves
- 2 (6-inch) fresh rosemary sprigs
- ¼ cup packed chopped fresh flat-leaf parsley
- 1½ tsp. grated lemon zest plus 1½ Tbsp. fresh lemon juice, divided
- 6 cups cooked mixed beans (such as cannellini, kidney, or cranberry)

1 Heat ½ cup oil in a large Dutch oven over medium-high. Add onion, carrots, and celery. Cook, stirring occasionally, until tender, 15 to 20 minutes. Stir in tomatoes, half the garlic, 2 teaspoons salt, and 1 teaspoon pepper. Cook, stirring often, until garlic is fragrant and tomato juices begin to caramelize, 4 to 6 minutes. Stir in lentils, bay leaves, rosemary sprigs, and 5 cups water. Bring to a boil over medium-high. Reduce heat to medium-low, and simmer, uncovered, stirring occasionally, just until lentils are tender, 20 to 25 minutes.

2 Meanwhile, stir together parsley, lemon zest, ½ teaspoon salt, and remaining garlic. Let mixture stand 10 minutes. Stir in remaining ½ cup oil, and season with salt to taste.

3 Add beans, remaining 4 teaspoons salt, and remaining 1 teaspoon pepper; stir to combine. If needed, stir in additional water to thin stew. Cook over low, uncovered, stirring occasionally, until beans are heated through and lentils are tender, 10 to 15 minutes. Stir in lemon juice, and season to taste with salt and pepper. Spoon gremolata over servings of stew. —MARIA SINSKEY

MAKE AHEAD Stew may be stored in an airtight container in refrigerator up to 5 days.

WINE Tart, earthy, natural Italian white: 2018 Cascina degli Ulivi IVAG

NOTE Find French green lentils at ranchogordo.com.

MUSHROOM-CHICKPEA POZOLE

Traditional pozole is made by creating a rich broth by cooking a whole pig head with some neck bones with dried hominy, then adding either red or green salsa for color and flavor. In this vegan pozole, mushrooms provide earthy flavor and heartiness.

TOTAL 45 MIN; SERVES 8

4 dried guajillo chiles

2 ancho chiles

2 chile de árbol

5 garlic cloves

1 white onion, quartered

2 roma tomatoes

¼ tsp. ground cumin

1½ tsp. kosher salt, divided, plus more to taste

8 cups vegetable stock

6 cups sliced baby portobello mushrooms

2 cups roughly chopped shitake mushrooms

3 (15-oz.) cans chickpeas

1 cup shredded green cabbage

¾ cup thinly sliced red onion

½ cup thinly sliced radishes

Crumbled dried oregano and chile oil, for garnish

Lime wedges, for serving

1 Add dried chiles and 3 cups water to a large Dutch oven. Cook over medium-high until water boils; reduce heat to medium and simmer 5 to 7 minutes. Remove chiles from water and place in a blender. Discard water. Add garlic, onion, and tomatoes to blender. Process until mixture reaches a paste-like consistency, about 1 minute. Transfer to a bowl; season with cumin and ½ teaspoon salt; set aside.

2 Heat stock in Dutch oven over medium-high. Add chile mixture and mushrooms; bring to a boil. Reduce heat to medium-low; add chickpeas and remaining 1 teaspoon salt. Cook, stirring occasionally, until mushrooms are tender, 25 to 30 minutes.

3 Top servings of pozole with cabbage, red onion, radishes, oregano, and chile oil. Serve with lime wedges. —MARCELA VALLADOLID

ROASTED CAULIFLOWER SOUP WITH CUMIN

For this deeply satisfying soup, chefs Anna Trattles and Alice Quillet roast cauliflower with cumin seeds and curry powder to intensify flavor, then simmer with onion and water to make an unfussy, spice-inflected puree.

ACTIVE 25 MIN; TOTAL 1 HR; SERVES 4 TO 6

1 medium head of cauliflower (1½ lb.), halved, cored and cut into 1½-inch florets

1 tsp. cumin seeds

1 tsp. curry powder

¼ cup sunflower or grapeseed oil

Kosher salt and black pepper

1 small onion, diced

3 Tbsp. unsalted butter

1 bay leaf

¼ cup whole milk

1 Preheat oven to 375°F. Toss cauliflower with cumin seeds, curry powder, and 3 tablespoons oil on a large rimmed baking sheet; season with salt and pepper. Roast just until tender, turning occasionally, about 25 minutes.

2 Heat remaining 1 tablespoon oil in a large saucepan. Add onion; cook over medium, stirring occasionally, until softened but not browned, about 5 minutes. Add roasted cauliflower, butter, bay leaf, and 4 cups of water; bring to a simmer. Cook over medium until liquid is reduced and cauliflower is soft, about 15 minutes. Remove and discard bay leaf.

3 In a blender puree soup in 2 batches until very smooth. Return soup to saucepan; stir in milk. Heat over medium, adding additional water for thinner consistency, if desired. Season soup with salt and pepper. —ALICE QUILLET AND ANNA TRATTLES

LENTIL AND SMOKY EGGPLANT STEW

You could make this stew with any kind of lentil. The advantage of using the small, almost round green kind called French (or Puy), as chef Fernanda Milanezi does here, is that they hold their shape very nicely even when fully cooked.

ACTIVE 20 MIN; TOTAL 1 HR 30 MIN; SERVES 12

¼ cup extra-virgin olive oil, plus more for drizzling

1 medium onion, finely chopped

1 celery rib, finely chopped

5 garlic cloves, finely chopped

1 bay leaf

3 cups green Puy lentils (20 oz.), rinsed and picked over

1 (14½-oz.) can chopped tomatoes

2 qt. vegetable stock

2 medium eggplants (1½ lb.)

2 Tbsp. harissa

⅓ cup chopped fresh flat-leaf parsley, plus more for serving

Salt and black pepper

Greek yogurt, chopped walnuts, small fresh mint leaves, and pomegranate molasses, for serving

1 Preheat broiler. Heat 2 tablespoons oil in a large saucepan. Add onion, celery, garlic, and bay leaf. Cook over medium until softened. Add lentils, tomatoes, and stock; bring to a simmer over medium-high. Reduce heat. Simmer, covered, stirring occasionally, until lentils are tender but still hold their shape, about 45 minutes.

2 Meanwhile, place eggplants on a foil-lined baking sheet and rub with remaining 2 tablespoons olive oil. Broil 6 inches from heat, turning occasionally, until completely blackened and tender, about 20 minutes. Let cool.

3 Cut eggplants in half lengthwise and scoop flesh into a colander set over a bowl; discard skins. Let eggplant flesh drain 5 minutes, then transfer to a bowl and mash until smooth.

4 Stir harissa and half the eggplant flesh into lentils until heated through. Stir in ⅓ cup chopped parsley; season with salt and pepper. Ladle stew into bowls; top with remaining eggplant. Garnish with yogurt, chopped walnuts, parsley, and mint leaves; drizzle with pomegranate molasses and olive oil. —FERNANDA MILANEZI

WINE Medium-bodied Pinot Noir: 2012 Chehalem Three Vineyard

SLOW-COOKER VEGETABLE-FARRO STEW
WITH FIGS AND PINE NUTS

ACTIVE 30 MIN; TOTAL 6 HR 30 MIN; SERVES 6

2 fresh rosemary sprigs

5 fresh oregano sprigs

5 fresh thyme sprigs

2 small artichokes

1 cup farro

¼ cup extra-virgin olive oil, plus more for drizzling

1½ cups tomato juice

½ cup water

2 tsp. kosher salt, plus more for seasoning

1 tsp. crushed red pepper

2 heads garlic, ¼ inch cut off tops

1 lemon, sliced ⅛ inch thick

1 Cubanelle pepper, sliced ⅓ inch thick

½ red bell pepper, sliced ⅓ inch thick

½ yellow bell pepper, sliced ⅓ inch thick

1 medium onion, quartered

1 large Japanese eggplant, cut into 6 wedges

1 cup dried Black Mission figs (5 oz.), stemmed

½ cup golden raisins

1 fennel bulb, trimmed and cut into 6 wedges

½ lb. large cherry tomatoes, halved

1 small zucchini, cut into 2-inch pieces

1 small yellow squash, cut into 2-inch pieces

1 bunch kale (6 oz.), stemmed and leaves quartered

Toasted pine nuts, chopped fresh oregano, lemon wedges, freshly grated Parmigiano-Reggiano cheese, and sherry vinegar, for serving

1 Using kitchen twine, tie rosemary, oregano, and thyme sprigs into a bundle. With a serrated knife, cut off the top third of the artichokes. Snap off small leaves from around artichoke stem. Cut artichokes in half lengthwise. With a spoon, scrape out and discard hairy chokes.

2 Turn a 6- or 6½-quart slow cooker to high and set timer for 6 hours. Add artichokes and the next 17 ingredients, up to and including cherry tomatoes. Add herb bundle; spread ingredients evenly. Cover and cook 4 hours.

3 Stir stew gently and add zucchini, yellow squash, and kale, stirring to submerge in the cooking liquid. Cover and cook 2 hours.

4 Discard herb bundle; season with salt. Serve with pine nuts, oregano, lemon wedges, cheese, and vinegar. —GRANT ACHATZ

WINE Herb-scented, light-bodied Italian red: 2012 Allegrini Valpolicella

HARISSA WHITE BEAN STEW WITH TURMERIC YOGURT

Cookbook author Sarah DiGregorio adds depth and heat to hearty white bean stew by adding harissa twice: first for the long simmer in the slow cooker, then at the end to finish the dish with bright heat.

ACTIVE 30 MIN; TOTAL 6 HR 45 MIN; SERVES 4 TO 6

- 3 Tbsp. unsalted butter
- 1 large red onion, finely chopped
- 5 garlic cloves, finely chopped
  Kosher salt
- ¼ cup plus 3 Tbsp. harissa
- 3 Tbsp. tomato paste
- 1 tsp. ground cumin
- 1 tsp. sweet paprika
- 1 lb. dried cannellini beans
- 2 large carrots, sliced ½ inch thick
- 3 fresh thyme sprigs plus 1½ tsp. thyme leaves
- 2 fresh bay leaves
- 1 (3-inch) strip lemon zest plus 3 Tbsp. fresh lemon juice
- 2 tsp. ground turmeric
- 1½ cups full-fat Greek yogurt
- ½ cup finely chopped fresh parsley, plus leaves for garnish
- ½ preserved lemon, pulp discarded and rind thinly sliced

1 Melt 2 tablespoons butter in a large skillet. Add onion and garlic; season generously with salt. Cook over medium-high, stirring occasionally, until onion has softened and is starting to brown, about 8 minutes. Stir in ¼ cup harissa and the tomato paste. Cook, stirring, until fragrant, about 1 minute. Stir in cumin and paprika; add 2½ cups water. Bring to a simmer, scraping any browned bits on bottom of pan. Transfer to a 6-quart slow cooker along with dried beans, carrots, thyme sprigs, bay leaves, and lemon zest and juice. Add 1 tablespoon salt and 3½ cups water. Cover and cook on high until beans are tender, about 6 hours.

2 Meanwhile, melt remaining 1 tablespoon butter in a small nonstick skillet. Add turmeric and cook over medium-low, stirring constantly, until it dissolves, about 30 seconds. Transfer to a medium bowl; let cool slightly, about 5 minutes. Slowly whisk in yogurt until smooth. Season with salt.

3 Discard bay leaves and thyme sprigs from stew. Just before serving, stir in thyme leaves, chopped parsley, and remaining 3 tablespoons harissa; season with salt. Ladle into bowls, and garnish with preserved lemon and parsley leaves. Serve with turmeric yogurt. —SARAH DIGREGORIO

MAKE AHEAD Turmeric yogurt can be refrigerated for 2 days. The stew can be refrigerated for 4 days; reheat gently before serving.

WINE Peppery Mediterranean Monastrell: 2015 Bodegas Volver Tarima Hill

BURMESE SAMUSA SOUP

This vegan soup from Desmond Tan's Burma Superstar in San Francisco features a broth that's seasoned with black mustard seeds, cumin, and turmeric. Fresh cabbage, herbs, and chiles top each ample bowl, contrasting tender lentils and potatoes with a pleasing crunch.

TOTAL 45 MIN; SERVES 4

- 1 tsp. cumin seeds
- 1 tsp. black mustard seeds
- ⅓ cup vegetable oil
- 3 to 4 small chiles de árbol or other dried chiles
- 2 bay leaves
- 1 medium onion, finely chopped
- ¼ cup finely chopped garlic (about 12 garlic cloves)
- 1 Tbsp. kosher salt
- 1½ tsp. paprika
- 1 tsp. ground turmeric
- ¼ cup toasted chickpea flour (besan)
- 2 qt. vegetable broth (such as Zoup!)
- ½ cup tamarind water (see Note)
- ½ cup dried yellow lentils
- 1 medium russet potato, peeled and chopped
- 2 red Thai chiles or ½ jalapeño, chopped
- ½ tsp. garam masala
- Chopped fresh mint, thinly sliced cabbage, fresh cilantro leaves, thinly sliced red Thai chiles, and lime wedges, for serving

1 Toast cumin and mustard seeds in a large dry saucepan over medium, stirring often, until fragrant, about 30 seconds. Remove from heat and grind into a coarse powder. Add oil to pan and heat over medium-high. Add cumin mixture, chiles de árbol, and bay leaves; cook, stirring constantly, until fragrant, about 25 seconds. Reduce heat to medium, and stir in onion. Cook, stirring occasionally, until onion softens, about 15 minutes. Stir in garlic, and cook, stirring often, until fragrant, about 2 minutes. Stir in salt, paprika, and turmeric.

2 Whisk together ½ cup water and chickpea flour in a small bowl until well combined. Add chickpea flour mixture, broth, tamarind water, lentils, and potato to pan. Stir to combine; bring to a boil over medium-high. Reduce heat to medium-low and simmer until lentils and potato are tender, about 20 minutes. Stir in Thai chiles and garam masala.

3 Garnish servings with chopped mint, sliced cabbage, cilantro leaves, sliced Thai chiles, and lime wedges. —DESMOND TAN

NOTE To make tamarind water, combine ¾ cup boiling water and 1 heaping tablespoon tamarind pulp. Let steep 1 minute. Mash with a fork, then let steep 3 minutes. Pour through a fine wire-mesh strainer into a bowl; discard solids.

CARAMELIZED ONION AND BREAD SOUP
WITH BRÛLÉED BLUE CHEESE

In their book Wine Food, *sommelier Dana Frank and recipe developer Andrea Slonecker pair funky, bright wines with flavorful, vegetable-forward dishes. In this vegetarian version of classic French onion soup, blue cheese and oloroso sherry bring new layers of flavor and depth. Notes of toasted nuts and fruit compote in the sherry pair well with caramelized onions, and its briny acidity cuts through the richness of the cheese.*

ACTIVE 1 HR 20 MIN; TOTAL 1 HR 40 MIN; SERVES 6

4½ lb. mixed onions (such as 2 large yellow onions, 2 large red onions, and 2 large sweet onions), halved and thinly sliced lengthwise (about 16 cups)

2 Tbsp. extra-virgin olive oil

2 Tbsp. unsalted butter

¼ cup oloroso sherry

6 cups homemade or store-bought low-sodium vegetable broth

8 fresh thyme sprigs

1 Tbsp. kosher salt, plus more to taste

¾ tsp. freshly ground black pepper, plus more to taste

2 tsp. sherry vinegar

6 day-old whole-grain rustic bread slices, halved

4 oz. Stilton cheese, thoroughly chilled and thinly sliced with a wire cheese slicer or crumbled

1 Combine onions, oil, and butter in a stockpot over medium-high; toss together. (Tongs are an ideal tool to toss this many onions.) Cook, stirring occasionally, until onions start to caramelize, about 20 minutes. Reduce heat to medium, and continue to cook, stirring and scraping any browned bits from bottom of pot with a wooden spoon, until onions are tender and caramelized, about 25 minutes.

2 Add sherry, and cook, stirring to scrape up any remaining browned bits. Simmer over medium, stirring constantly, until sherry is mostly evaporated, 2 to 3 minutes. Stir in broth, thyme, salt, and pepper. Increase heat to high and bring to a boil. Reduce heat to medium-low and simmer, partially covered, until flavors marry, 20 to 25 minutes. Stir in vinegar, and cook 1 minute; add salt and pepper to taste.

3 Preheat oven to broil with oven rack 6 inches from heat. Remove and discard thyme sprigs from soup. Divide hot soup evenly among 6 ovenproof crocks or bowls, then place on a rimmed baking sheet. Place 2 bread pieces on each bowl, and gently press them down to submerge halfway into soup. Add cheese to each bowl. Broil until melted, bubbly, and browned in spots, 2 to 3 minutes.
—ANDREA SLONECKER

NOTE The soup, cooked through Step 2, will keep, covered, in the refrigerator up to 3 days. It can be frozen in an airtight container up to 3 months.

POTATO SOUP WITH SAGE BUTTER AND RYE CRUMBS

The sour rye crumb contrasts with the creamy, rich soup. Slather extra sage butter on a slice of bread. Verjus, made from the juice of unripened wine grapes, is acidic but gentler than vinegar and balances the richness of this soup. Look for it online or in gourmet grocery stores.

ACTIVE 25 MIN; TOTAL 40 MIN; SERVES 4

- 2 (2½-oz.) 100%-rye bread slices, crumbled into ¼-inch pieces
- 3½ tsp. medium-grind sea salt, divided
- 1 lb. Yukon Gold potatoes, peeled and cut into ¾-inch pieces
- 4 cups sliced leek bulbs (from 4 large leeks)
- 2 Tbsp. fresh sage leaves
- 1 cup high-quality unsalted butter (8 oz.), softened
- 1 tsp. white verjus
- ½ cup heavy cream (optional)

1 Preheat oven to 300°F. Spread bread pieces in a single layer on a rimmed baking sheet. Bake until dry and crispy, 20 to 30 minutes.

2 Bring 3 cups water and 2¾ teaspoons salt to a boil in a large saucepan over high. Add potatoes and leeks; return to a simmer. Reduce heat to medium-low; cover and simmer until tender, about 30 minutes.

3 While soup simmers, pulse sage in a food processor until finely chopped, about 10 times. Add butter, verjus, and remaining ¾ teaspoon salt. Process until smooth, about 1 minute.

4 When soup has finished simmering, transfer to a blender. Secure lid on blender, and remove center piece of lid to allow steam to escape. Place a clean kitchen towel over opening. Process until smooth, about 1 minute. Stir in heavy cream, if desired.

5 Sprinkle bowls of soup evenly with rye crumbs; top with about 2 teaspoons sage butter each, reserving remaining sage butter for another use. —SPIKE GJERDE

WINE Earthy, rich Alsace Pinot Blanc: 2016 Domaines Schlumberger Les Princes Abbés

SHORBAT JARJIR (ROCKET SOUP)

A blend of spinach, cilantro, and arugula anchors this delicate, vegetal soup from Yasmin Khan, author of Zaitoun. Warming spices like nutmeg, allspice, and turmeric amplify the flavor of the greens. Potato adds light, silky texture, and a drizzle of olive oil and dollop of yogurt enrich the soup while keeping it light.

TOTAL 40 MIN; SERVES 4

- 2 Tbsp. light olive oil
- 1 medium yellow onion, roughly chopped (about 2 cups)
- 4 garlic cloves, crushed
- 1 tsp. ground turmeric
- 1 tsp. sea salt
- ½ tsp. black pepper
- ½ tsp. grated fresh nutmeg
- ¼ tsp. ground allspice
- 1 medium russet potato, chopped
- 4 cups homemade or low-sodium chicken or vegetable stock
- 7 oz. arugula
- 5¼ oz. fresh spinach
- 1 oz. fresh cilantro sprigs (about ½ packed cup)
- Plain whole-milk Greek yogurt, for serving
- 2 Tbsp. extra-virgin olive oil

1 Heat light olive oil in a large saucepan over medium. Add onion and garlic, and cook, stirring often, just until tender, about 5 minutes. Stir in turmeric, salt, pepper, nutmeg, and allspice; cook, stirring often, 2 minutes. Add potato and stock, and bring to a simmer. Cook until potato is tender, about 10 minutes.

2 Reserve a handful of arugula for garnish. Add spinach, cilantro, and remaining arugula to pan. Bring to a simmer over medium, and cook 10 minutes. Working in batches, transfer soup to a blender. Secure lid on blender, and remove center piece of lid to allow steam to escape. Place a clean kitchen towel over opening. Process until smooth. Taste and adjust seasonings, if needed, then divide soup among 4 bowls.

3 Top each serving with a generous spoonful of yogurt, some of the reserved arugula, and a drizzle of extra-virgin olive oil. —YASMIN KHAN

WINE Lime-scented dry Riesling: 2017 Penfolds Bin 51

VEGETARIAN TORTILLA SOUP WITH SWEET POTATO

This hearty vegetarian tortilla soup pulls its flavor from plenty of seasonings and bright and tender sweet potatoes. To make this soup vegan, substitute vegan sour cream and cheese.

ACTIVE 45 MIN; TOTAL 1 HR; SERVES 4 TO 6

¼ cup extra-virgin olive oil

1 medium onion, finely chopped

2 bell peppers, finely chopped

1 jalapeño, seeded and chopped

1 clove garlic, minced

1 Tbsp. chili powder

1 tsp. cumin

1 tsp. unsweetened cocoa powder

½ tsp. Mexican oregano

½ tsp. paprika

½ tsp. cayenne pepper

Pinch of crushed red pepper

½ tsp. kosher salt

Freshly ground black pepper

1 (28-oz.) can diced tomatoes

4 cups vegetable broth

1 large sweet potato, chopped into ½-inch pieces

1 (15-oz.) can black beans, rinsed

1 (15-oz.) can dark red kidney beans, rinsed

Vegetable oil, for frying

6 (4-inch) corn tortillas, cut into ½-inch strips

2 lime wedges, plus 4 to 6 more for serving

¾ cup fresh corn kernels (from 2 medium ears)

Diced avocado, sour cream, chopped fresh cilantro, shredded Monterey Jack or crumbled queso fresco, for serving

1 Heat olive oil in a large pot. Add onion and bell peppers; cook, stirring occasionally, over medium-high until onions are soft and translucent, 5 to 7 minutes. Add jalapeño and garlic; cook 1 minute. Add chili powder, cumin, cocoa, oregano, paprika, cayenne, red pepper, ½ teaspoon salt, and a few turns black pepper. Cook until fragrant, about 1 to 2 minutes.

2 Stir in tomatoes and broth; bring to a boil. Add potatoes; reduce heat. Simmer 10 minutes. Add beans and simmer until potatoes are tender, 20 to 25 minutes.

3 Heat ½ inch vegetable oil in a skillet over medium until shimmering. Fry tortilla strips in batches until crispy, about 3 minutes per batch. Transfer to a paper towel and immediately sprinkle with salt and squeeze with lime.

4 Gently stir corn into soup. Taste and adjust seasonings if desired. Ladle soup into bowls and serve with tortilla strips, lime wedges, diced avocado, sour cream, fresh cilantro, and shredded Monterey Jack or crumbled queso fresco. —MOLLY YEH

MAKE AHEAD The soup and tortilla strips can be made the day before. Garnish directly before serving.

TOMATO AND QUINOA SOUP

Drizzle this soup with olive oil and/or stir in tender greens, such as arugula or baby spinach. Serve a bowl of the soup on its own, or make it a heartier meal alongside a grilled cheese sandwich.

ACTIVE 20 MIN; TOTAL 1 HR 10 MIN; SERVES 12

- 1 medium onion, cut into 8 wedges with root end intact
- 4 garlic cloves, peeled
- 4 large carrots, peeled and cut into 1-inch pieces (12 oz. whole)
- 1 tsp. fresh thyme leaves
- ¼ cup olive oil, divided
- 1 tsp. kosher salt, plus more to taste
- ½ tsp. freshly ground black pepper
- 2 Tbsp. tomato paste
- 2 fresh or dried bay leaves
- 1 (28-oz.) can diced tomatoes
- 1 (28-oz.) can crushed tomatoes
- 1 cup uncooked quinoa, rinsed if desired
- 3 Tbsp. agave nectar, plus more to taste
- 1 tsp. cider vinegar, plus more to taste

1 Preheat broiler with rack about 5 inches from heat. On a large rimmed baking sheet toss onion, garlic, carrots, and thyme with 2 tablespoons oil, the salt, and pepper. Broil vegetables, tossing every 2 minutes, until golden brown in spots and tender when pierced, about 10 minutes. Transfer vegetables to a blender with 1 cup water; blend, cracking lid and covering with a towel to release steam, until smooth. Reserve vegetable purée.

2 In a large heavy pot heat remaining oil. Carefully stir in tomato paste (it will spatter); cook, stirring, until oil and paste are brick red, about 3 minutes. Stir in vegetable purée, scraping bottom and sides of pot with a wooden spoon to release any caramelized tomato. Stir in bay leaves, diced and crushed tomatoes, quinoa, and 4 cups water. Simmer soup, uncovered, until thickened and quinoa is cooked, about 30 minutes. Stir in agave and vinegar. Season soup with additional salt, agave, and vinegar to taste. —CAROLINE WRIGHT

NOTE Adapted with permission from Soup Club © by Caroline Wright (2021)

SHEET PAN

SHEET PAN CHICKEN WITH SOURDOUGH AND BACON (P. 239)

SAUSAGE-AND-POTATO PAN ROAST

For a cold-weather weeknight dinner, Food & Wine's *Justin Chapple serves this one-pan dish: roasted sweet sausages with potatoes and shallots, tossed with brightly flavored arugula and lemon.*

ACTIVE 20 MIN; TOTAL 50 MIN; SERVES 4-6

- 2 large red potatoes, cut into 1½-inch pieces
- 2 Yukon Gold potatoes, cut into 1-inch wedges
- 1 large baking potato, cut into 1½-inch pieces
- 10 medium unpeeled shallots, halved
- ⅓ cup extra-virgin olive oil, plus more for brushing
- Kosher salt and black pepper
- 1½ lb. sweet Italian sausage, cut into 3-inch lengths
- 1 (8-oz.) bunch arugula, stemmed and chopped
- 1 Tbsp. fresh lemon juice

1 Preheat oven to 425°F. On a large rimmed baking sheet, toss all the potatoes with shallots and ⅓ cup olive oil. Season generously with salt and pepper. Roast until potatoes are lightly browned, about 15 minutes. Brush sausage with olive oil; add to baking sheet. Roast until potatoes are tender and sausage is cooked through, 20 to 25 minutes.

2 Transfer potatoes and sausages to a platter. Fold in arugula; drizzle with lemon juice, and season with salt and pepper. —JUSTIN CHAPPLE

WINE Reserva and gran reserva Rioja

SHEET PAN HANGER STEAK AND BOK CHOY
WITH LEMON-MISO BUTTER

The mix of softened butter, umami-packed miso, and zippy lemon zest transform this elevated weeknight meal into a showstopper.

ACTIVE 30 MIN; TOTAL 3 HR 30 MIN; SERVES 4

½ cup unsalted butter, softened

2 Tbsp. red miso paste

1½ Tbsp. grated lemon zest

5 Tbsp. extra-virgin olive oil, divided

2 Tbsp. rice vinegar

1 small clove garlic, grated on a microplane

1 tsp. kosher salt, divided

1 (1-lb.) hanger steak, membrane removed

4 medium baby bok choy, halved lengthwise, rinsed, and thoroughly patted dry

¼ tsp. freshly ground black pepper

1 Stir together butter, miso paste, and lemon zest in a medium bowl until combined. Let stand at room temperature at least 20 minutes. (Mixture can be made ahead and stored in an airtight container up to 2 weeks.)

2 Whisk together 3 tablespoons olive oil, vinegar, garlic, and ½ teaspoon salt in a small baking dish. Add steak, and turn to coat. Cover and refrigerate 1 to 4 hours, flipping steak once or twice to ensure even coverage.

3 Preheat oven to broil with oven rack 8 inches from heat source. Remove steak from marinade; discard marinade. Rub with 1 tablespoon lemon-miso butter. Place steak on a rimmed baking sheet lined with aluminum foil. Broil 6 minutes. Flip steak; broil 5 to 6 minutes for medium-rare (depending on thickness of steak) or until a meat thermometer registers 130°F. Place steak on a cutting board. Dollop steak with 2 tablespoons lemon-miso butter. Let meat rest 10 minutes; thinly slice meat against the grain and transfer to a serving platter.

4 While steak rests, heat oven to 425°F. Place bok choy in a large bowl, drizzle with remaining 2 tablespoons olive oil, and season with pepper and remaining ½ teaspoon salt; toss to coat. Arrange bok choy in a single layer, cut-sides down, on hot baking sheet. Roast until stems are crisp-tender and leaves are browned and crisp at edges, 9 to 10 minutes. Transfer bok choy to platter with steak. Serve remaining lemon-miso butter on the side. –LEAH KOENIG

HERBES DE PROVENCE-CRUSTED BRANZINO AND FINGERLINGS

Herbes de Provence, a blend of spices including lavender, thyme, and fennel, is a traditional French ingredient. Williams Sonoma has a particularly aromatic blend, which, when combined with softened butter and spread on fish and potatoes, results in a simple and delicious weeknight meal.

ACTIVE 10 MIN; TOTAL 40 MIN; SERVES 2

1 lb. fingerling potatoes, halved lengthwise

2 Tbsp. extra-virgin olive oil

2 Tbsp. plus 2 tsp. herbes de Provence, divided

Kosher salt and freshly ground black pepper

¼ cup unsalted butter, softened

1 Tbsp. Dijon mustard

2 (12-oz.) butterflied branzino or trout

1 Preheat oven to 375°F. Line a rimmed baking sheet with aluminum foil.

2 Toss together potatoes, olive oil, 2 tablespoons herbes de Provence, 1 teaspoon salt, and ½ teaspoon pepper on prepared baking sheet. Roast until potatoes are golden around edges and nearly tender, about 20 minutes.

3 Meanwhile, mash butter, mustard, remaining 2 teaspoons herbes de Provence, and 1 teaspoon salt together with a fork in a small bowl. Arrange fish, flesh-sides up; season with salt and pepper, and spread butter mixture evenly on fish.

4 Flip potatoes and arrange around edges of pan to accommodate fish. Add fish to baking sheet, flesh-sides up, and roast until fish is opaque and flaky and potatoes are cooked through, about 10 minutes. —FOOD & WINE

SHEET PAN CHICKEN WITH SOURDOUGH AND BACON

PHOTO P. 233

Food & Wine's Justin Chapple developed this recipe for roast chicken legs that drip meaty, delicious fat onto a smoky, peppery bed of potatoes, red onion, and crispy croutons.

ACTIVE 20 MIN; TOTAL 1 HR 5 MIN; SERVES 6

½ lb. sourdough boule, cut or torn into 2-inch pieces

½ lb. slab bacon, cut into 1- × ½-inch lardons

1 large baking potato, scrubbed, halved crosswise, and cut into ¾-inch wedges

1 large red onion, cut into 1-inch wedges

2 Tbsp. cold unsalted butter, diced

4 fresh oregano sprigs

½ tsp. crushed red pepper

¼ cup extra-virgin olive oil

Kosher salt and black pepper

6 whole chicken legs

1 Preheat oven to 400°F. On a large rimmed baking sheet toss bread, bacon, potato, onion, butter, oregano, and crushed red pepper with olive oil; season generously with salt and black pepper. Spread in an even layer. Season chicken with salt and black pepper, and arrange on bread mixture.

2 Roast until the bread is crisp and a thermometer inserted in chicken legs registers 160°F, about 45 minutes. —JUSTIN CHAPPLE

WINE Luscious, herb-scented Russian River Valley red: 2015 Limerick Lane Syrah-Grenache

SHEET PAN CHICKEN AND MUSHROOMS
WITH PARSLEY SAUCE

Cookbook author Julia Turshen amps up the flavors in her simple chicken and mushroom pan roast with roasted lemons followed by a bright fresh parsley sauce that's made in minutes.

ACTIVE 15 MIN; TOTAL 45 MIN; SERVES 4

1½ lb. boneless, skinless chicken thighs
   Kosher salt and black pepper

½ cup plus 2 Tbsp. extra-virgin olive oil

1 lb. mixed mushrooms, such as shiitake and cremini, stemmed and halved if large

1 lemon, thinly sliced, plus slices for garnish

½ cup finely chopped fresh parsley, plus more for garnish

2 Tbsp. red wine vinegar

1 large garlic clove, minced

1 Preheat oven to 450°F. Place a large rimmed baking sheet in oven to heat. Season chicken generously on both sides with salt and pepper. Drizzle 2 tablespoons olive oil onto hot baking sheet. Arrange chicken in a single layer on hot baking sheet. Roast until chicken begins to brown, about 5 minutes.

2 Toss mushrooms and lemon slices in a medium bowl with 2 tablespoons olive oil; carefully scatter evenly around chicken. Roast until mushrooms and lemon are browned and an instant-read thermometer inserted in chicken reads 160°F, about 30 minutes.

3 Meanwhile, in a small bowl mix remaining 6 tablespoons olive oil with ½ cup parsley, the vinegar, and garlic. Season with salt.

4 Transfer chicken, mushrooms, and lemon slices to a platter. Drizzle with some of the sauce, and garnish with lemon and parsley. Serve with remaining sauce.
—JULIA TURSHEN

WINE Earthy New Zealand Pinot Noir: 2014 Ata Rangi

SHEET PAN CHICKEN WITH ZUCCHINI AND GARLICKY TOMATO RELISH

This all-in-one roasted dinner begins minimalist—chicken pieces, zucchini, and shallot chunks tossed with olive oil, salt, and pepper. While the chicken and vegetables brown beautifully in the oven, there's time to prep a herb-packed, garlic-studded cherry tomato relish.

ACTIVE 20 MIN; TOTAL 50 MIN; SERVES 4

- 1 (3- to 3½-lb.) whole chicken, patted dry and cut into 6 pieces, or 3 lb. bone-in, skin-on chicken drumsticks and/or thighs
- ½ cup plus 2 Tbsp. extra-virgin olive oil, divided
- 2½ tsp. kosher salt, divided
- ½ tsp. freshly ground black pepper, divided
- 4 medium shallots, halved lengthwise
- 3 medium zucchini, diagonally cut into 1-inch-thick rounds
- 2 cups halved cherry tomatoes
- ¼ cup white wine vinegar
- 2 Tbsp. chopped fresh tarragon
- 2 medium garlic cloves, grated (about 1 tsp.)

1 Preheat oven to 450°F. Rub chicken all over with 2 tablespoons oil. Season all over with 1 teaspoon salt and ¼ teaspoon pepper. Place on a rimmed baking sheet. Toss together shallots, zucchini, 2 tablespoons oil, ½ teaspoon salt, and remaining ¼ teaspoon pepper in a medium bowl. Scatter zucchini mixture around chicken.

2 Bake 25 minutes, rotating baking sheet halfway through bake time. Increase oven temperature to broil. (Do not remove baking sheet from oven.) Broil until chicken is cooked through and skin is lightly browned, 2 to 4 minutes.

3 While chicken roasts, stir together tomatoes, vinegar, tarragon, garlic, and remaining 6 tablespoons oil and 1 teaspoon salt.

4 Transfer chicken and zucchini mixture to a platter. Immediately add tomato mixture to hot baking sheet (alternatively, scrape pan juices from baking sheet into a medium saucepan, then stir in the tomato mixture), and place over medium. Using a flat wooden spoon or spatula, scrape up browned bits from bottom of baking sheet while tomatoes release their juices. Immediately pour tomato relish over chicken and vegetables. —ROBIN BASHINSKY

ANCHO-RUBBED TURKEY BREAST WITH VEGETABLES

To enhance the flavor and moistness of turkey, and to create an exceptionally crisp skin, Food & Wine's *Justin Chapple rubs the bird with a salt, sugar, and spice mix before roasting.*

ACTIVE 30 MIN; TOTAL 2 HR 45 MIN; SERVES 6

1½ Tbsp. ancho chile powder

1 tsp. ground coriander

1 tsp. onion powder

½ tsp. granulated sugar

1½ tsp. chopped fresh oregano, plus 6 oregano sprigs

1 3¾-lb. boneless whole turkey breast with skin, patted dry

¼ cup plus 2 Tbsp. extra-virgin olive oil

Kosher salt and black pepper

3 large baking potatoes, cut lengthwise into 1-inch wedges

3 poblano chiles, halved lengthwise

3 medium red onions, peeled and cut into 1-inch wedges through the core

1 Whisk together chile powder, coriander, onion powder, sugar, and chopped oregano in a small bowl. Set turkey breast, skin-side down, on a work surface. Drizzle with 1 tablespoon olive oil, season generously with salt and pepper, then rub with half the spice mixture. Fold in sides and tie turkey breast with twine to make a neat roast. Season outside of turkey breast with salt and pepper, then rub with remaining spice mix. Drizzle with 1 tablespoon olive oil. Let stand at room temperature 1 hour.

2 Preheat oven to 425°F. On a large rimmed baking sheet toss potatoes, poblanos, onions, and oregano sprigs with remaining ¼ cup olive oil. Season vegetables with salt and pepper, then spread evenly. Set turkey breast, skin-side up, on vegetables. Roast until a thermometer inserted in the thickest part of the turkey registers 155°F, about 1 hour; tent with foil if it browns too quickly. Transfer turkey breast to a carving board and let stand 20 minutes. Untie roast and thinly slice crosswise. Serve with roasted vegetables. —JUSTIN CHAPPLE

WINE Smoky, meaty Syrah from Washington state: 2012 Corvidae Lenore

SAUSAGE AND RED ONION SHEET PAN QUICHE

At Convivial in Washington, D.C., Cedric Maupillier's foot-long quiche takes this breakfast classic to the next level. This version, prepared in a rimmed baking sheet, makes plenty for the whole family.

ACTIVE 1 HR 50 MIN; TOTAL 4 HR 20 MIN; SERVES 12

CRUST

- 3½ cups all-purpose flour (about 14⅞ oz.), plus more for work surface
- 1 Tbsp. kosher salt
- 1 tsp. black pepper
- 1¼ cups unsalted butter (10 oz.), cut into ½-inch pieces and chilled
- 8 to 10 Tbsp. ice water, as needed

FILLING

- 1 Tbsp. canola oil
- 8 oz. bulk breakfast sausage
- 18 large eggs
- 2¼ cups half-and-half
- 1 Tbsp. kosher salt
- 1½ tsp. black pepper
- 9 oz. Gruyère cheese, shredded (about 2¼ cups)
- 1 small red onion, cut into ¼-inch rings
- 2 Tbsp. fresh thyme leaves
- 1 cup loosely packed baby arugula

1 **Make the crust:** Pulse flour, salt, and pepper in a food processor until combined, about 4 pulses. Scatter butter pieces over flour mixture; pulse in 1-second bursts until butter is the size of small peas, 9 to 10 pulses. Drizzle ice water into mixture, 1 tablespoon at a time, pulsing until mixture resembles coarse meal. Turn out dough onto a work surface; knead just until dough comes together. Using your hands, flatten to a 1-inch-thick rectangle. Wrap in plastic wrap, and chill 1 hour.

2 Line an 18- × 13-inch rimmed baking sheet with parchment paper. Unwrap dough, then roll out on a floured work surface to a 20- × 15-inch rectangle. Gently roll dough around rolling pin; unroll onto prepared pan. Press dough into corners and up sides of baking sheet. Trim excess dough to about ¼ inch above rim of pan. Crimp edges of dough as desired. Freeze 45 minutes.

3 Preheat oven to 400°F with rack in upper third of oven. Line crust with 2 large sheets of parchment paper; top with dried beans or pie weights to cover. Bake until bottom is set and edges are light golden brown, 35 to 40 minutes. Remove weights and parchment. Return crust to oven; bake until crisp and browned, 15 to 20 minutes. Gently press crust down if needed. Let cool completely.

4 **Make the filling:** Heat oil in a medium-size skillet over medium. Add sausage; cook, breaking into medium-size pieces with a wooden spoon, just until cooked through, about 6 minutes. Remove from heat.

5 Whisk eggs in a large bowl until smooth. Whisk in half-and-half, salt, and pepper. Sprinkle cheese, sausage, and about half the onion rings on crust. (Reserve remaining onion for another use.) Gently pour egg mixture over crust; sprinkle with thyme.

6 Bake until slightly puffed and just set, 30 to 35 minutes. Remove from oven; let stand 10 minutes. Top with arugula just before serving. —JUSTIN CHAPPLE

WINE Rich rosé sparkling wine: NV Gloria Ferrer Rosé Brut

ROASTED MERGUEZ SAUSAGE
WITH APPLES AND ONIONS

For this dinner, use Honeycrisp or Pink Lady apples, which hold their shape better during roasting that other varieties. Plus, their pleasant sweetness balances the intensely spiced merguez sausage.

ACTIVE 15 MIN; TOTAL 40 MIN; SERVES 4 TO 6

1½ lb. thin merguez sausage coil or links

3 (10-oz.) Honeycrisp or Pink Lady apples, cut into 1½-inch wedges

3 (6-oz.) red onions, cut into ¾-inch wedges

6 thyme sprigs

¼ cup extra-virgin olive oil

8 medium garlic cloves, coarsely chopped

1 tsp. lemon zest

1½ tsp. kosher salt

1 tsp. black pepper

½ cup chopped fresh flat-leaf parsley

1 Preheat oven to 425°F. Insert 2 skewers into sausage coil in an X shape. Place sausage coil in center of a large rimmed baking sheet. (If using links, arrange in a single layer on baking sheet.)

2 Toss together apples, onions, thyme, olive oil, garlic, and lemon zest in a large bowl; season with salt and pepper. Scatter apple mixture around sausage on baking sheet. Roast until sausage is cooked through and apples are tender but not falling apart, about 25 minutes. Remove skewers and cut sausage into large pieces. Sprinkle with parsley. —JUSTIN CHAPPLE

WINE Rich Lebanese red: 2015 Massaya Cap Est.

SPRING ONION AND SALAMI SHEET PAN PIZZA

When making sheet pan pizza, bring the dough to room temperature before shaping. This ensures that the gluten is relaxed and the dough doesn't shrink away from the pan edges.

ACTIVE 20 MIN; TOTAL 45 MIN; SERVES 8

¼ cup extra-virgin olive oil, plus more for drizzling

2 (1-lb.) fresh prepared multigrain or plain pizza dough balls, at room temperature

1 cup jarred pizza sauce (such as Rao's)

10 oz. shredded mozzarella cheese (about 2½ cups)

4 oz. salami, soppressata, or spicy Italian sausage

1 small spring onion or fennel bulb, thinly sliced (about 1¾ cups)

2 oz. Parmesan or pecorino Romano cheese, grated (about ½ cup)

½ tsp. fennel seeds, crushed

Flaky sea salt (such as Maldon)

Fresh baby greens or herb leaves (such as flat-leaf parsley or basil)

1 Preheat oven to 500°F with oven rack in lower third of oven. Grease an 18- × 13-inch rimmed baking sheet with ¼ cup oil. Place 1 dough ball on one side of pan. Using your hands, gently stretch dough outward until it covers half of the baking sheet. (If dough springs back, let it rest 10 minutes before stretching again.) Repeat procedure with remaining dough ball on opposite side of baking sheet. Press seam together in center to seal, creating 1 large sheet of dough. Spoon pizza sauce over dough; sprinkle with mozzarella, and top with salami, spring onion, Parmesan, and fennel seeds.

2 Bake until crisp and brown on bottom and edges, about 25 minutes. Remove from oven and sprinkle with salt. Top with greens; drizzle lightly with additional oil.
—SARAH COPELAND

WINE Lively, dark-fruited southern Italian red: 2015 Cantele Salice Salentino Riserva

SHEET PAN SALMON WITH BRUSSELS SPROUTS

This recipe combines three simple elements that cookbook author Klancy Miller enjoys when cooking solo: seafood, an assortment of vegetables, and a mini sheet pan. When dinner's done, she has just one pan to wash, and she can unwind with her favorite music and a well-deserved glass of wine.

ACTIVE 15 MIN; TOTAL 35 MIN; SERVES 1

¼ cup hoisin sauce

3 Tbsp. fresh lime juice (from 2 limes)

3 Tbsp. olive oil, divided

1 Tbsp. minced peeled fresh ginger (from 1 [2-inch] piece)

2 garlic cloves, minced (about 1 tsp.)

¼ tsp. cayenne pepper

6 medium Brussels sprouts, trimmed and cut into ¼-inch-thick slices (about 1¼ cups)

1 small red bell pepper (about 6 oz.), cut into ¼-inch-thick strips (about 1 cup)

1 cup thinly sliced red onion

½ tsp. flaky sea salt, divided

⅓ lb. skin-on salmon fillet (about 1 inch thick)

½ tsp. sesame seeds

1 Preheat oven to 375°F. Line a quarter sheet pan with parchment paper. Whisk together hoisin sauce, lime juice, 1½ tablespoons oil, the ginger, garlic, and cayenne pepper in a small bowl; set aside.

2 Toss together Brussels sprouts, bell pepper, onion, ¼ teaspoon salt, and remaining 1½ tablespoons oil. Place salmon on prepared sheet pan. Arrange vegetable mixture around salmon. Drizzle ⅓ cup hoisin mixture over all; reserve remaining hoisin mixture. Sprinkle salmon with sesame seeds.

3 Bake until salmon is cooked to desired degree of doneness and vegetables are tender, 16 to 20 minutes. Drizzle 2 tablespoons reserved hoisin mixture over salmon and vegetables; sprinkle salmon with remaining ¼ teaspoon salt. Serve with remaining hoisin mixture. —KLANCY MILLER

SHEET PAN EGGPLANT PARMESAN

A quick broil followed by a longer bake makes this no-fry recipe hands off enough to put together on a Tuesday, with results delicious enough for a weekend dinner party. Be sure to let the eggplant drain to achieve the best charred eggplant texture.

ACTIVE 15 MIN; TOTAL 1 HR 15 MIN; SERVES 8

- 3 Tbsp. kosher salt, divided
- 2 large eggplants (about 14 oz. each), cut into ½-inch-thick rounds
- ¼ cup olive oil, divided
- 2 cups sourdough bread crumbs (from 2 [3-oz.] day-old sourdough bread slices)
- 2 garlic cloves, minced
- 1 Tbsp. lemon zest (from 1 lemon)
- 1 tsp. fresh thyme leaves
- 1 tsp. black pepper
- 4 plum tomatoes (about 4 oz. each), sliced
- 1 lb. fresh mozzarella cheese, sliced
- 1 (24-oz.) jar marinara sauce (about 3 cups)
- 4 oz. Parmesan cheese, grated (about 1 cup)
- 1 cup loosely packed fresh basil leaves, torn

1 Sprinkle 2 tablespoons plus 2 teaspoons salt on both sides of eggplant rounds. Place rounds on a wire rack lined with paper towels. Let liquid drain from eggplant 30 minutes.

2 Meanwhile, preheat broiler to high with oven rack 6 inches from heat. Heat 3 tablespoons olive oil in a large skillet over medium-high. Add bread crumbs, and cook, stirring often, until lightly browned, 5 to 6 minutes. Add minced garlic, lemon zest, and thyme. Cook, stirring often, until fragrant, 1 to 2 minutes. Remove from heat and set bread crumb mixture aside.

3 Pat eggplant dry. Drizzle both sides of eggplant rounds with remaining 1 tablespoon olive oil, and sprinkle with pepper and remaining 1 teaspoon salt. Place in a single layer on a rimmed baking sheet. Broil until lightly golden brown, about 4 minutes per side. Let cool 10 minutes.

4 Reduce oven temperature to 425°F. Layer tomatoes and mozzarella slices between eggplant rounds, slightly overlapping, on baking sheet. Drizzle with marinara sauce. Sprinkle with Parmesan, top with bread crumb mixture. Bake until cheese is melted and golden brown, about 15 minutes. Sprinkle with basil and serve.

DESSERTS

**RED, HOT, AND COOL
STRAWBERRIES (P. 271)**

APRICOT KUCHEN WITH LABNEH WHIPPED CREAM

Kuchen is a simple sweet cake—here studded with juicy, tart apricots and served with tangy labneh whipped cream. Frozen apricot halves will work when fresh are unavailable, as will other fruits as the seasons change. Also try grapes, apples, or nectarines.

ACTIVE 35 MIN; TOTAL 1 HR 30 MIN; SERVES 8

1¼ cups all-purpose flour (about 5⅜ oz.)

½ cup plus 2 Tbsp. granulated sugar, divided, plus more to taste if apricots are tart

1 Tbsp. fine cornmeal or semolina

2 tsp. baking powder

¼ tsp. fine sea salt

½ cup unsalted butter (4 oz.), at room temperature

1 large egg

1 lb. fresh apricots (about 8 small or 6 medium), halved or quartered

⅔ cup heavy cream

½ cup labneh or plain whole-milk Greek yogurt

1 Tbsp. powdered sugar

1 Preheat oven to 350°F. Sift flour, ½ cup sugar, cornmeal, baking powder, and salt into the bowl of a stand mixer fitted with paddle attachment. Add butter and beat on medium until ingredients are mostly incorporated, about 1 minute. Add egg; beat on medium-high until ingredients are completely incorporated and dough starts to form a ball, about 30 seconds.

2 Transfer dough to a work surface and gather into a ball. Press about 1¼ cups dough into a lightly greased 9- to 10-inch tart pan with removable bottom, pressing evenly onto bottom and up fluted sides. (Use a straight-sided measuring cup or a small straight rolling pin lightly coated with cooking spray to make a smooth and even surface on bottom.) Wrap remaining dough in plastic wrap, and chill with dough in pan 15 minutes. Arrange apricots, cut-sides up, on chilled tart dough in bottom of pan, pressing slightly. Unwrap remaining dough; divide into 8 portions. Shape each dough portion into a ball (about 1½ teaspoons each), and arrange dough balls on apricots in pan. Sprinkle with remaining 2 tablespoons sugar.

3 Bake until golden and dough is crisp, about 35 minutes. Transfer kuchen to a wire rack and let cool 30 minutes.

4 Meanwhile, beat cream in a stand mixer fitted with whisk attachment on medium-high until soft peaks form, about 1 minute. Add labneh and powdered sugar; beat just until combined, about 10 seconds.

5 Remove pan rim from kuchen. Cut kuchen into slices. Serve with labneh whipped cream. —ADEENA SUSSMAN

BROWN SUGAR CAKE
WITH RICOTTA AND BLUEBERRIES

Chef Joe Flamm cinched the season 15 Top Chef *win with this brown sugar cake, which he learned to make from the late pastry chef Todd Kunkleman at Stephanie Izard's Girl & the Goat in Chicago. The chewy, dense confection is a cross between a cake and blondie. It's delicious both by itself and dressed up with Ricotta Mousse and Blueberry Sauce.*

ACTIVE 20 MIN; TOTAL 1 HR 45 MIN; SERVES 12

Nonstick cooking spray

1½ cups packed light brown sugar

¾ cup (6 oz.) unsalted butter

3 large eggs

1½ cups all-purpose flour (about 6⅜ oz.)

2 tsp. baking powder

Ricotta Mousse (recipe follows)

Blueberry Sauce (recipe follows)

1 Preheat oven to 375° F. Coat a 10½- × 15½-inch rimmed baking sheet with cooking spray.

2 Place brown sugar and butter in a medium saucepan over medium; cook, stirring often, until butter melts and mixture is combined, about 6 minutes. Remove from heat and let cool 10 minutes.

3 Whisk together eggs and brown sugar mixture in a medium bowl. Whisk in flour and baking powder until combined.

4 Pour batter into prepared baking sheet. Bake in preheated oven until edges are browned and begin to pull away from sides of pan, 20 to 22 minutes. Remove from oven and cool completely, about 45 minutes.

5 Cut cake into 24 rectangles. Smear Ricotta Mousse on each plate. Place 2 cake rectangles on mousse. Top with Blueberry Sauce to serve. —JOE FLAMM

RICOTTA MOUSSE

TOTAL 5 MIN; MAKES 2 CUPS

2 cups ricotta cheese

1 tsp. granulated sugar

1 tsp. vanilla bean paste or seeds
   from 1 vanilla bean

Combine the ingredients in a food processor. Process until smooth, about 30 seconds. —JF

BLUEBERRY SAUCE

TOTAL 10 MIN; MAKES 2 CUPS

½ cup granulated sugar

2 Tbsp. fresh lemon juice

2 thyme sprigs

3 cups blueberries, divided

1 Stir together sugar, lemon juice, thyme, and 1½ cups blueberries in a large saucepan over medium; bring to a simmer. Reduce heat to medium-low; continue to simmer until blueberries are very tender, about 10 minutes. Let sauce cool. Discard thyme sprigs.

2 Transfer blueberry mixture to a blender; process until smooth, about 30 seconds. Pour sauce into a medium bowl; fold in remaining 1½ cups blueberries. —JF

BROWN SUGAR CAKE WITH
RICOTTA AND BLUEBERRIES

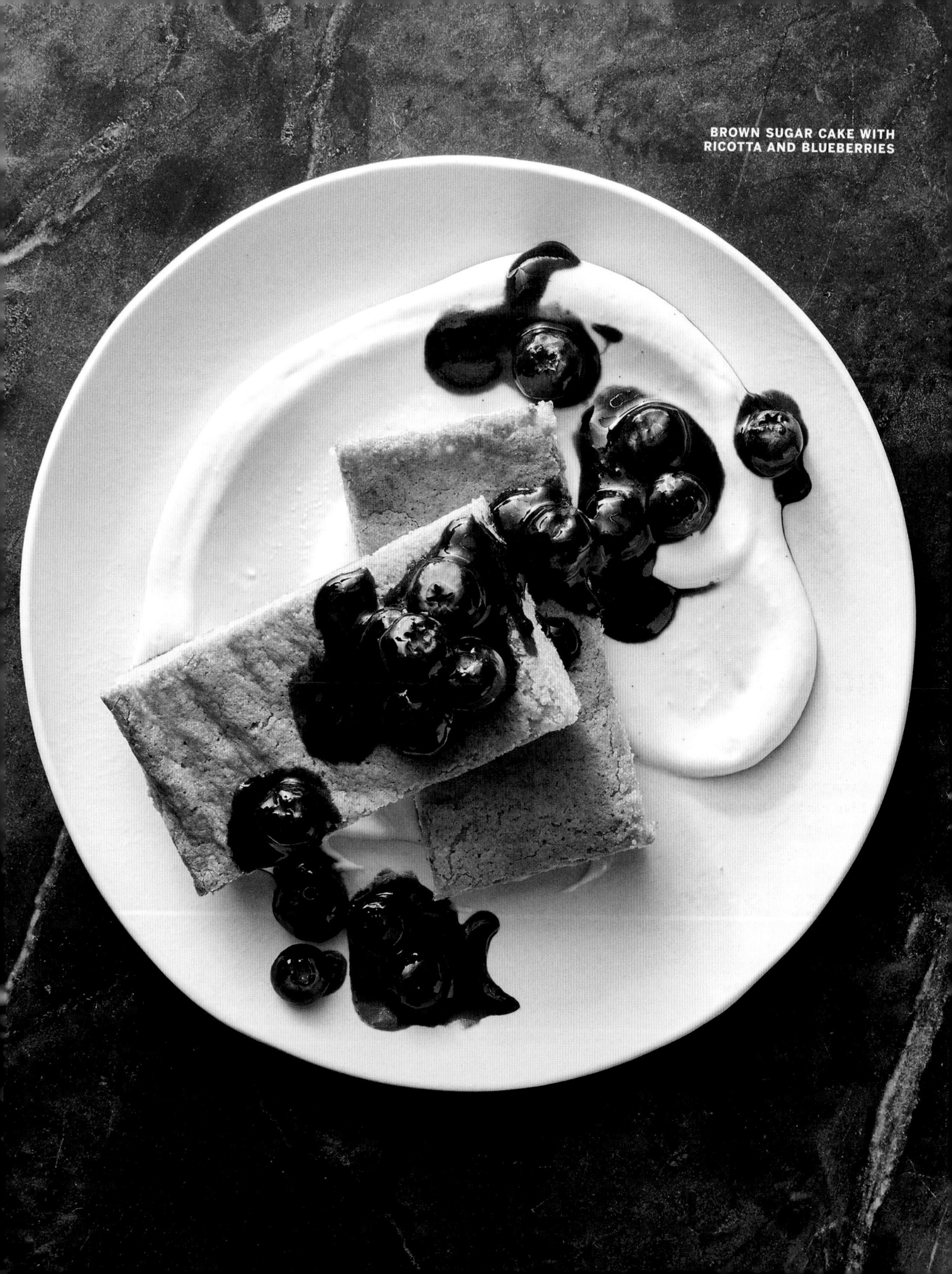

OLIVE OIL CAKE WITH HONEY-YOGURT CREAM AND STRAWBERRIES

This is no featherweight spring cake: Olive oil and almond flour keep it dense and moist to hold plenty of juicy macerated strawberries. An infusion of lime in the cake batter and tangy yogurt whipped cream brighten each slice.

ACTIVE 20 MIN; TOTAL 1 HR 30 MIN; SERVES 6

- ½ cup fruity extra-virgin olive oil, plus more for greasing
- 1½ cups almond flour (about 5¼ oz.)
- ½ cup all-purpose flour (about 2⅛ oz.)
- 1 tsp. baking powder
- ½ tsp. baking soda
- ½ cup plus 1 tsp. granulated sugar, divided
- 4 large eggs
- 2 tsp. lime zest, divided
- 3½ Tbsp. plus 1 tsp. fresh lime juice (from 2 limes), divided
- 1 tsp. vanilla extract
- 2 qt. fresh strawberries, hulled and quartered
- 1 cup plain whole-milk Greek yogurt
- ¼ cup heavy cream
- ¼ cup honey

1 Preheat oven to 350°F. Lightly grease the bottom and sides of an 8-inch springform pan with oil. Line bottom of greased pan with parchment paper, then lightly grease parchment; set pan aside.

2 Whisk together flours, baking powder, and baking soda in a medium bowl.

3 In the bowl of a stand mixer fitted with whisk attachment, or in a large bowl with an electric mixer, beat ½ cup sugar and eggs on medium-high speed until pale yellow and slightly thickened, about 3 minutes. Beat in ½ cup oil, 1 teaspoon lime zest, 3½ tablespoons lime juice, and vanilla. With mixer running on low, gradually add flour mixture just until incorporated.

4 Pour batter into prepared pan. Bake until top is dark golden brown and a toothpick inserted in center comes out clean, 40 to 45 minutes. Cool in pan on a wire rack 10 minutes. Remove outer ring, and invert cake onto wire rack. Remove bottom of pan and parchment; cool cake completely, about 1 hour.

5 Stir together strawberries, remaining 1 teaspoon zest, and remaining 1 teaspoon sugar in a medium bowl. Let stand at room temperature 30 minutes to 1 hour.

6 Whisk together yogurt, cream, honey, and remaining 1 teaspoon lime juice until incorporated.

7 Top cake slices with large spoonfuls of honey-yogurt cream and strawberries.
—SARAH HELLER

ORANGE TORTA

Made with almond flour, chef Hillary Sterling's cakes are dairy-free, gluten-free and extra moist. Juices from lemons and oranges, plus orange wedges from jammy orange mostarda contribute citrusy scent, sweetness, and moistness.

ACTIVE 20 MIN; TOTAL 45 MIN; SERVES 10

Baking spray

1 cup drained orange pieces from Orange Mostarda, plus liquid for drizzling (recipe follows)

6 Tbsp. fresh orange juice

3 Tbsp. fresh lemon juice

6 large eggs, separated

1 cup plus 2 Tbsp. granulated sugar, divided

½ tsp. kosher salt

2 cups almond flour (about 7 oz.), sifted

Almond gelato or nondairy frozen dessert, for serving

Chopped toasted almonds, for garnish

1 Preheat oven to 350°F. Coat 10 cavities of 2 (6-cavity) mini fluted tube pan molds with baking spray; set aside. Process drained orange pieces, orange juice, and lemon juice in a blender until smooth, about 2 minutes, stopping to scrape down sides as needed. Set aside.

2 Beat egg whites in a stand mixer fitted with whisk attachment on high until foamy, about 2 minutes. Gradually add ½ cup sugar, beating until stiff peaks form, 3 to 5 minutes. Transfer mixture to a large bowl.

3 Place egg yolks and remaining ½ cup plus 2 tablespoons sugar in stand mixer bowl. Beat on high until pale yellow and creamy, about 2 minutes. Gently stir egg yolk mixture, orange mixture, and salt into egg white mixture. Gently fold in almond flour.

4 Spoon batter evenly into the 10 prepared pan molds (about ¾ cup per mold). Tap pans gently on counter to release any air bubbles.

5 Bake until cakes are golden brown and edges pull away from sides, 22 to 25 minutes. Let cool in pans 10 minutes. Invert cakes onto a wire rack; let cool completely, about 20 minutes. Serve cakes with almond gelato; drizzle with mostarda liquid, and garnish with chopped toasted almonds. —HILLARY STERLING

ORANGE MOSTARDA

A long simmer yields tender orange rinds that contribute the jammy texture spiced condiment in a spiced condiment.

ACTIVE 1 HR 40 MIN; TOTAL 10 HR 40 MIN; SERVES 10

1 lb. Cara Cara oranges (about 2 oranges), unpeeled, cut into 8 wedges each

3 cups granulated sugar, divided

1 Tbsp. mustard seeds

1 Tbsp. fennel seeds

½ bunch fresh thyme (about ¼ oz.), tied with kitchen twine

5 bay leaves

1 Stir together orange wedges, 2 cups sugar, and ½ cup water in a medium bowl until combined. Cover and let stand at room temperature 8 hours or overnight.

2 Transfer orange mixture to a medium saucepan. Add mustard seeds, fennel seeds, thyme bundle, bay leaves, remaining 1 cup sugar, and 1 cup water; stir to combine. Bring to a boil over medium-high. Boil, stirring occasionally, until liquid becomes syrupy and orange wedges become translucent, about 1 hour and 30 minutes. Remove from heat; let cool completely, about 1 hour. Remove and discard thyme bundle and bay leaves. Store, covered, in refrigerator up to 2 weeks. —HS

SKILLET BROWNIES ON THE GRILL

Brownies take on deliciously smoky flavor on the grill while "baking" in a skillet set over hot coals. Top them with ice cream for a showstopping dessert at your next cookout.

ACTIVE 10 MIN; TOTAL 1 HR 10 MIN; SERVES 8

¾ cup (about 3¼ oz.) plus 1 Tbsp. all-purpose flour

½ tsp. kosher salt or fleur de sel

¼ tsp. baking soda

7 oz. unsweetened chocolate, chopped

½ cup (4 oz.) salted butter, plus more, melted, for greasing skillet

2 Tbsp. canola oil

3 large eggs

1 cup packed light brown sugar

1 cup granulated sugar

2 tsp. vanilla bean paste or vanilla extract

Vanilla ice cream (optional)

1 If using a charcoal grill, open bottom vent of grill completely. Light charcoal chimney starter filled with briquettes. When briquettes are covered with gray ash, pour onto bottom grate of grill, then push to one side. Adjust vents as needed to maintain a temperature of 350°F to 400°F. If using a gas grill, preheat to medium (350°F to 400°F) on one side. If using an oven, preheat to 350°F.

2 Whisk together flour, salt, and baking soda in a small bowl; set aside. If grilling, place a heatproof bowl on unoiled grates over the side without coals (or the unlit side of a gas grill). Heat a medium saucepan over low. Add chocolate, butter, and oil to bowl or saucepan; cook, stirring constantly, until melted and smooth. Remove from heat. Let cool slightly, about 5 minutes. Add eggs, brown sugar, granulated sugar, and vanilla to chocolate-butter mixture; stir together until smooth and thoroughly incorporated. Add flour mixture; stir gently just until combined.

3 Grease a 10-inch cast-iron skillet with melted butter. Pour in batter, spreading evenly.

4 If grilling, place skillet on grates over the side without coals (or the unlit side of a gas grill). Grill, covered, until a wooden pick inserted in center of brownies comes out almost clean (it will have crumbs but should not be wet), 40 to 45 minutes. If using an oven, bake 35 minutes. Remove from heat; cool in skillet 10 minutes. Cut into wedges and serve with ice cream, if desired. —VALERIE GORDON

QUICK APPLE CRUMBLE WITH LABNEH

The blend of flavors and textures here—crunchy, smooth, nutty, sweet, tart—makes this easy dessert irresistible. Opt for labneh or another soft, slow-to-melt fresh cheese that won't melt quickly beneath the warm apples.

TOTAL 20 MIN; SERVES 4

6 Tbsp. unsalted butter

2 large Granny Smith apples, peeled, halved, cored, and thinly sliced (see Note)

¼ cup plus 2 Tbsp. light brown sugar

½ tsp. ground cinnamon

Pinch of freshly grated nutmeg

1 Tbsp. fresh lemon juice

2 cups labneh (16 oz.), Greek yogurt, or quark

1 cup granola

1 Heat butter in a large skillet. Add apple slices and cook over high, stirring occasionally, just until tender and lightly browned, 5 to 6 minutes. Add brown sugar, cinnamon, nutmeg, and lemon juice. Cook, stirring and shaking skillet, until sugar is melted and apples are lightly caramelized, about 5 minutes. Add ¼ cup water and stir gently until a sauce forms.

2 Spoon labneh into bowls; spoon apples and sauce on labneh. Sprinkle apples with granola and serve. —GRACE PARISI

MAKE AHEAD The recipe can be prepared through Step 1 up to 6 hours ahead. Rewarm before assembling.

NOTE Firm, ripe peaches, nectarines, and plums, cut into wedges, would be delicious in place of apples.

GRAND MARNIER SOUFFLÉ

This ethereal soufflé recipe from Jacques Pépin turns out just as good today as it did 40 years ago.

ACTIVE 20 MIN; TOTAL 1 HR 15 MIN; SERVES 6

3 Tbsp. granulated sugar

3 Tbsp. all-purpose flour

Unsalted butter, softened, for greasing

Crème Pâtissière (recipe below), at room temperature

2 Tbsp. Grand Marnier

1 Tbsp. orange zest

6 large egg whites, at room temperature

Powdered sugar, for garnish

1 Preheat oven to 375°F with oven rack in lower third of oven. Stir together granulated sugar and flour in a small bowl; set aside. Cut a 24- × 12-inch piece of parchment paper; fold lengthwise 3 times (letter-style). Wrap paper around outer top of a 1-quart soufflé dish to form a collar extending 2 inches above rim; secure tightly with string or tape. Rub inside of soufflé dish and parchment collar with butter. Dust with flour-sugar mixture, shaking out excess. Chill dish at least 15 minutes.

2 Stir together crème pâtissière, Grand Marnier, and orange zest in a large bowl. Beat egg whites in bowl of a heavy-duty stand mixer on medium until glossy and stiff peaks form, about 4 minutes. Whisk about one-third of egg whites into crème pâtissière mixture until well incorporated. Gently fold in remaining egg whites just until incorporated. Pour mixture into prepared dish. Place dish on a rimmed baking sheet. Bake until soufflé is puffed and golden brown, 40 to 45 minutes. Sprinkle with powdered sugar. Serve immediately. —JACQUES PEPIN

CRÈME PÂTISSIÈRE

ACTIVE 15 MIN; TOTAL 1 HR 15 MIN; MAKES 1⅓ CUPS

⅔ cup granulated sugar

3 large egg yolks

1 tsp. pure vanilla extract

3 Tbsp. all-purpose flour

1 cup whole milk

1 Whisk together sugar, egg yolks, and vanilla in a medium bowl until mixture is pale yellow and makes ribbons, 3 to 4 minutes. Add flour; whisk until smooth.

2 Bring milk to a boil in a medium saucepan over medium, about 3 minutes. Gradually add milk to egg yolk mixture, whisking constantly. Return mixture to saucepan. Bring to a boil over medium, whisking constantly, about 3 minutes. Boil mixture, whisking constantly, 1 minute. Transfer mixture to a medium bowl; press plastic wrap directly onto surface. Let cool to room temperature, about 1 hour. —JP

MAKE AHEAD The custard can be chilled, covered, up to 3 days.

GRILLED PEACH AND PINEAPPLE MELBA SUNDAES

Justin Chapple's spin on peach Melba takes advantage of the smoky flavor that grilling lends to fruit. The sauce is also reinvented with grilled sugared raspberries. The fruit for this sundae can be grilled outdoors on a gas or charcoal grill.

ACTIVE 30 MIN; TOTAL 50 MIN; SERVES 6

12 oz. fresh raspberries

2 Tbsp. granulated sugar

1 Tbsp. fresh lemon juice

Pinch of flaky sea salt, plus more for serving

2 medium peaches, cut into thin wedges

2 (½-inch-thick) fresh pineapple slices

2 pt. vanilla bean ice cream, for serving

1 Preheat grill to high (450°F to 550°F). Layer 2 medium sheets of heavy-duty aluminum foil. Toss together raspberries and sugar on foil. Slide foil onto the grill grate, and grill, uncovered, stirring once or twice, until juicy, about 8 minutes. Transfer raspberries and any juices to a blender, and let cool completely. Add lemon juice and a pinch of flaky sea salt; puree until very smooth. Transfer raspberry sauce to an airtight container and refrigerate until chilled, about 30 minutes.

2 Meanwhile, grill peach wedges and pineapple slices, uncovered, until lightly charred, 3 to 4 minutes per side. Transfer to a work surface; let cool completely. Dice pineapple.

3 Decoratively layer ice cream, pineapples, peaches, and raspberry sauce in each of 6 (8-ounce) glasses. Sprinkle with flaky sea salt and serve immediately.
—JUSTIN CHAPPLE

MAKE AHEAD The raspberry sauce and the grilled pineapple and peaches can be prepared and refrigerated overnight.

DARK-CHOCOLATE PUDDING WITH CANDIED GINGER

"For me, ginger should be everywhere," says Jean-Georges Vongerichten. "It's as good in marinades and vinaigrettes as it is in dessert." In this dessert, candied ginger garnishes dark-chocolate pudding.

TOTAL 15 MIN; SERVES 8

½ cup plus 1 Tbsp. granulated sugar

½ cup unsweetened cocoa powder

5½ Tbsp. cornstarch

¼ tsp. salt

1 qt. half-and-half

1 (3.5-oz.) bar bittersweet chocolate, chopped

1 tsp. vanilla extract

Lightly sweetened whipped cream and sliced candied ginger, for serving

1 Sift together sugar, cocoa powder, cornstarch, and salt in a medium bowl. In a large saucepan add half-and-half then whisk in cocoa-powder mixture. Cook over medium, whisking constantly, until pudding begins to bubble and thicken, about 4 minutes. Remove from heat; stir in bittersweet chocolate and vanilla.

2 Pour pudding into 8 (6-ounce) ramekins; let cool. Cover and refrigerate until chilled, about 1 hour. Top each pudding with whipped cream and candied ginger.
—JEAN-GEORGES VONGERICHTEN

BISCOFF BANANA PUDDING

The subtle spice of Biscoff cookies balances the sweetness of each luscious layer of creamy custard and fresh bananas in this tall and impressive banana pudding for a crowd. The recipe is inspired by one made by 2019 F&W Best New Chef Kwame Onwuachi's aunt Yolanda, of Beaumont, Texas, which he tasted on a trip to connect with his roots in Louisiana and Texas.

ACTIVE 20 MIN; TOTAL 3 HR 20 MIN; SERVES 20

- 1 (5.1-oz.) pkg. instant vanilla pudding and pie filling mix
- 2 cups whole milk
- 1 qt. heavy cream
- ½ cup powdered sugar
- 1 (14-oz.) can sweetened condensed milk
- 1 Tbsp. vanilla extract
- 1 (11-oz.) pkg. vanilla wafers, divided
- 1 (8.8-oz.) pkg. crisp gourmet cookies (such as Biscoff), divided
- 10 medium bananas, cut into ¼-inch-thick slices (about 10 cups), divided

1. Beat pudding and pie filling mix and whole milk in a medium bowl with an electric mixer on low speed until combined and slightly thickened, about 2 minutes. Let stand at room temperature until soft-set, about 5 minutes.

2. Beat together cream and powdered sugar in a large bowl with electric mixer on medium-high speed until stiff peaks form, about 5 minutes. Carefully fold in sweetened condensed milk, vanilla, and pudding mixture just until combined.

3. In separate zip-top plastic bags, coarsely crush 5 vanilla wafers and 4 gourmet cookies; set aside for garnish. Reserve 16 of the remaining vanilla wafers.

4. Arrange another 16 remaining vanilla wafers and 7 remaining gourmet cookies in a single layer in a 4½-quart trifle dish, alternating vanilla wafer and cookie rows, breaking as needed to fit dish. Evenly layer 2½ cups banana slices on cookies. Spread 3 cups vanilla custard in an even layer over bananas. Repeat layering process 3 times with remaining vanilla wafers, gourmet cookies, banana slices, and vanilla custard. Sprinkle crushed cookies over top layer of custard. Insert reserved 16 vanilla wafers around edge of dish. Loosely cover with plastic wrap and refrigerate at least 3 hours or up to 12 hours before serving. —KWAME ONWUACHI

MAKE AHEAD Pudding can be prepared through Step 2 and stored in an airtight container in refrigerator up to 1 week.

RED, HOT, AND COOL STRAWBERRIES

PHOTO P. 255

The chile-induced heat in this dish doesn't kick in until the last moment, creating a gentle afterburn that is cooled by sweet strawberries and a smooth bed of tangy cream. Look for chiles de árbol at Latin grocers.

ACTIVE 25 MIN; TOTAL 50 MIN; SERVES 4

1 chile de árbol or similar chile, stemmed and seeded

7 oz. strawberries, hulled and chopped into ½-inch pieces

¼ cup superfine sugar

1 Tbsp. fresh lemon juice

⅔ cup plain whole-milk Greek yogurt

⅔ cup cream cheese, softened

Fresh mint leaves, for garnish

1 Heat a small skillet over high; add chile and cook, tossing occasionally, until toasted and a nutty aroma is released, 3 to 5 minutes. Remove from skillet; crush in a mortar and pestle.

2 Stir together crushed chile, strawberries, sugar, and lemon juice in a heavy-bottomed saucepan. Bring to a boil over high, and cook, stirring occasionally, until thickened and syrupy, about 15 minutes. (Strawberries should mostly keep their shape; if they start collapsing, remove from heat sooner.) Remove from heat and let strawberry mixture cool completely, about 25 minutes.

3 While strawberry mixture cools, whisk together yogurt and cream cheese in a medium bowl until smooth. Cover and chill until ready to serve.

4 Divide yogurt mixture among 4 bowls; top evenly with strawberry mixture. Garnish with mint leaves and serve. —CAROLINE EDEN

STICKY TOFFEE AND EARL GREY PUDDING

One bite of chef Merlin Labron-Johnson's take on this dessert and you'll understand why he earned a Michelin star at the tender age of 24 at Portland. Labron-Johnson steeps dates—a regular player in sticky toffee pudding—in Earl Grey tea, infusing them with the bright, aromatic lift of bergamot.

ACTIVE 35 MIN; TOTAL 1 HR 30 MIN; SERVES 9

- 2 cups pitted Medjool dates, finely chopped
- 2 Earl Grey tea bags
- 1 tsp. baking soda
- 1¼ cups boiling water
- 2 cups all-purpose flour (about 8½ oz.)
- 2 tsp. baking powder
- 1¼ tsp. sea salt, divided
- ¾ cup vegetable shortening
- 1 cup light muscovado sugar, divided
- ¾ cup dark muscovado sugar, divided
- 3 large eggs
- 1 cup unsalted butter (8 oz.), plus more for greasing
- 1 cup heavy cream
  Vanilla ice cream or clotted cream, for serving

1 Preheat oven to 350°F. Place dates, tea bags, and baking soda in a medium bowl. Add 1¼ cups boiling water and let stand 15 minutes. Remove and discard tea bags. Stir mixture with a fork to break apart dates.

2 Stir together flour, baking powder, and ¾ teaspoon salt in a medium bowl; set aside. Combine shortening, ¼ cup light muscovado sugar, and ¼ cup dark muscovado sugar in the bowl of a stand mixer. Beat on medium speed until no lumps remain, about 1 minute. Add eggs, 1 at a time, beating well after each addition. With mixer running on low speed, gradually add flour mixture just until incorporated. Stir in date mixture. Lightly grease a 9-inch square baking pan with butter. Pour batter into prepared pan. Bake until a wooden pick inserted in center of pudding comes out clean, 30 to 32 minutes.

3 While pudding bakes, combine butter, heavy cream, remaining ¾ cup light muscovado sugar, remaining ½ cup dark muscovado sugar, and remaining ½ teaspoon salt in a large saucepan. Bring to a boil over medium-high, whisking often. Boil, whisking constantly, until sauce reaches 218°F on an instant-read thermometer, about 3 minutes. Remove from heat.

4 Remove pudding from oven. Immediately prick all over with a wooden or metal skewer, piercing all the way to the bottom of pan. Pour 1½ cups warm toffee sauce evenly over pudding; let stand until sauce is absorbed, about 30 minutes. Cut warm pudding into 9 (3-inch) squares. Drizzle servings evenly with remaining ½ cup toffee sauce; top with ice cream or clotted cream. —MERLIN LABRON-JOHNSON

SIMMERED PLANTAINS WITH COCONUT MILK AND PALM SUGAR

The key to this recipe is selecting perfectly ripe plantains: Choose fruits that are dull yellow-orange and blackened in spots. They should still feel slightly firm when you squeeze them, like an unripe banana. Alternatively, purchase unripe plantains and let them ripen a few days at room temperature.

ACTIVE 25 MIN; TOTAL 35 MIN; SERVES 4

- 2 very ripe plantains (about 1¼ lb.), peeled and cut diagonally into ½-inch-thick slices
- 1½ cups well-shaken and stirred unsweetened coconut milk
- ¼ cup palm sugar or firmly packed dark brown sugar, plus more for garnish
- ¼ tsp. kosher salt
- 2 fresh or thawed frozen pandan leaves, each tied into a knot, or 1 Tbsp. vanilla extract

Place plantains, coconut milk, 1½ cups water, palm sugar, salt, and pandan leaves in a large saucepan. Bring to a boil over medium-high, stirring often. (Don't let the coconut milk boil for more than a few seconds; it might curdle.) Immediately reduce heat to low; simmer gently, stirring occasionally, until plantains are fork-tender but still hold their shape, 3 to 6 minutes. Remove from heat; set aside to cool until liquid is just warm. Discard pandan leaves; ladle mixture evenly into 4 shallow bowls. Sprinkle with palm sugar to garnish, and serve warm.

—JAMES OSELAND

NOTE Pandan leaves are often used to flavor desserts with sweet almond and vanilla flavor. The fresh leaves , which can be chopped or tied into knots and boiled, are often used in rice, curries, and as wrappers for barbecued dishes. Find them at amazon.com.

WINTER CITRUS WITH FROZEN YOGURT AND PISTACHIOS

Suzanne Goin, the chef at the famed Lucques in Los Angeles, marked 20 years of business in 2018 with a dinner that celebrated her now-classic blend of French cuisine and California produce. This light winter dessert celebrates citrus and dresses it up with browned butter, frozen yogurt, and sbrisolona.

TOTAL 25 MIN; SERVES 6

- 4 lb. mixed citrus (such as blood oranges, Cara Cara oranges, and tangerines)
- 2 Tbsp. unsalted butter
- ¼ cup pistachios, slightly crushed
- 2 cups vanilla frozen yogurt
- 2 Tbsp. wildflower honey
- Pistachio Sbrisolona (recipe follows)
- Flaky sea salt

1 Using a paring knife, cut away and discard peels from citrus. Slice half of citrus crosswise into rounds. Cut remaining citrus into sections. Chill fruit until ready to serve.

2 Melt butter in a small skillet over medium, stirring often, just until butter begins to brown, 2 minutes 30 seconds to 3 minutes. Add pistachios, and toast, stirring constantly, until pistachios are golden brown, about 30 seconds. Remove from heat. Remove pistachios from skillet, and set aside.

3 To serve, divide citrus segments and rounds evenly among 6 chilled shallow bowls, leaving a well in center of each. Place ⅓ cup frozen yogurt in center of citrus in each bowl. Spoon 1 teaspoon honey over frozen yogurt in each bowl; place 1 slice of Pistachio Sbrisolona in each bowl. Scatter toasted pistachios over and around frozen yogurt and citrus. Sprinkle servings with salt. —SUZANNE GOIN

PISTACHIO SBRISOLONA

Somewhere between dense cake and chewy shortbread cookie, Italian sbrisolona with orange zest and pistachios is a gorgeously contrasting accompaniment to fresh citrus.

ACTIVE 25 MIN; TOTAL 1 HR 35 MIN; SERVES 8

- ¾ cup raw pistachios (about 3½ oz.)
- 1 cup plus 2 Tbsp. all-purpose flour (about 4¾ oz.)
- 6 Tbsp. fine yellow cornmeal (about 1⅞ oz.)
- ½ tsp. kosher salt
- 7 Tbsp. cold unsalted butter (3½ oz.), cut into small cubes, plus more for greasing
- ⅓ cup granulated sugar
- 3 Tbsp. light brown sugar
- 1 extra-large egg yolk
- 1 Tbsp. orange zest
- ½ tsp. vanilla extract

1 Preheat oven to 350°F. Spread pistachios in a single layer on a rimmed baking sheet. Toast until golden brown, 8 to 10 minutes, stirring every 3 to 4 minutes. Remove from oven, and let stand until cool, about 10 minutes. Coarsely chop pistachios.

2 Stir together flour, cornmeal, and salt in a large bowl until blended. Add butter; using your fingers, rub butter into flour mixture until a coarse meal is formed. Stir in granulated sugar, brown sugar, and chopped pistachios until blended.

3 Stir together egg yolk, orange zest, and vanilla in a small bowl. Make a well in center of flour mixture, and pour in egg yolk mixture. Using your hands, gently combine mixture until a dry, crumbly dough forms.

4 Grease an 8-inch springform pan with butter. Transfer dough to prepared springform pan; very lightly press dough into pan, being careful not to pack tightly. (Top will be uneven.) Bake until set and golden brown, 30 to 40 minutes. Remove from oven. Let sbrisolona cool 20 minutes before slicing. —SG

ZABAGLIONE WITH CHAMPAGNE-GLAZED STRAWBERRIES

ACTIVE 10 MIN; TOTAL 40 MIN; SERVES 6

1 lb. strawberries, hulled and thinly sliced

3 Tbsp. granulated sugar

2 cups Zabaglione (recipe follows)

1 In a bowl stir together strawberries and sugar. Let stand at room temperature 30 minutes to 1 hour.

2 Arrange a single layer of macerated strawberries in the bottoms of 6 crème brûlée dishes. Top with enough zabaglione to cover (about ⅓ cup). Broil on high 3 to 4 inches from heat until zabaglione is bubbly and browned, 2 to 3 minutes.
—JODY WILLIAMS & RITA SODI

ZABAGLIONE

Chef Umberto Creatini flavors his sauce with a "shepherd's liqueur," a Tuscan specialty unavailable in the U.S. Zabaglione is also delicious served on its own or as a sauce for fresh fruit.

TOTAL 10 MIN; MAKES 4 CUPS

6 large egg yolks

½ cup granulated sugar

Pinch of kosher salt

½ cup sweet wine, such as Marsala, Moscato, or Vin Santo

1 Beat yolks in a heat proof bowl (preferably copper) until combined. Add sugar and salt, whisking constantly, until combined.

2 Pour wine into yolk mixture; whisk until sugar is dissolved, about 30 seconds.

3 Heat mixture over a saucepan of barely simmering water, whisking vigorously to incorporate air into mixture.

4 Whisk until custard is warm, tripled in volume, and dragging the whisk across it leaves a ribbon on the surface, 8 to 9 minutes. Remove from heat. Serve immediately, or whisk over an ice bath until cooled. —JW & RS

MOSCATO MASCARPONE CREAM For a stabilized zabaglione that can be chilled for a few hours before serving, chefs Jody Williams and Rita Sodi of New York City's Via Carota share tips. Make Zabaglione using Moscato. Let mascarpone come to room temperature, and stir until creamy with no lumps. Fold mascarpone into an equal part cooled Moscato Zabaglione.

STRACCIATELLA SEMIFREDDO

ACTIVE 20 MIN; TOTAL 3 HR 20 MIN; SERVES 8

Cooking spray

⅓ cup toasted sliced almonds

4 cups Marsala Zabaglione (recipe above)

3 cups whipped heavy cream

½ cup chocolate shavings

Coat a 9-inch loaf pan with cooking spray, then line pan with plastic wrap. Sprinkle bottom of pan with toasted sliced almonds. Fold cooled Marsala Zabaglione with whipped heavy cream and chocolate shavings; scrape into loaf pan, cover, and freeze until firm, at least 3 hours. To serve, invert onto a plate and slice. —JW & RS

FRESH FRUIT WITH ZABAGLIONE

RECIPE INDEX

Page numbers in **bold** indicate photographs.

PHOTO CREDITS

MEASUREMENT GUIDE

BASIC MEASUREMENTS

GALLON	QUART	PINT	CUP	OUNCE	TBSP	TSP	DROPS
1 gal	4 qt	8 pt	16 c	128 fl oz			
½ gal	2 qt	4 pt	8 c	64 fl oz			
¼ gal	1 qt	2 pt	4 c	32 fl oz			
	½ qt	1 pt	2 c	16 fl oz			
	¼ qt	½ pt	1 c	8 fl oz	16 Tbsp		
			⅞ c	7 fl oz	14 Tbsp		
			¾ c	6 fl oz	12 Tbsp		
			⅔ c	5⅓ fl oz	10⅔ Tbsp		
			⅝ c	5 fl oz	10 Tbsp		
			½ c	4 fl oz	8 Tbsp		
			⅜ c	3 fl oz	6 Tbsp		
			⅓ c	2⅔ fl oz	5⅓ Tbsp	16 tsp	
			¼ c	2 fl oz	4 Tbsp	12 tsp	
			⅛ c	1 fl oz	2 Tbsp	6 tsp	
				½ fl oz	1 Tbsp	3 tsp	
					½ Tbsp	1½ tsp	
						1 tsp	60 drops
						½ tsp	30 drops

US TO METRIC CONVERSIONS

The conversions shown here are approximations. For more precise conversions, use the formulas to the right.

VOLUME			WEIGHT			TEMPERATURE			CONVERSION FORMULAS
1 tsp	=	5 mL	1 oz	=	28 g	475°F	=	246°C	tsp × 4.929 = mL
1 Tbsp	=	15 mL	¼ lb (4 oz)	=	113 g	450°F	=	232°C	Tbsp × 14.787 = mL
1 fl oz	=	30 mL	½ lb (8 oz)	=	227 g	425°F	=	218°C	fl oz × 29.574 = mL
¼ c	=	59 mL	¾ lb (12 oz)	=	340 g	400°F	=	204°C	c × 236.588 = mL
½ c	=	118 mL	1 lb (16 oz)	=	½ kg	375°F	=	191°C	pt × 0.473 = L
¾ c	=	177 mL				350°F	=	177°C	qt × 0.946 = L
1 c	=	237 mL	LENGTH			325°F	=	163°C	oz × 28.35 = g
1 pt	=	½ L	1 in	=	2.5 cm	300°F	=	149°C	lb × 0.453 = kg
1 qt	=	1 L	5 in	=	12.7 cm	275°F	=	135°C	in × 2.54 = cm
1 gal	=	4.4 L	9 in	=	23 cm	250°F	=	121°C	(°F − 32) × 0.556 = °C

More books from
FOOD&WINE

Holiday

Celebrate the joy of the season with this collection of more than 300 recipes that will become holiday favorites at gatherings large and small. Whether hosting a festive holiday party, preparing a cozy family brunch, or baking tempting cookies for platters, you'll find trusted recipes to share.

Cocktails

This book features more than 150 of our best recipes for cocktails and mocktails from innovative bartenders across the country. A must-have collection for the home bartender, inside you'll find essential tips, tools, and techniques, and 24 menu ideas for drinks and bites. Join the editors of *Food & Wine* as they showcase the art of mixing a proper cocktail and offering hospitality with the finest in food and drink. Cheers!

Grilling

This must-have grilling book features luscious recipes with full-color photographs to inspire you, grilling basics to guide you, and essential tools, plus tips and practical advice from all-star chefs. It's the definitive book for grilling enthusiasts that goes beyond the basics to get the most out of every fire.